Daniel Lane is an award-winning sports journalist. His previous books include *Rugby League Rebel – The Mark Geyer Story* (1994), *Laurie and Clyde, Young Guns of Rubgy League* (1995), *A Family Betrayal* with Jarrod McCracken (1996), *Sirro! Tales From Tigertown* (1997) and *Pacemaker* with Glenn McGrath (1998).

Lane spent time training with the Waters boys on their Kulnura property when he prepared to fight as an amateur heavyweight. However, he earned the wrath of Ces Waters when he openly supported Guy's move to Johnny Lewis' stable of boxers at the Newtown Police Boys Club.

Lane lives in Sydney but he likes to travel overseas as much as possible to such places as the coast of Kenya or Cairo with his girlfriend Camille.

raging waters

the life of an innocent killer

dean waters

with daniel lane

Pan Macmillan Australia

First published 1998 in Macmillan by Pan Macmillan Australia Pty Limited
St Martins Tower, 31 Market Street, Sydney

Reprinted 1998

National Library of Australia
Cataloguing-in-Publication data:

Waters, Dean.
Raging Waters.

ISBN 0 330 36122 8.

1. Waters, Dean. 2. Waters, Ces, 1927–1989. 3. Boxers (Sports) – Australia – Biography. I. Lane, Daniel (Daniel Q.). II. Title.

796.83092

Typeset by Midland Typesetters
Printed in Australia by McPherson's Printing Group

'What is hateful ... is not rebellion but the despotism which induces rebellion. What is hateful are not rebels but the men, who, having the enjoyment of power, do not discharge the duties of power. They are the men who, having the power to redress wrongs, refuse to listen to petitioners that are sent to them; they are the men who, when they are asked for a loaf, give a stone ...'

Wilfrid Lauren

I dedicate this book to any man, woman or child who has been a victim of any form of abuse. I beg you not to suffer in silence. Tell someone of your problems and accept whatever help is made available to you. *No-one* – not even a parent – has the right to hurt you.

Contents

THE FORGOTTEN YEARS

Chapter One

'I am not a saint, I don't profess to be a saint, but for everything I've done in my life I had a reason for doing it ... and if I had my time over with my children again I wouldn't do anything different. I'll tell you one thing, and I have to be forgiven for this, but if I had my time to go over again I would probably not have any children because I've been terribly disappointed in the way my children have treated me ...'

Ces Waters on life's regrets

I was always my father's 'special boy'. I was the oldest and strongest of his children and Dad said he loved me most of all. And I adored my dad in return.

I remember when I had a bad dream once I climbed into his bed and was comforted by an immediate sense of security just by being with him. In my child's mind I knew he'd protect me from the (imaginary) monsters which scare kids in the dead of night.

Dad was my hero. He'd acted in movies, he'd been a British soldier at fifteen, he'd boxed, he could fly aeroplanes and he'd even done time in the toughest prisons in Britain. But most of all, Dad bowed to no-one. Not to our busybody neighbours, not to the London Child Welfare Unit or even the military brass when he was a soldier.

When I was little he'd tell me stories about his life and I thought he was quite brave to join the English army back in 1942. Dad was only a boy and fresh from the mean streets of Manchester when he signed on to fight Adolf Hitler's troops. However, Private Cecil 'Titch' Waters didn't get past basic training – the camp commander gave him his marching orders once he learned Dad had lied about his age. Nevertheless, tucked away in his kitbag was the trophy he won during the Derbyshire army camp's boxing tournament. Even though he was a boy in a man's world Dad was good – and tough – enough to beat men twice his age.

He was back in khaki in 1945 but this time his fighting was with the officers who didn't think he had the right attitude – or character – to serve in the King's army. They tried to break his spirit by sentencing him to long stints in the 'clink' and they ordered him to do extra details. However, Dad refused to buckle.

He liked to talk of the time he was locked up after another run-in with the officers. I'd sit in wide-eyed awe as he told his story.

In army prison, son, they gave you the choice of either cocoa or soup for your evening meal. When you had soup they gave you as much as you wanted, so I gulped it all down, only to find out it was laced with Epsom Salts! I was on the toilet all night and I was as sick as a dog.

As soon as I got out, Dean, I vowed to get my revenge. And you know what I did? I got hold of some fifteen centimetre nails and hammered them into the officer's latrine doors. Then I sneaked in and filled the cauldrons of their stew with Epsom Salts – the officers had to crap in full view of the enlisted men on the parade ground! It was a blast.

On another occasion after I served time in the prison for going absent without leave I surprised the officers by volunteering to maintain the camp's prized cannon from the Crimean War. It belonged to the Lancashire Fusiliers and they doted on it, son. When I said I'd like to look after it they were surprised, boy, they were surprised, but they complimented me on my new attitude.

I went out, got the ugliest green paint possible and painted the thing! Ha! They had enough and kicked me out.

While Dad always seemed to have a terrible temper – it was a powder keg, actually – there were times when he could be fun to be around. Like the day when Guy and I dug a big hole in our backyard and filled it with water so it became a big, messy bog. Anyway, Dad ran out into the backyard and slid into my pond of goo. He was covered in smelly mud like the Creature from the Black Lagoon and he didn't look very happy at all. At first I thought I was in for a hiding, but after a few seconds Dad sat back and roared with laughter. He laughed his head off. It was nice. Yeah, Dad loved me back then. I knew he wouldn't mind me sleeping in his bed when I got scared.

Unfortunately, that's one of the few good memories I have of Ces Waters, the father. Most of my early childhood years are a blank and the other incidents I'm able to recall centre around brutal acts of violence.

Some psychiatrists believe such blank spots occur as a safety valve in the minds of people who have been mentally or physically abused. They believe the victim's mind shuts down because it's the only way they can cope with the stresses they've been subjected to.

But that isn't any comfort to me when I try to remember our life in North London during the late 1960s and early 1970s, though I do have memories of two Christmasses.

I can clearly remember the day I peeked out of our front window to see the cause of a commotion outside our place. A crowd had gathered around a man who was lying dead on Wilberforce Road. He had lost his grip on the back of a double-decker bus as it went around the corner, and his head had crashed onto the bitumen. Blood was everywhere and some had even splattered over the presents he was taking home to his family.

Then there was a Christmas morning in 1969 when we were pushed out the back door as snow fell from the sky. While the other children around Finsbury Park unwrapped their presents and waited to tuck into their roast turkey and plum pudding lunches, we Waters boys were issued with pairs of second-hand boxing gloves and advised to keep warm the best way possible. We threw punches at one another and, as the hours passed by and the temperature dropped, we fought even harder.

I've often thought about my childhood and I'm sure that Guy, Troy and I were being bred to be either soccer players or prize fighters. Our sister Tracey was spared from a life in the boxing ring because she was born a girl. Though, Dad did the next 'best' thing and forced her to take up running. Who knows? Perhaps he thought she'd do her bit to bring him some fame by winning an Olympic gold medal.

We aren't the only kids who had been 'engineered' to be athletes – I've heard about an American guy who was born to be a quarterback and he lived a life of deprivation and sacrifice. Ours was the same sort of upbringing and our apprenticeships started at an early age.

Tracey was seven, I was six, Guy was five and Troy – the baby – was only three when Dad forced us to do road runs around the Finsbury Park recreation area. It's a huge green belt in grimy old North London and I can still picture the bleak fields blanketed in snow. However, the last thing on our minds on our early morning runs was the scenery – we were more interested in keeping our little legs moving to try and stay warm.

It didn't matter if it was howling a blizzard or pouring rain, we were made to run for miles at a time. In Dad's mad mind we were running towards an FA Cup victory lap or world boxing and running titles.

I was always the slowest and whenever I lagged too far behind the others Dad would drive his car up on the footpath and revive me by blasting his horn and shouting at me. Then, when I slacked off he would nudge me with the car's bumper ... I can't properly explain the terror I felt when he did that. However, it was great enough to push me along even though there were times when I would be crying and vomiting at the same time. And I didn't dare stop because I wasn't sure if Dad would hit his car's brakes.

The few people who were out exercising in that ungodly weather would stop dead in their tracks when they saw us. Four toddlers running for their lives in front of a car driven by a wild-eyed maniac. It must have seemed like a scene straight out of the *Twilight Zone*.

I couldn't understand why we had to run every morning

and I can still hear Dad's answer the time I asked him why he made us run until we were sick.

'It's my way of getting the bad out of you, Dean.' I didn't quite understand what he meant. After all, I was only seven! But Dad's lessons were always tough ones.

For instance, sometimes when Troy was on the point of exhaustion after a road run, Dad would trip him over. It hurt him, and when Troy asked Dad why he pushed him to the ground, he replied, 'You have to learn to pick yourself up in life because no-one else will.'

And we've all been trying to do just that ever since. It was interesting to hear Dad's recollections of those enforced runs on a tape he posted to Tracey not long before his death. His memories were so skewed and so typically Dad.

> *I used to get up of a morning and light that fire and warm the room and warm the tracksuits in the freezing cold weather. I'd warm the tracksuits up and call you down from bed and you'd get your tracksuits on and off we'd go to the park. I was building up a cardio-respiratory system for my children that I knew would probably hold them in good stead one day. And in those days I was thinking of athletics for you and soccer for the boys. The boys liked soccer. I'm a lover of soccer myself and I thought, you know, this could be so. I thought there might be a future for the boys in soccer . . .*

When he wasn't training us Dad was always keeping himself busy. He ran a driving school, but he spent a lot of time with his 'associates'. North London was a pretty tough part of the world where criminal activity was rife. If you smiled for a few seconds too long someone would steal the gold fillings from out of your teeth! No joke.

I'm not sure what activities Dad got up to but I suspect they were no good. He liked to brag he spent time in some of Britain's toughest prisons, including Dartmoor, where he was the youngest inmate. And he'd often talk about his 'contacts' who lived in the shadowy nooks and crannies of North London.

By Dad's own account, he'd rubbed shoulders with some of the London underworld's heaviest characters, including the Kray twins, Ronnie and Reg, and one of their associates, Noel Gallagher. He also claimed to know the great train robbers – Ronnie Biggs, Tommy Whisby and Jim Hussey – and he'd talk about them for hours at a time.

Whenever Dad was trying to intimidate someone without actually threatening them he'd casually drop their names in conversation. For instance, he'd tell them when he first befriended Ronald Biggs in prison he was only a petty criminal. According to Dad, the mastermind behind the £2,500,000 robbery of a Royal Mail train en route from Glasgow to London did not appear then to be a criminal genius. 'If anything, I thought he was a family man.'

And to reinforce his image as a 'hard bastard', Dad would divulge what he called 'undisclosed' details about the robbery. He'd delight in telling how one of the robbers died of severe head injuries when he was struck by a train as he crossed the tracks. He said the police hadn't found his body because two of Biggs' villains were ordered to double back and bury the dead man in a trench near the railway line before the coppers arrived.

It was probably just an urban myth, but Dad made it sound to strangers as if he'd heard the story from Biggs himself! Dad also revealed the police showed plenty of 'interest' in him after the robbery because he was certain they wanted to somehow implicate him in the crime.

When he wasn't socialising with the likes of the Krays in one of their nightclubs Dad said he could be found down at the exclusive Fifty Club in Frith Street. It was said to be a swish place where actors, poets, lawyers, politicians and doctors of all sexual persuasions could hide behind a haze of blue cigar smoke and sink whisky. An actor friend named Shaw introduced Dad to the jet set and, if it is true, I'm sure the old man's motive would have been to befriend one of the rich members to 'touch' them for a loan that would never be repaid.

Apparently Dad would enjoy long conversations with an osteopath named Stephen Ward and his beautiful girlfriend, Christine Keeler. Unbeknown to Dad, and most of his cronies at the time, Christine was sleeping with some of the most influential men in Britain and he nearly dropped the paper in shock the morning he read Ward and Christine were linked in the political sex scandal that would become known as the Profumo Affair.

While Dad was sorry to learn Ward committed suicide in the Old Bailey for his part in the scandal, he said the doctor was no different from a debauched priest he knew of in Manchester in the sense he had serious sexual deviances. Apparently Dad learned in the turkish baths of the Fifty Club that Ward would pay dirty old men to 'defile' Keeler for his own stimulation. 'No matter how powerful or respectable a man might seem, his true animal nature comes out behind closed doors.'

However, as for theft or getting into trouble with the law, Dad made it clear he'd tolerate nothing untoward from any of us. One time he took a cucumber from a bowl and placed it on a chopping board, telling us to watch and see what he'd do to any of us if he ever caught us stealing. He lifted a small axe, like a tomahawk, over his head and brought it down fast and hard. One half of the vegetable rolled from the board and onto the ground and Dad waited a few extra seconds for dramatic effect before saying, 'I'll cut your hands off.'

Our mother, Gloria Newman, left us when we were infants. For years Dad said she deserted us.

'She was a good time girl, she liked to drink, she liked to smoke and she liked to gallivant about.' He'd say that kind of thing over and over again until it sunk in.

'What kind of woman would abandon her babies? A woman *never* leaves her children, it doesn't matter how bad things might be.'

As we grew older Dad derived plenty of pleasure from blackening her name by telling us that Gloria enjoyed affairs during their sexually 'open' marriage. Worse still he told us she worked as a prostitute, 'a working girl on Euston Road'. They were dad's words, not ours.

And for a while he poisoned our minds towards Mum. He painted her as a wicked woman who hated her kids and ran off with a younger bloke. However, he didn't mention a few other facts, such as that she had spent years being Dad's punching bag and that when she couldn't take it any more she left for the laundromat one night and never returned.

Whenever I think about my mother I have a memory flash of a tormented woman who'd been smashed over the head with a milk bottle. Her face was masked with blood and she moaned in agony. I'm certain that was Mum, and I regret that it is one of the few early memories I have of her. It actually brings tears to my eyes if I dwell on it for too long.

When Mum disappeared, word quickly spread about

Finsbury Park that Dad had necked her. All of Mum's clothes and personal papers – like her driver's licence – were found scattered at Hampstead Heath and the early indications suggested she'd met foul play. The rumours grew so strong Scotland Yard launched an investigation into her disappearance. They went over the house with a fine-tooth comb and when they saw that bits of clothing had been mixed into the plaster Dad used to brick up the chimney they made plans to knock it down.

It was a traumatic time for us kids. We were always crying and asking where Mum had gone, but Dad had no answers. However, he lapped up the attention and even phoned the *News of the World* tabloid to talk to them about the 'anguish' he was suffering.

He'd called the papers on a previous occasion, during the garbage men's strike in the late 1960s. He asked for a journalist and a photographer to be outside the Prime Minister's residence at 10 Downing Street at a certain time to see him make a statement.

Dad made his statement all right. He dumped a truckload of rubbish outside the gates to let Prime Minister Harold Wilson know what the 'common' folk had to live with. The headline of the *Evening News* on 8 October 1969 screamed: 'A Load of Rubbish on Harold's Doorstep' and the paper reported Dad was upset that we kids couldn't eat our meals properly because of the stench from the rubbish near our homes. Dad would have loved to have believed his message to Mr Wilson had sent shivers of fear down Britain's corridors of power when he said, 'I voted for the last time in my life at the last general election – and I voted Labour. *Never* again!'

If only Mr Wilson could have seen the filth we grew up in when we moved to a remote farm in Australia! *That* would have made London during the great garbage strike resemble a cleaning drive!

On this particular occasion – Mum's disappearance – the following morning's newspaper featured a photograph of the old man on the front page with the headline: 'Husband's amazing statement – THEY SAY I'VE WALLED UP MY WIFE IN THIS CHIMNEY'. Dad painted a brilliant picture of a wronged husband and he even brought some kindly old ladies to the brink of tears when he told them about the many trials and tribulations of being a single parent – a father, at that – with four hungry kids. By Dad's account in his tape to Tracey, even our local doctor thought he had been hard done by Mum.

When she visited Australia (in 1988) she said I used to bash her up but there is no case on record that I brutalised her. There's nothing in the police station, there's nothing in the doctor's report. Nothing. Oh yeah, we had our fallouts and I whacked her – of course I did – but not to the extent she made out. The doctor said many years later just before we left for Australia – because I needed to get a medical examination for us to go to Australia – that he knew who the baddie was. 'I'll tell you one thing, Ces,' said the doctor, 'she can say what she likes but I know who the offender is. She left you and those children. You stuck around with those children all these years. So I know who the baddie is.' That's what the doctor said . . .

Not everyone was sympathetic, though, and many of Dad's customers abandoned his driving school because they thought he was a murderer. For years Dad was to blame a 'smear' campaign for forcing him to close his business down.

However, the truth is my mother's disappearance and the

seemingly suspicious circumstances surrounding it spoke volumes for Dad's street cunning. Mum did run off and as I've said it was for her own safety. However, what angered Dad most of all was he had no idea of where she was hiding out and he was adamant she'd stolen money, a silver Gurkha dress knife and a half-sovereign gold ring his mother had given him. He wanted to track her down and because he couldn't afford a private detective he got the police involved by making it appear as if she'd met with foul play.

Dad threw all Mum's personal belongings over a hill and the police were called. For years he'd laugh at the fact he had the coppers do all the legwork for him and track down our mother at the 'right price'. As it turned out, Mum heard about the police investigation and came forward to the *News of the World* office a week later to say she was still alive, though we didn't see her again until I tracked her down twenty-odd years later. Indeed, we Waters kids grew up believing our mother was dead and buried in a London cemetery.

However, we did see a lot of a man and a woman from the Child Welfare Unit. They didn't think Dad could raise four kids on his own and were always knocking on the door. Dad tolerated them for a while until the day they arrived with applications for him to sign so we could be fostered out to what they termed 'good' families. They said if we were lucky it might be possible for us to grow up knowing where each other lived.

Well, that set Dad off on a rampage. He shouted the house down and threatened to kill them.

'What do you mean, adopt my kids out?' he screamed. 'Go! You have one minute to go before I kill you stone dead.'

Dad was smart. He knew he'd won *that* battle against

the authorities, but realised it would only be a matter of time before the welfare officers came back with the police. If it took a day, a week or a month he knew they'd return.

So he hatched a plan with a young woman he'd had an affair with while he was married to Mum. Her name was Christine Hicks and Dad had met her when she was only seventeen and he'd taught her how to drive.

Dad always said he and Christine could do their 'little thing' with clear consciences because of an understanding which meant Mum had her boyfriends, Christine had hers and Dad, well, he had other lady friends. His association with Christine turned out to be a handy liaison because in a bid to keep the Child Welfare authorities at arm's length, Dad married Christine, knowing that a woman's touch would convince the authorities we kids would be brought up properly.

But there was an extra incentive for Dad to get hitched a fourth time. He wanted to start a new life in Australia and part of the conditions for his immigration was that he had to be married. Christine came to his rescue. They planned to make the boat trip together, spend a few months as a man and wife, get divorced and, while we hit the road in search of a home, Christine would return to England to study at university to become a vet.

Somewhere along the way that plan must have fallen apart because, while it wasn't much of a life for her, we grew up with Christine as our mother figure.

We were under strict instructions from Dad not to call Christine 'Mum'. For her troubles, she spent seventeen years being beaten up by Dad and thirteen selling her body to 'Johns' at sleazy Kings Cross in Sydney's Eastern Suburbs.

I imagine I would have been excited to be going on the big boat, the SS *Australis*, to a sunny land on the other side of the world but I don't remember too much about our leaving England except for the fact that a lady was waiting for us on the docks to say goodbye to Dad. It wasn't our natural mother; instead, it was one of Dad's earlier wives named Doreen McCarthy. She had born Dad a son named Arnold, my half-brother, and I'm certain she was the only woman he really had any affection for. Doreen used to smuggle contraband such as sweets and tobacco, which were currency on the inside, into the prison for Dad whenever he served time to help make his life easier.

Dad remembered Doreen as a real 'mate' but the reason I can vaguely recall her is because she gave Troy, Guy, Tracey and me a pound each before we boarded the boat. I think she kissed us farewell as well, but I can't really remember if she did or not.

As it turned out her three quid was invaluable because Dad added it to the measly seven Australian dollars he'd saved up for us to start our new life on the other side of the world.

When we reached Australia, Dad received word that poor Doreen had committed suicide. I'm sure he felt sorry for her until his ego eventually took over because in later years he'd brag about the fact he was such a good man, such a good lover, that a woman gassed herself in an oven over him. And when I grew older Dad would ask me, 'How many women have killed themselves over you, Dean?'

A FAMILY MADNESS

Chapter Two

'My father's advice about women has always stuck by me. He said if ever you get a good woman, shoot her before she turns bad so she'll have died a good woman . . .'

Ces Waters' advice to his three sons on the opposite sex

I only met my great-grandmother, Granny Gilbert, once and even in her ancient years she was a tough old bird. She smoked a clay pipe packed with twist-tight tobacco and the fumes were foul enough to clear a room. And she talked tough, really tough. There wasn't much tenderness in her harsh Manchester accent and she scared the tripe out of me.

In her younger days Dad's grandmother made extra money by knocking men out in the boxing booths at carnivals in northern England. And even old age didn't slow her down because legend has it that even when she was seventy-five this amazon from England's industrial north would lug a sixty-pound roll of linoleum around the neighbourhood's streets and sell it door-to-door.

'Fighting has always been in our blood, ever since my old grandmother used to knock men out in Manchester', Dad told the press when we first gained media attention in 1983.

Indeed, I had received a painful insight into just how short Granny's temper really was when I did something to annoy her during that early childhood visit. Bang! The old woman cracked me over the shoulders with her walking stick and it hurt like crazy! I ran off crying and hid from her for the rest of her stay. She wasn't impressed and I think she might have dismissed me as a bit of a cry baby. 'The lud's a bit soft, Ces.'

Tracing our bloodlines is a monstrous task for Tracey, Troy, Guy and me because we have to fossick our way through the fact and fiction Dad raised us on. For instance, he maintained the actor John Wayne was a distant relative of ours. He said Wayne, whose real name was Marion Morrison, was somehow related to my grandfather's Gipsy family and Dad took great pride in telling people he had some claim to the Hollywood hero's name. I have no idea if it is true or not. However, I am certain 'the Duke' didn't ever appear in a movie with as bizarre a plot as our family's history.

Our great-grandfather Cecil Waters Senior arrived in England as a member of a travelling troupe from America. Cecil, one quarter Negro and part Ute Indian, liked the English way of life so much he stayed in Manchester long after the cast of *Savage South America* returned to the USA.

Before abandoning them ten years later, Cecil had a family and one of his offspring, John Darkie Waters, was to become our grandfather. John was dark by complexion – and even darker by nature. Indeed, Dad told me his other grandmother, Granny Ada, had to boot Darkie out onto the street when he was only fourteen because he was out of control. He would attack his sisters during violent fits of rage and, though they'd be left bloodied and bruised, Granny Ada was even more concerned by the fact her son seemed to *enjoy* making the girls cry.

Apart from possessing a sadistic streak Darkie was also mechanically-minded and he scratched out a living as a mechanic and chauffeur for the wealthy. He enjoyed some fame in his youth as 'Muddy' Waters, a thrill-seeking motorcycle racer, but he turned his back on that sport after his best friend was killed in an accident.

He then became the driver for a Gipsy woman named Mary-Jane Gilbert who had made a fortune buying and selling Irish horses. Mrs Gilbert's life was governed by all the old Gipsy superstitions – like not crossing knives or putting shoes on tables – so I'm amazed she didn't sense the danger when Darkie appeared on her doorstep.

Darkie took an instant shine to Mrs Gilbert's daughter, Nancy, and it was a recipe for disaster. Nancy was much older than him and married with seven kids but, from all accounts, that didn't worry Darkie because she was a real 'looker'. (While I haven't seen a photo of my grandmother in her prime, Dad claimed the actress Deborah Kerr was a dead-ringer for her.) While Darkie did his utmost to win my grandmother over, he didn't succeed until the night she got drunk and dropped her guard. It was a bad mistake because once their misdemeanour became common knowledge my grandmother's life took a terrible turn. When Nancy confessed to her crime of passion, and that she was carrying Darkie's baby, she was banished to live amid the filth with Manchester's dead-beat poor. She was ordered to leave her husband, an alcoholic ex-soldier, and children behind to start a wretched life with Darkie in the worst of Manchester's slum areas, Chorlton-on-Medlock.

My grandparents never married, but nine months after their drunken liaison my father entered the world, a wailing bastard, full of wind. I have no idea what Nancy expected her life to be like with Darkie, though I'm certain the squalor would have been a huge shock to her system after being raised among finery and lace.

Manchester had once been a thriving city where beautiful textiles and carpets were manufactured. However, the mills and factories had been forced to shut down when Britain was flooded with cheap imports from such places as India. The owners of the mills couldn't compete with the cheaper items and they laid their workers off as part of their cost-cutting measures. As more people became unemployed a sense of desperation set into Manchester and the standard of living plummeted. Houses crumbled through neglect, people went hungry and rats as big as cats bred in plague proportions. There was no escaping the thick black smoke that spewed out of the hundreds of chimneys which dotted the skyline. Dad remembered their fumes as 'poisonous' and said they not only choked the air but they also scattered soot all over the place. In some places he reckoned the soot could be up to an inch deep!

Any hope Nancy might have had of making a go of her new life with Darkie, despite such a miserable backdrop, must have been shattered once my grandfather's true nature surfaced a week before my father's birth. He came home from a late-night drinking binge in a foul mood and he repeatedly punched his partner in the belly. It was the first of a lifetime's worth of beatings and by the time Dad turned three his again-pregnant mother could take the abuse no longer.

On a visit to the city one afternoon she held Dad tight in her arms and leaped into a murky canal in a suicide bid. While a passer-by saved them from drowning no-one could rescue my grandmother – or Dad, for that matter – from Darkie's terrible temper.

He was a brute who made extra drinking money on weekends by participating in prize fights down at the old railway yards. They were contests in which mercy was never asked for, and none was offered.

I can only imagine the fights were a reflection of the frustrations which must have existed in poverty-stricken northern England. Dad always philosophised that people adapt to their environment to survive and in old Manchester that meant people battered one another for a few pennies. They stole. They lied. They struggled and they found ways to escape their plight.

Old Man Waters escaped the drudgery by going out on binge drinking sessions which either ended in someone's teeth getting knocked out or his spending a night in a cheap brothel. (My grandmother escaped by making her kids the focus of her life.)

When he wasn't boozing, brawling or whoring my grandfather would while away a Sunday morning by watching clog-kicking bouts down at the railway yards. The rules were painfully simple – two combatants held one another by the shoulders and took it in turns to kick the other person in the shins with steel-capped shoes. The first to scream 'No more!' lost the bout and any claim to the small purse. Punters won and lost money on an individual's pain threshold and while today we would bracket clog-kicking alongside cockfighting as inhumane Dad said the best contestants – scrappers with names like Clodhopper Moof and Pankey White – were idolised in much the same way as are our football stars.

It should now be obvious that my father lived hand in hand with violence. If he wasn't being bashed by his father – like the time he had a fire poker smashed over his head – there were bullies and thugs to sidestep on every corner. Dad said people walked on eggshells whenever they passed any of Manchester's hundreds of pubs because it was so easy to be dragged into a brawl. There were no such things as innocent bystanders, and the fights normally ended with the loser being served a large slice of 'toe pie' – having the boot laid into them.

So it was tough and Dad was cursed to have to wear callipers on his legs as a child because he suffered from rickets. His handicap initially made him a sitting target for schoolyard bullies, but Dad quickly gained their respect – and fear – by grabbing any antagonist by the head and biting their face whenever they picked on him.

Even the neighbourhood's toughest kids were terrified of Ces Waters because they knew he'd resort to animal-like behaviour when necessary, such as the afternoon he was cornered in a back alley by a gang-leader and his lackeys. Dad would have only been about eight at the time, but he was still crazy enough to pick up a brick and repeatedly smash it into the other boy's face.

Chorlton-on-Medlock was that kind of place, and if what Dad said was true there was no relief from the violence. For instance, as a toddler Dad couldn't understand why his little playmate, a girl named Nancy, didn't come outside one afternoon when he yelled for her.

Nancy was in the newspaper headlines the following day.

Her father had returned home with a bellyful of grog and in his drunken stupor, thought a battalion of devils was attacking him with their little pitch-forks. He was scared witless; however, he lashed out at them and even 'caught' one! He picked the 'demon' up and threw it head-first from the second floor window and onto the cobblestone street. His infant daughter died instantly and the judge sent him away to a mental institution.

On another occasion, Dad was sitting on the front doorstep when a neighbour called in to visit his mother. Just as she was about to enter my grandmother's front door the lady's drunken husband ran at her, abused her and then slashed her throat with a razor. While Dad said the woman survived the attack, he remembered it took months of hard scrubbing with an old monkey stone to remove the bloodstains from the front step.

Amid the madness of the slums stood my grandmother, a woman who Dad said was the closest he'd ever come to hugging a saint. Even after suffering the most severe hidings which left her face puffed up and her body swollen, Grandma Nancy did her best to bring her kids up properly. I think it always burned away at my Dad's conscience that he was never strong enough to stand up to his father and protect her. Apparently Darkie only had to raise his voice and my father would cringe like a dog – and that was a feeling my father in turn forced onto me and my siblings.

There was one time he tried to make a stand. After seeing my grandmother receive a terrible beating Dad threatened to break a bottle of acid over Darkie's face if he laid another hand on her. Unfortunately his courage gave way when Darkie threatened to make him drink the liquid. He dropped the bottle and ran for his life out the back door!

Despite my grandmother's best attempts, Dad drifted into a life of petty crime and thuggery. At fourteen he helped put bread on the family table by stealing the contributions from the local church's poor plates; he'd spend the remainder in the local brothels where he received discount rates on account of his youth.

But even at the lowest points of his life – and there were quite a few of them – the old man never forgot his mother's efforts to raise him the best way possible. 'A very rough childhood,' he told *Sydney Morning Herald* journalist John Huxley. 'Knew what it was like to be cold, but not hungry. Mum used to always find something. She could make a stew out of a sixpence.'

While Guy, Troy and I were not allowed to mix with women when we lived on the farm at Kulnura many years later, the old man didn't mind sowing his own wild oats as a young man. By his own admission he was a useless student – he left school unable to read or write – but he said he learned plenty about the facts of life from his teacher when he was only twelve. On finding Dad with a pornographic magazine hidden up his jumper she kept him back after school and fondled his penis until he orgasmed.

Dad liked his first taste of sex. He was immediately hooked and tried to find ways to satisfy his urges. At first he'd do such things as spy on his naked sisters and cousins when they bathed. He played doctors and nurses with them and then, until he found ways of making enough money to pay, he'd peek through the local prostitutes' windows and watch as they serviced their customers.

Within two years of that experience at the back of the schoolroom he was a regular at Manchester's most notorious brothels, much to his half-sister Mary's disgust. Mary was a well-known female wrestler who fought under the name of 'Miss England' and whenever she heard her little 'bastard brother' was out 'spending dosh' she'd barge into the whorehouse and whack the hookers over the head with a heavy stick. Then Mary would bellow abuse at Dad as she dragged him home by the lobe of his right ear!

While Dad's perversions must have broken my grandmother's heart, such antics made him a local legend among his peers. Within time he was the leader of a group of youngsters he liked to refer to as 'villains' and they loved mischief. For instance, when Hitler's airforce, the Luftwaffe, attacked Manchester during the Second World War, Dad and his mates used the bombing raids as a diversion to steal goods from a variety of warehouses and storage yards!

It was madness, and while Dad thought he was bulletproof I sometimes feel sad to think he spent his entire life trying to prove he was a better man than anyone else – and that insecurity even extended to his dealings with his own sons. I can only hazard a guess that these feelings stretched back to his childhood when he watched helplessly as his mother was beaten mercilessly by Darkie. The only victory Dad really enjoyed over my grandfather was when he reached a stage where he refused to cry, no matter how badly Darkie battered him.

As Dad grew older, he'd try to prove his mettle by doing such daring things as robbing closely guarded warehouses and bashing people. He enjoyed fighting and when we were kids he'd boast about the time he gnawed an ear off an opponent in a dogfight. And, rather than show any remorse whenever he saw the listener's look of horror, he'd sneer such brutal acts stemmed from the law of the jungle. 'I was living among animals so I acted like one!'

In another incident Dad claimed he torched a boarding

house run by a West Indian bloke after a bad business transaction. Apparently the black man and his friends conned Dad and an associate (it may have been his half-brother) out of some stolen goods. When the West Indians returned to their home the old man dished out his idea of back alley justice by splashing petrol under their front door and setting the building alight. His mate waited outside the back door to crack the West Indians over the head with a tyre lever as they ran for their lives. From all reports Dad thought it was a great hoot, and the old man justified his actions by saying he had to show the West Indians that he was someone not to mess with. Fear, he said, was his way of gaining their respect and he'd warn us the world would eat us alive if we were weak.

I remember the stories he'd tell around the family dinner table when we were just kids. His conversations usually centred around murders, bashings, whores and rapes. Dad didn't mind rapists as people, and in 1960 he even staged a one-man protest outside the American embassy in London when the US authorities announced they were going to execute a high-profile serial rapist. The bloke had preyed on couples in lovers' lanes; after he overpowered them the rapist would tie the male up and assault the girl. News of his execution made international headlines.

As a sign of support for the condemned man, Dad stood outside the American embassy with a placard which proclaimed: 'Shame on you, USA!'. In later years he took plenty of heart from the fact that a professor from Oxford University stopped to shake his hand and wish him well. Others would have dismissed Dad as a crackpot, because there's no doubt the rapist committed some sick deeds and the old man was adamant the death penalty was too extreme. 'No-one was murdered, were they?' he'd reason.

I can't ever recall any of us being told fairytales when we were kids, nor did we know anything about such movies as *Mary Poppins* or *Willie Wonka and the Chocolate Factory*. Instead, we were told about 'snuff' flicks, films in which people are killed – really killed – and their agony captured on celluloid. Dad saw one in the 1950s and he often spoke about the shock he felt once he realised the woman's hysterical screams wasn't a case of good acting.

While we didn't see a snuff film with Dad, he often played an old 16mm film of the Nazi concentration camps to us from a young age. I remember seeing hundreds of dead Jews being bulldozed into mass graves by the German troops and to this day I can't work out why he showed them to us.

Before – and after – the Allan Hall shooting in 1988, the old bloke would tell the media he migrated to Australia because he feared the only future Troy, Guy and I had in London was an iron cot in a cold prison cell. Dad liked to say he knew the dangers and temptations young men faced in depressed environments and he didn't want us exposed to them.

And Dad would tell anyone who cared to listen about the incident which made him go on the straight and narrow. It centred around the execution of a Manchester lad named Teddy Devline. He was condemned for his part in a murder which occurred during a bungled robbery. There are a number of versions of this story but Dad said a policeman's elderly mother had her skull crushed in and, even though he swore he didn't do it, Teddy swung alongside his accomplice on the gallows. Apparently Teddy was one of the street urchins who looked upon my old man as some sort of role model and Dad said it broke his heart to see him sitting in the condemned cell at Walton Jail, Liverpool.

'I wondered what I had done to contribute to this', he asked many times over. 'When they hanged him I was shattered. It left a bad taste in my mouth and a feeling of guilt. This kid had looked up to me. I was his example, and look at the way he finished up . . .'

Dad knew the British penal system well. He wasted his youth in some of the United Kingdom's toughest prisons and was happy to mix with the scum of society. He even said the prisoners were a better breed of humans than the white collar creeps who stole from the poor or that hypocritical priest he knew who paid a prostitute to urinate in his shoes while he masturbated. 'And then he'd go back and preach about heaven and hell! What a joke!'

Dad made numerous friends on the inside and he enjoyed making the authorities wonder whether or not he was the full quid. To emphasise how street-smart he was, Dad would occasionally tell us of the time he saved himself from a terrible beating by a group of 'screws'. Apparently when Dad heard the prison officers heading towards his cell to teach him a lesson after yet another violent run-in he feared they might really do him over and kill him. In his panic, Dad's bowels loosened and he used the mess to his advantage. He painted himself with his shit and when the heavy iron door finally swung open the wardens were repulsed by the stench – and the sight – of him. Even though he taunted them to attack him the wardens just shook their heads in disbelief, called him an animal and slammed the door shut.

However, covering himself in his own crap wasn't the worst activity Dad engaged in behind bars. He also dabbled in homosexuality. While it embarrasses me to reveal this side of my father's character, I believe it has to be mentioned to explain my life story fully. I was shocked by his admission because Dad constantly warned us as we grew up that he wouldn't tolerate any of his sons turning out queer. Yet when he was in prison he'd pay the 'pretty young boys' in prison currency – tobacco and sweets – to smother his genitals in margarine and massage them until he orgasmed. He said the prisoners used margarine as a lubricant because it would have been a dead giveaway what they were up to if they purchased Vaseline from the prison store. However, Dad stressed he wasn't bent, it was nothing more than a case of him adapting to his environment, like thieving and fighting in poverty-stricken Manchester.

While my dad definitely preferred to have sex with females he also had a deep hatred – even loathing – for them. Dad made it a point throughout his life never to mix with decent women. He preferred what he called 'bad eggs'. He liked the women he associated with to be without the slightest thread of decency because that way he could treat them like animals. 'I wanted bad eggs because I myself was a bad egg', he'd say and he'd tell us such things as he never caught venereal disease from a whore. Dad had caught gonorrhoea when he was a teenager and attributed that painful experience to a liaison with 'what society calls a good girl, can you believe it!'.

There was only one exception to his preference for rotten apples, his first wife Peggy Ashworth. Dad met Peggy when he was a kid of seventeen. She was eighteen, beautiful and blessed with a head of fiery red hair. Her parents didn't approve of the relationship – because they knew the sort of person Dad was – so they eloped. However, on their wedding night Dad could not help himself and sneaked off to a local pub to have sex with a prostitute. He chose one particular whore because he knew his father favoured her above the others.

While Peggy was said to have adored Dad, her parents

convinced her to have the marriage annulled when he did another stint in prison. 'Peggy was a lovely girl. She didn't use bad language. She didn't drink. She didn't smoke. She was the closest thing to perfect and much too good for me. It was lucky for that girl her mother had that marriage dissolved, annulled.'

The next woman in Dad's life was Doreen McCarthy. They met at a dance hall when he was on leave from the army and she was only fourteen. As it turned out they had a mutual friend named McMahon and, after talking for a few hours, 'We went to her house and because her grandmother had locked her out we stayed at a friend's house. I slept with her.'

Dad lovingly described Doreen as a villain who even helped him escape from the army watch-house when he was detained for being AWOL. 'When I'd go and rob trains of packages and silk in the goods yards Doreen would stand watch for me and help me spend the money. It was exciting. If I needed to steal a car she'd help.'

However, Dad also used Doreen to satisfy his perverted pleasures. In the final years of Dad's life, he would tell people how he and Doreen used to scour the cafes and bars of London's West End district to find a third partner – male or female, it didn't matter – to join them in the cot. Doreen bore Dad his first known son, Arnold, but when the responsibilities of providing a roof over their heads became too much of a constraint, Dad did the bolt. Though I should mention Doreen didn't stick parenthood out all that much longer because Dad said that not long after he took off she passed Arnold onto a kindly West Indian couple to raise!

I think poor Doreen never stopped loving Dad even after he left her stranded with a baby. As I've already mentioned she was down at the wharves to farewell us on our way to Australia by pressing a crinkled pound note into each of our hands. However, after he learned she'd committed suicide Dad lamented the fact Doreen had always battled a terrible addiction to cigarettes and alcohol.

Dad's third partner, Joan, was seventeen, just half his age, when they met. Despite her tender years, Dad said she was definitely 'trouble' and that thrilled him. Joan worked as a prostitute in North London and their de facto relationship ended on a tube station platform after she shacked up with a client for three days. Dad was frantic because he feared she had been murdered by a creep. However, after he tracked her down to a house on the other side of the city, the old man realised he was being taken for an idiot so he followed her to the tube station and lost his temper when she smirked at him. Dad punched Joan to the ground and waited for a train to come along so he could throw her in front of it. Thankfully the train was delayed and, because a crowd had gathered, Dad left Joan spread-eagled and bleeding on the platform.

The police arrested him a few weeks later and charged him with grievous bodily harm. He was placed in the notorious Brixton prison for a week and rubbed shoulders with some mean hombres as he waited to be tried. While the case was eventually dismissed because Joan couldn't recall anything of the incident, Dad said it was one sentence he would have been happy to have served because the 'bitch deserved a good thrashing'.

My mother Gloria, wife number three, was only eighteen when she met Dad in a rundown cafe in Harrogate. He was bowled over by the attractive, blonde teenager and he did his best to charm her. I can understand that a lot of people – women especially – would wonder what young girls saw in Dad, especially in light of his character. However, photos of my father as a younger man show a good-looking bloke; added to which was the fact Dad not only had a certain charisma but he was also blessed with plenty of front.

He impressed some of Britain's top movie directors and gained bit-part roles in such British movies as *Shadows of Fear*, *The Hijackers* and in the television series *The Saint* with Roger Moore. While Dad met numerous stars, including Elizabeth Taylor and Richard Burton, he claimed the highlight of his acting career was being asked to audition for the James Bond movie *Goldfinger*.

Despite believing he had loads of ability Dad said he dropped out of the film industry because the majority of people he rubbed shoulders with in studios and out on location were 'plastic' and he couldn't tolerate their nature. If I try hard enough I can picture Dad using that line as an ice-breaker whenever he met a young and impressionable woman, like my mother.

Apparently Mum and Dad had a 'rip-roaring affair' before they settled down. But while she bore him four children Dad could never forgive Mum for leaving him after enduring years of abuse. He did his utmost to make us feel ashamed of her as we grew up by saying terrible things. For instance, he would skite about the times they attended nudist camps in southern England to participate in wife-swapping parties.

In keeping with his preference for younger women his fourth wife, Christine Hicks, was twenty-four years Dad's junior when they first met. According to Dad, Christine had a bad reputation around the neighbourhood in Finsbury Park because she was supposed to be having affairs with the fathers of the children she babysat. (I don't know if that claim is true either.)

When she supposedly told Dad about her 'little secrets' during their driving lessons it drove him crazy with lust. He *had* to have her and she eventually migrated to Australia with us as Dad's wife and our step-mother.

While none of Dad's relationships lasted the distance, he took great comfort in the fact *he* showed *them* the door. 'I think it is important none of them divorced me – I divorced them!'

Dad hated them. He hated *all* women. He even hated his first child with Gloria because she was born a girl. He would often tell Tracey how he seriously considered dropping her on the concrete floor as they walked out of the maternity hospital because he was so disgusted at being 'burdened' with a female.

My father's advice about women has always stuck by me. He said if ever you get a good woman, shoot her before she turns bad so she'll have died a good woman ... I have found women to be the downfall of good men.

This geezer who lived near me in England, well, he and his wife didn't want children but she didn't want the operation. She said she was scared, so the bloke went under the blade and she thanked him by sleeping with other men. He caught her and killed her and you know what? The court cleared him because of the circumstances. Take it from me women are a bad invention.

You know what I really hate? It's when a woman goes out to make herself out to be a saint and me a big, bad wolf. How many women in the world today goad men on and then scream 'rape'? Even in the workplace they dress in such a way to attract a man by showing their bosoms and backsides and then when a man approaches them they scream 'sexual harassment'.

We weren't the only kids to suffer as a result of the Waters' family 'madness'. Two of our cousins – Cicero and Fidel – who were raised in northern England, near the famous Rugby League town of Wigan, didn't escape the violence we were subjected to. For example, one time when they were sorting out a difference of opinion with their fists in their backyard my aunt – Dad's sister, Sylvia – threw a claw hammer at their feet and screamed: 'Hit him, kill him, kill him!'.

She wasn't playing favourites, my mad aunt just wanted to see blood – and plenty of it! And the old battle-axe wasn't disappointed because one week later Fidel woke from a coma to find a Catholic priest administering his last rites.

This violent streak in our family hasn't just been a sickness, you know. It has been a terrible curse.

TOUGH LOVE

Chapter Three

'Children will do your bidding if you show them how to. Your children will depend on you to teach them how to do everything and you can show them and get them to do what you want them to do . . .'

Ces Waters on the joys of fatherhood

One of the best memories I have from my childhood is the time Dad drove us across the Nullarbor Plain from Perth to Sydney in the old motorised Bedford caravan we brought over from England. It was the most wonderful adventure for a kid who'd only ever known a concrete jungle like North London.

It was also a heart-in-the-mouth trip because the van was an old banger which threatened to fall apart every time we drove over a bump on the tar track which passed for a road. Actually, it's still a great mystery to me how we crossed the vast Australian continent without any major mechanical problems especially when the van had broken down just ten minutes into our trip from Fremantle!

After spending six weeks at sea, our welcome to Australia was a mixed one. Not long after we disembarked from the ship a drunken Aboriginal woman punched Christine flush on the jaw for reasons I can't really remember. Though I do vividly recall how the screaming black woman scared the wits out of me. I wondered what kind of godforsaken place Dad had brought us to.

That incident aside, I loved the wide open spaces of our new country and I can still recall the thrill I felt one evening during the three-thousand kilometre trek, when the sun had just started to sink behind us and I saw a kangaroo hop across the road. The creature looked so proud and majestic I shouted at everyone to take a look and they were just as impressed by it. Of all my childhood memories the image of that kangaroo silhouetted against the sun has stayed with me as if it had only just happened.

As I have already said there is Gipsy blood coursing through our veins and for the first couple of months after our arrival down under we lived like our forefathers who'd travelled from town to town in horse-drawn caravans. Towns with funny names like Boulder, Kalgoorlie and Mildura became our temporary homes as Dad looked for work to keep us going.

I can only guess our nomadic way of life sparked something which was buried deep within the old man because he'd take time out along the way to teach us a few phrases in Romany, the universal Gipsy language. He learned them from his mother when he was a little boy and wanted to share them with us.

While I didn't get all that good a grip on the weird lingo, Troy picked it up and reverts to it whenever he wants to tell me a secret. For instance, if a pretty girl walks past with her male friend Troy might hit me on the arm and say,

'Deek the reckler with the moosh, chavvy!'.

It isn't as rude as it sounds because once translated it simply means, 'Look at the girl with the man, boy'.

While Dad entertained us along the way by playing the ukulele, singing songs and telling some great stories it was a bloody tough existence. There were many times when we didn't know where our next meal would come from. Sometimes we'd be enrolled in schools throughout the outback so the teachers could babysit us while Dad and Christine tried to find work – or hatch scams to obtain money.

We were the only children I can remember who never took a packed lunch to school and when the dinner bell went at noon Troy, Tracey, Guy and I would stand at the front gate in the hope Dad had made enough money to buy us lunch. As Troy told the journalist Steve Crawley on the eve of his 1989 world title bout against Italy's Gianfranco Rosi, there was no better sight than the old man running up the track with a couple of brown paper bags in his hands. Needless to say, we went hungry when he didn't.

While Dad was always an advocate for fitness, he didn't enjoy physical labour and that trait did little to endear him with the people who employed him as we crawled towards the eastern seaboard.

Apart from being bone lazy and always looking for shortcuts, Dad had no qualms whatsoever about stealing from his employers. It didn't matter how badly they themselves might have been travelling, Dad would often rip them off before he even did a minute's work. I can only suppose Dad thought Australians were too trusting a race and needed a few lessons in life courtesy of a graduate of

Manchester's school of hard knocks and setbacks!

Dad would play on the sympathy and sense of decency of tough goldminers and old Greek cafe-owners that he had a family to feed and he needed work, any work, to put food on the table. Back in the early 1970s there was a great demand for manpower of any kind in the outback, so they would not only take Dad on board with open arms but some even advanced him a few dollars to help tide him over. The old man reckoned it was the easiest money he ever earned because soon after he pocketed an advance we'd pack the camper up and continue on our way towards Sydney.

These days I feel bad that my father abused the trust of so many people. I can vaguely remember one bloke, an old goldminer, who lived a hermit-like life outside Kalgoorlie. If I remember the details correctly, this bloke was happy just to pay someone to do a few chores and to hang around for company, yet Dad had no scruples about ripping him off. Indeed, he'd justify his actions in later years by saying the first Aussies he came across, the frontiersmen, were crude alcoholics who swore too much for his liking, as if their gruff manner meant they weren't entitled to any common decency.

Our training for Dad's future glories didn't stop during the trek. Every couple of hours, Dad would stop the van and tell us to stretch our legs by running towards Sydney. Despite the heat it wasn't too bad, and I can still remember shaking what seemed to be tonnes of red desert sand out of my shoes before climbing back into the van.

Dad seemed to be quite happy with our change in life, but he still went into the manic rages which frightened us all when we lived in Finsbury Park. I've never worked out why Dad got so angry that he had to attack us. There were times when he would just snap and would make us pay by beating us with a piece of rubber hose. We grew to hate that frigging hose pipe and Dad would sometimes brag to journalists that it was his magic wand! 'I only have to pick it up and they do what they're told.' In their ignorance, the journalists would laugh, thinking it was all a great joke. Well, it wasn't.

It was easy to tell when Dad was about to lose his temper. He would strut backwards and forwards like a peacock, with his veins popping out of his neck, his eyes bulging and face turning purple. And then everything would explode like fireworks and he would flay into us. He didn't know when to stop.

Sometimes we'd be so badly beaten we could not walk properly for days at a time; however, we quickly learnt to stem our flow of tears because if he caught us 'blubbering like babies' Dad accused us of trying to make him feel bad and he'd launch into another attack.

Tracey copped it worst of all. It wasn't her fault. Dad said he could see a lot of our mother Gloria in her and he made her pay for her genes. She was whacked for trivial things with everything from the hose pipe to his clenched fists to heavy wooden tomato stakes. Poor Tracey would sometimes end up with such bad bumps on her head it would be impossible for her to brush her hair properly.

Guy, Troy and I didn't know how to stop Dad and his violence. We were all programmed to accept it as part of the day, like eating breakfast or having a shower. We were all bashed; there wasn't a day that went by during our life with Dad in which someone wasn't abused.

I think Tracey was the first to cop it not long after the SS *Australis* docked at Fremantle. She failed to perform to Dad's expectations in a crappy junior athletics carnival and he was furious. She finished second in her race and when we returned to the caravan park he locked us in the old Bedford, then dragged Tracey by her hair into the car and drove back to the running track. He not only beat her with the hose pipe, but also subjected her to hours of torture by trailing her in the car as she ran around the course. When it grew dark, Dad would stop at different points along the track and beat Tracey to help 'keep her mind on the job'. She was bashed whenever she slowed down.

As she grew older, Dad noticed men would look at her in a certain way and he would punish her for it, saying she was leading them on by standing in provocative positions. I didn't think she was doing anything to attract the men's attention but as he battered her Dad would scream at the top of his voice: 'You're a *trollop* just like your *mother*. You'll *never* amount to *anything*. *Don't* have kids, Tracey, because you'll *abandon* them like your *mother* did us.'

As kids we were smart enough to realise when it came to beatings it was a case of every man – or woman – for themselves. We turned a blind eye to the other person's suffering and made sure we didn't get beaten up as well. I've heard a similar mentality existed in Japanese prisoner of war camps because the prisoners' basic survival instincts outweighed any rage they may have felt on behalf of others.

I copped it – and badly – soon after Tracey's hiding when a boy in the caravan park at Kalgoorlie cheated against me in a game of marbles. The incident didn't worry me in the slightest but Dad said the fact I didn't stand up to the boy was a sign of cowardice. He beat me for that 'crime' over a period of days and in between blows he screamed such things as, 'You're yellow. You don't have a man's blood in your veins!' Whack, Whack, Whack.

*

The old man needed just one brief look at bustling Sydney to say it reminded him too much of what he had left behind in England to want to stay there. We hit the road again, this time to a place called Terrey Hills in Sydney's beautiful northern beach suburbs. Dad had heard there was a nudist camp there and decided it was as good a place as any for us to drop anchor.

Our first home was a rat-infested hovel not too far from the camp and my memories of that joint aren't very pleasant. I was much happier when we moved to an acreage at nearby North Narrabeen.

However, it was there Dad started some weird practices. For instance none of us – Christine included – were ever allowed to use the toilet. Instead, we had to relieve ourselves in a small bucket he placed in the middle of the lounge-room. I have no idea why Dad did this; perhaps it satisfied some sexual bent or it was a domination thing, but he watched as we urinated into the bucket. If I wanted to pass water he would hold my penis.

I didn't like it, but I accepted it as a part of every-day life. However, it was still humiliating and I couldn't understand why we were not allowed to go into the bathroom and lock the door like Dad. At night when I lay in bed, I'd shut my eyes and pretend to be asleep when Christine and Tracey squatted over the bucket because I knew it must have been embarrassing for them to urinate like that.

In later years, a team of psychiatrists told me the toilet trick was Dad's way of exerting power over his family by degrading and humiliating us.

Once we reached puberty Dad would make us trim our pubic hair with scissors or even shave under our arms with a razor before we went to the nudist camp. I didn't think much of it at the time but in later years when I heard paedophiles do not like to see hair on kids it made me want to vomit.

I hated going to the nudist camps because I was at an awkward age. First I had hair growing in strange places and secondly I had started to have 'funny' feelings about girls. But as much as I loathed going I never baulked at another trip to the camp because enforced nudity was a lot less painful than being flogged with the hose pipe for rebelling.

I lived in constant fear of getting bashed by Dad and one of my greatest regrets as a big brother to Guy was the day I broke the wheel off a cheap toy car Dad had bought me. He demanded to know how it broke and I could tell he was ready to erupt because all the danger signs were there – the popping veins and the bulging eyes. In my panic I blamed Guy and I cried my eyes out as he was belted because our unwritten law had always been not to allow anyone to take another person's punishment. Poor Guy said over and over that he didn't break the toy but each denial resulted in yet another barrage of blows. When I finally admitted it was me, not Guy, Dad battered me and then dragged us to the kitchen table where he slammed down two glasses of water. He told us each to pick a glass and warned us that whoever was lying would die as soon as they sipped it because the water had a deadly poison which was activated by lies.

Dad did other things which have since made me wonder about his thoughts towards kids. For instance, he took Tracey down to Kings Cross on a couple of occasions when she was just twelve years old and forced her to pose naked with an older woman in sordid photo sessions. Troy, Guy and I would be made to sit behind a screen so we couldn't see what was happening but I can recall Tracey's face would be bright red and tears would build in the corner of her eyes when we left for home. None of us know what has happened to those full-frontal photos, but I pray to God they were destroyed years ago.

For quite a few years Dad would take in handicapped kids for what he called 'adventure weekends' on our properties at North Narrabeen and then at Kulnura. The kids would ride horses and play with the animals. Dad's motives seemed honourable enough to even the most wary parent – he would tell them how lonely it had been when he had to wear callipers as a boy. He said it was dreadful to have no-one take an interest in him and he didn't want other kids to feel neglected.

The parents initially thought Dad was great, however, one by one they refused to allow their children to stay with us anymore and their hostility towards us surprised me. I thought they were being terribly unfair until I learned, many years later, the reason why the mothers and fathers of those kids called my Dad terrible names was because he had molested the children in our spare bedroom. Rather than view them as unfortunate, my father saw handicapped children as easy targets.

Needless to say, I hated school. I not only had an unnatural fear of the other children but I also had a deep terror of not being near my father so he could protect me. There was another loner in my class named Steven Dawes and together we would hide from the other kids at lunchtime in empty classrooms, or behind the school buildings if the teachers ordered us back out into the playground. Even though I was much bigger and stronger than the other kids I was also afraid of them. If I wanted to I could have bullied them – especially the one who made fun of Dad by calling him Cecil the Sausage – but Dad had me so scared of the world I cringed whenever anyone spoke to me.

Not everyone was an enemy and I befriended one of my school teachers, a former Rugby League and Rugby Union star named Stephen Knight. He took an interest in me when I was only thirteen and heaved one hundred and sixty pounds worth of metal above my head in the school gym. While it felt as if the strain had ripped my guts from out of me, Mr Knight made me feel good when he said the lift was a great feat. But I remember the terror I felt one morning when I did something wrong and I was ordered to go to a classroom and wait until Mr Knight worked out my punishment. The only disciplinary measures I was familiar with were Dad's brand and I had no intentions of copping the hose pipe at school.

I sprinted for my life but Mr Knight, a former Australian representative, caught up with me in no time at all. He asked why I was so scared but I couldn't tell him; I just burst into tears. I guess he sensed I was a troubled kid because he told me everything would be all right and not to worry.

In retrospect I'm certain our teachers knew something was very wrong because we turned up to school with only one exercise book, our clothes were never ironed and, compared with the other kids, we were a withdrawn and shy mob. But unlike now where everyone is watched very closely when it comes to a child's welfare, the general rule back in the 1970s regarding children with family problems seemed to be for the teachers to turn a blind eye to them.

All the teachers had to do was make sure their pupils could read and write. Our report cards were shocking, but Dad didn't seem too worried about them. All he insisted on was for us to behave, to excel at sport and to keep an arm's length from trouble. He obviously realised we would cast an unwelcome spotlight on him if we were regulars outside the principal's office or placed on detention so we kept our noses clean.

I can clearly remember how I went into a terrible spin the day a teacher wrote on my report card that I had disrupted her class throughout the term. She may as well have handed Dad the strap to belt me! In my mad panic I ripped my report card up and threw the tiny pieces of paper down the back drain – it still amazes me that Dad never asked to see it.

Nevertheless, I was more terrified of having to go to school than I was of my father and I'm certain that is exactly the frame of mind he wanted us to be in. Dad wanted mind control over all of us, which he proved by not only driving us to and from school every day but also refusing to allow any of us to go on school excursions. When we asked why we had to stay at school while our friends went to places like Newcastle and Sydney as part of the education process, Dad just shook his head and told us of the dangers the teachers could expose us to.

'What would happen if the bus crashed, rolled and exploded into flames, Dean? Who would save you? I wouldn't be able to. And it happens, son, school buses always crash. Do you want to die in a bus crash? No? Then do as you're told and stop being stupid.'

So I went to school terrified that the world was a dangerous place and, as a result, I was a wreck of a kid. When Dad finally dragged me from the classroom to work on our new farm on Mangrove Mountain north of Sydney after I completed Year Eight I felt an enormous sense of relief and gratitude towards him because I figured he had rescued me. It felt like the time when I was a kid seeking refuge in my dad's bed whenever a dream demon scared me.

CES'S KINGDOM OF THE DAMNED

Chapter Four

'The lads stay on the property almost all the time ... they spend six days a week training hard and haven't even got time for girlfriends ...'

Ces Waters on the most successful crops he grew at Kulnura

On one of the windows at our Ma and Pa Kettle-like farm in beautiful Kulnura was a sticker which said: 'Welcome to the funny farm'. Believe me, it wasn't a joke, it was a dead-set warning.

The place, which Dad secured with $10,000 stolen from the safe of a Sydney gardening centre, was a nut house. The farm was Dad's escape from reality because it was one place where he didn't have to answer to anyone, and an environment where his word was law. We had a couple of neighbours, but they also lived in fear of the old man and he thrived on knowing they were frightened of him.

At one stage we had forty-five broken-down horses, two hundred and seventy-four stray dogs, a mob of twenty-seven lost and mangy cats and dozens of chickens acquired from some nearby battery egg farms, all living on the farm and their collective noise jabbed the stillness of some of Australia's most serene countryside. Our neighbours didn't appreciate Dad's idea of a farm and whenever they gathered at our gate to complain about the stench and the incessant noise of the animals Dad screamed at them like a man possessed: 'Ahhhhhhhhhhhhhhhh! Ahhhhhhhhhhhhh! Ahhhhhhhhhhhh!'.

The neighbours, who were basically decent people, didn't know how to handle his rage because it wasn't the behaviour of a normal person. They would walk away red-faced and shaken.

On one occasion – and I will never forget it because it highlighted the level of contempt Dad held for the law – a sheriff arrived at the farm to issue a summons for some minor offence, maybe an unpaid parking fine. I stopped working on a broken piece of machinery as I saw the sheriff open the gate and waddle down towards the old house – he was a fat, balding bloke who was sweating profusely in the heat. The sheriff looked as if he'd have preferred to have been in the local pub, and by the time he'd finished with Ces Waters that day the poor bugger deserved a few beers!

When Dad saw the summons he was about to be presented he lost it. He charged up the slight hill which led to the road screaming, shouting and cursing. The big bloke could sense the impending danger and he wisely dropped the envelope, turned tail and ran for his life. I couldn't help but admire how fast he moved for a big heap – he literally rolled over the closed gate and hit the ground running. And snapping at his heels like a little terrier was the old man, who threatened to do all sorts of terrible things to this officer of the court if he dared to ever return!

Adding extra pepper to the sheriff's final humiliation was the sight of Dad throwing rocks at his retreating back and screaming 'giitttt outta here, you!' as if he was yelling at a pesky dog. Dad didn't even bother to look at the summons which had been dropped on the ground – I watched him rip the paper up and throw it into the bin. Like I said, on our ten hectares of land at Kulnura, Ces Waters' word was law.

We moved onto the farm three years after arriving in Australia with those seven bucks in our kitty, and I'm sure his signing the contract to buy the property was one of the crowning moments in Dad's life. He was a landowner, and if you listened to him crow about it you'd have sworn he had joined the English gentry.

The property he went into $39,000 debt for was very rough and ready. When we first moved in it was covered in blackberry bushes while the grey, concrete-block house was another rat-infested hovel. An old Italian bloke had it on the market for eighteen months because most people who saw it bolted.

But not Dad. Unlike the other parties, he saw the sweeping views of the mountains and he was also sold on the idea there were springs of mineral water bubbling under the ground. Last, but not least, he loved the sense of freedom the place offered.

Dad was later to call the farm his slice of heaven but he certainly didn't tell too many people how he made the money to buy the property in the first place. Dad liked to tell people he saved the $10,000 deposit – which was a substantial amount then – by buying and selling old cars and through borrowing cash from friends. The truth is he obtained the money by breaking into the safe at the plant nursery where Christine worked in Warringah, near the Sydney beachside suburb of Manly. 'The old Manchester lessons sometimes come in handy, son!'

It took plenty of gut-busting work to clear the land of the blackberry bushes which seemed to cover every bloody inch of it. And the old man didn't use farm machinery to help make our job any easier, either. Instead, he had all of us – Christine, Tracey, Guy, Troy and me – swinging mattocks from the crack of dawn until sunset to clear the land. It was back-breaking labour which suited Dad's fanatical way of doing things. I'm certain that our clearing the land until we had blisters form on our hands was another of Dad's ways of getting the 'bad' out of us.

Dad liked to run the farm as if we were slaves in the days of the Roman Empire. When we weren't training to fight in our rough and ready home-made gym we tended our farm duties, which could include anything from grooming the horses to clearing trees for fences or repairing broken-down and rusting pieces of machinery.

I'm certain Guy and Troy would agree with me when I say getting the timber from the deep forests in the Yarramalong Valley where the hill-billies and ferals lived was the biggest bastard of a job. Dad would drive us into the Ourimbah State forest and after he selected a tree he thought would be good for a fence post he'd order us out of the truck and we'd set about chopping it down with an axe if the chainsaw was broken. Once that task was completed he'd give us chains to strap to our bodies and we would sometimes drag the log sixty metres up a hill. It was as primitive as it was painful.

And it wasn't just a case of chopping down a tall tree alongside the road; sometimes, the old man would see a tree in the gully and we'd have to climb down the embankment, chop it down, connect the chains from the log to our torsos and then strain as we dragged what could easily be a four metre long log up the slope.

As Dad barked out orders to 'heave!' we boys could feel every muscle in our bodies strain – and then give – as we defied gravity. While Dad would sometimes lend a hand to drag the logs, we did this until the day he realised we could use our new tractor to drag the wood! I still can't believe how things worked back then.

I especially can't comprehend why Dad let the animals take over the house. Dad thought it was acceptable for hundreds of cats and dogs to stay in the house, to eat in it, piss in it, shit in it and vomit in it. And because Dad allowed it to happen we thought it was acceptable until we grew older and resented their mess and stench.

What also grated with me was that while Dad thought nothing of bashing us until welts formed on our bodies, he would lovingly pat the dogs on the head and say they were his 'children' and that he loved them with all his heart.

Just like in ancient Egypt, where cats were revered as gods, Dad's 'children' would be waited on by Christine and us kids. All of us took a backseat to Dad's adoration for a pack of half-starved mongrels and that thought hurts me a lot now.

As a teenager I could live with most of the things Dad subjected us to, but not the animals in the house. Sometimes when I trod in a puddle of cat piss or sloppy dog shit I'd explode in silent fits of rage. I didn't dare to scream at Dad because I knew the retribution, a beating, would be severe. Nevertheless, I would beg Dad to keep the animals out of the house – I told him they made me feel sick – and sometimes I would think I was getting through to him because he'd shepherd them outside into the paddocks. However, a couple of hours later when the sun sank over the mountains the dogs would be back indoors and I'd be reduced to tears because I knew I couldn't win this battle with Dad.

Like us, the animals were vegetarians. Their main diet was powdered milk and old, mouldy bread Dad bought in bulk – he'd buy up to four hundred loaves a week from a bakery in Wyong and it formed the staple diet for both dogs and us. The mixture of powdered milk and bread would play havoc with the animals' digestive systems and they'd leave pizza-sized puddles of gooey crap throughout the house and it stank.

Dad's way of combating this problem was to leave a shovel in the kitchen for us to scrape it up. And when the worm-riddled hounds would try and relieve their itch by rubbing their dirty backsides up and down on the fridge, stove, walls and doors, Christine would have to scour the brown stains away with a sponge and steel wool. We then had to wash the house out with sheep dip, and that stank too. It went from smelling like Old McDonald's frigging farm to a chemical factory.

It became even worse when we developed a media profile and the public learned of Dad's love for animals because people would dump their unwanted animals on our doorstep instead of taking them to the local pound. It all became too much but my protests fell on deaf ears. It seemed that God had told Dad it was his job to protect the dumb and helpless creatures of the world.

Troy echoed Dad's sentiments on that subject in an interview just before he fought Gianfranco Rosi for the world title in 1989. The journalist asked Troy about our obsession with animals and Troy's answer showed how brainwashed we were. It could have been Ces himself speaking when Troy replied, 'People call them dumb, but animals were here before we were. If we can't save the world, we can save the animals, maybe half of one percent.'

That 'divine' duty with which Dad said we were entrusted extended to an animal's death. If Dad passed a dead animal on the road he'd pull up and make us drag it into the bush. It didn't matter if the animal was freshly killed or a fly-blown carcass which had started to decompose, we had to remove it. If the animal's body had been ground into the road by car tyres, we had to get on our hands and knees and peel the pelt and bones out of the bitumen with our fingers. Sometimes the stench would be so over-powering we would dry-retch. But we did what Dad said had to be done.

I had my own dog, a purebred blue cattle dog named Toby I bought for a dollar. He was a great mate and a crazy bugger with it. He had the most amazing jaw muscles and I would laugh myself silly when Toby would entertain himself by swinging from a horse's tail for hours at a time. We were inseparable.

However, I taught him not to bite the hand of the human who fed him the day he latched onto me after I tried to take a bone from him. Toby sank his fangs deep into me and not only did it hurt like high hell, but he wouldn't let go. When I eventually wrestled the mutt free, I grabbed him and bit down on his snout. He yelped like nothing on earth but it certainly taught him a good lesson about respect.

I did not know much about the world outside Kulnura because Dad would not allow us to go into Gosford or Sydney unattended. He took us everywhere to protect us from what he called the 'poisoned fruits of society'. He warned us against drugs, alcohol, cigarettes, criminals, villains and immoral women and how they could be the undoing of clean-cut boys such as us. He said we would be easy prey and that we needed him to protect us.

I did not mind being confined to the farm because Dad had taught me about mechanics and I loved to tinker around with things like the tractor and our water pump, which had actually been an old Holden engine. It was Dad's invention and as simple as it was ingenious. We towed the Holden into place soon after we moved onto the farm and I jacked the back wheels of the car up and removed them. Under Dad's guidance I connected a belt from the pump onto the rim of a wheel, which meant whenever we wanted water someone simply had to start the car to make the rear wheel spin around!

However, these sorts of invention helped to give the farm a rundown look. Visiting journalists often referred to our farm as something out of a Ma and Pa Kettle movie because the place was littered with broken-down vehicles, an old caravan, a red telephone box, a boxing ring, bits and pieces of old machinery and a house prime for demolition. When I look back on the farm, I realise it was a pigsty which would look more at home in the Third World.

If ever I feel as though I am beginning to forget what the farm looked like, I only need to refer to this passage from an article written by Tony Maiden which was published in *Time* magazine in 1989.

A visitor must drag open a sagging steel gate with a red NO TRESPASSING sign, and bounce down a rutted track past a rusty abandoned bus, a demounted truck tray laden with junk, a disused trailer, an abandoned slasher, a battered caravan and a flaking red telephone box with waist-high weeds growing inside. Spreading out from a dusty main yard in no discernible pattern is an array of sheds, fences and pens.

A baying group of dogs, more than two dozen of them, mill menacingly around the yard. The dogs, mostly strays taken in by the family, are fed on biscuits and vegetables. Across the yard in the lee of a straggly row of pines, squats the Waters homestead. It is a wide, almost windowless bunker of concrete blocks and corrugated iron. One end is an open carport daubed with spray can graffiti, TNT IS DEAN, and filled with a clutter of old tyres and broken, oily machinery. In a final insane touch, the front verandah from which hang two heavy punching bags is supported by elegant doric columns. Inside, a small living room dominated by a vast trophy cabinet is clean and snug, though the smell of dogs pervades the property.

Around the side of the house and down a cluttered slope, an open iron-roofed boxing ring sits in a grassy field. It commands a magnificent view south-east down the smokey green blue folds of the Moonie Moonie valley . . .

The country air did nothing at all to soothe Dad's temper. If anything the isolation of our Springs Road property at Kulnura helped drag him inch by inch over the edge. The abuse continued on a daily basis, and because most of what Dad did was not seen by anybody else he sank further into madness.

For instance, when I was about sixteen and Guy and I were in trouble for something trivial, we had literally to run for our lives when the old man grabbed his .22 rifle and fired at us from the verandah! We fled to the safety of a neighbour's property and took refuge in a stormwater drain positioned under the road. That hole was our regular hiding spot and we stayed there until Troy came along a few hours later and said everything was okay, that the gun had been put away and Dad had calmed down.

Another time when I ran from Dad I heard Guy scream: 'Duck!'. I took his tip as a bloody tomahawk flashed past – in his rage the old goat had tried to kill me!

The best way to stay safe was to avoid eye contact with Dad and to throw ourselves into our chores. However, that didn't help our constant feelings of uncertainty – we never knew just what would trigger an explosion.

THE DEVIL WITHIN

Chapter Five

'You've got to prove to yourself you're a man; you have courage; you have guts and every time you step in that ring you have to prove you're made of the right stuff and the right mettle ...'

***Dean Waters on* Sixty Minutes**

One of my greatest faults has been that I have never been able to back away from a challenge. It did not matter how stupid the dare might have been I *had* to do it. Dad named me after the Hollywood idol James Dean and apart from his name I sometimes think I also inherited Jimmy's self-destructive streak.

While he never said it directly to me, Dad long feared I had suffered some sort of brain damage when, as kid of four, I held my breath until I turned blue in the face, collapsed and stopped breathing. He rushed me to a neighbour, a nurse, who revived me after I had not breathed for, according to Dad, a few minutes. The doctors at a nearby hospital apparently cleared me of any serious side-effects but in later years, when I spoke about Christianity and the guilt I felt about Allan Hall's murder, Dad told some people he wondered whether my 'madness' was a result of my brain being starved of oxygen when I was a child.

I did have problems – serious head problems – as a kid and one of them was the fact I felt as if I constantly had to prove myself to be a man. There were a number of times when proving myself has almost been the end of me and one of the craziest incidents occurred when I was a teenager with an infatuation for the sensation of speed and the power of guns.

I bought a 1979 Elasanor Chrome Boar motorcycle from a local boy named Mark Skaife who went on to find fame, and I guess fortune, as an ace motor car racing driver. Another 'suicide' machine in my garage was an old EJ Holden paddock-basher Dad allowed me to hoon around the farm in. I stripped the mudguard from it, whacked on a mean set of mag wheels, removed the bumper bars and gave it plenty of grunt as I tore around our ten hectares at a breakneck speed.

I didn't have a care in the world when I hit the one hundred and twenty kilometre an hour mark, but Dad was a different kettle of fish. He'd see me doing my stunts and would run down waving his arms around like a windmill as he sent me to my room for an hour or so to cool off. 'Get in there before you kill yourself, Dean!'

As for guns I was in love with the noise, the explosion, and their power. I once purchased an SKK semi-automatic weapon and when I didn't think it was a powerful enough I worked on the trigger mechanism and transformed it into a fully automatic job. When I finished my 'tinkering' – at about 2 am – I went deep into the Ourimbah State Forest and blasted some ancient, tall trees until the barrel started to smoke. All around me it rained thick, heavy, leafy branches, like the scene out of the Arnold Schwarzenegger movie *Predator* when Arnie's character fights an alien in the South American jungle. Anyway, as the ratta-ta-tatt of my weapon resounded around the valley like rolling thunder I got a mighty buzz out of thinking that the poor old farmers who lived up the way must have thought a war was being fought in their back paddock!

My English cousin from Wigan, Fidel, filmed me in action during his visit to Australia and the sight of me dressed in black, wearing a balaclava and going ballistic spooked him so much he dropped the video camera and ran screaming, 'You're mad, Dean – you shoot American presidents with a fucking gun like that!'. I laughed at his horror.

While my collection of guns symbolised a form of power I did not have around my father, the motorcycle gave me the sense of freedom I craved. When I first bought the machine I rode it so fast and so hard I suffered internal bleeding, but I didn't care because of the sensation of sheer speed. I'd dress in my leathers and pads, whack on my crash helmet and go full throttle along the back paddock, screaming as I went. I would constantly tempt fate by flying at one hundred kilometres an hour in fifth gear and I'd get off on the adrenalin rush.

Now I'm older – and just a little bit wiser – I realise I could have broken my neck a million times over. But I did not think like that back then. The motorcycle was my only real escape from Dad's constant bashings and verbal abuse so I refused to allow fear to interfere.

In time, however, I wasn't content to simply ride my motorbike fast and hard. I complicated matters by challenging myself to jump one of the longest dams on our property like the famous American daredevil Evel Knievel! It was up to twenty metres long and five metres wide and it took me weeks to summon the courage needed to attempt the stunt. I tried plenty of times but at the last moment I'd pull up metres from the dirt ramp I'd constructed with the tractor. Every time I failed to deliver I cursed out loud at myself. I considered my apprehension a sure-fire sign of cowardice and it infuriated me because it seemed to confirm Dad's reckoning that I didn't have a man's blood flowing through my veins.

Eventually the jump became a direct challenge to my manhood and it burned at me until the day I thought 'stuff it!' and gritted my teeth. I baulked at my first attempt but, even though my heart was beating like a piston in an old steam engine, I gave it another burl. This time, with a wild scream of defiance – raaaaaahhhhhhhhhhhh – I let rip. I was still screaming insanely as the bike commenced its flight over the brown water and for a few seconds I soared like an eagle. I'd conquered a fear and felt invincible.

However, my exhilaration, my heroic triumph, turned into white-knuckled terror once I realised my motorcycle was going to fall short of clearing the dam properly. The front wheel hit the edge of the dam – the bloody dirt wall wasn't steep enough for me to jump from – and I flew headfirst over the handlebars milliseconds before my motorcycle cartwheeled end over end away from the water!

While the bike needed a few days' worth of minor repairs it survived the sudden impact much better than me. I finished in a crumpled heap and the source of my agony was my bloody testicles! They were swollen up like tennis balls and it felt as if they were stuck in my throat and choking me! The pain was so severe I just wanted to die, it hurt to breathe, my bones ached, it felt as if an imaginary sledge-hammer was cracking my skull with heavy blows and my balls throbbed madly.

I don't know how long I was on my back for – maybe an hour, perhaps two – but when I finally summoned the willpower needed to climb to my feet I staggered towards the house as if I was John Wayne after a three-day bareback horse ride! I was in complete agony and as I lay on my bed for a few more hours I wondered if Dad would put me to work in one of those freak shows I'd heard about if my balls failed to shrink back to their normal size.

Dad can take the credit for instilling a love for speed in me when I was fourteen. He used to buy dilapidated 'bangers' from the car auctions in Bourke Street, Sydney and would fix them on the property, before selling them for a small profit to help pay for the hundreds of animals we were supporting. He had bought and sold motor vehicles back in England and one of his great regrets was the fact Al Capone's car slipped through his fingers when his business partner, a shady dude named Tony, sold it while Dad was either doing a stint in prison or hiding out from the law.

The Capone car was one of Dad's favourite talking points and we kids heard the tale over and over again as we grew up. In time I have come to realise it represented yet another of what my father called 'life's wasted opportunities' because whenever we did it tough on the farm – and that was more often than not – he rued the fact the old car's place in America's criminal history would have been more than enough to alleviate our financial woes. 'It's in a car museum in Las Vegas now, Dean, and it's priceless!'

It was one of a litany of 'if only's' but I liked it when he would tell visitors of the neglected vehicle which had spent weeks on display at the Manchester car auctions. The green Cadillac caught his attention because some of the panels were riddled with bullet holes and the back window could be lowered to fire a machine gun. He studied the car for hours at a time and the day the vehicle went under the hammer he and Tony outbid the few other people who turned out. I'm sure Capone, the notorious Chicago gangster of the 1920s, would have appreciated the fact my old man and Tony obtained the cash they used to buy his motor by flogging off a truckload of hot goods fresh from a poorly guarded warehouse! As Dad and Tony took possession of the car's keys a newspaper journalist approached them and asked for their thoughts on owning Capone's car!

Dad never found out how or why the gangster's car finished up in Manchester but he said the local authorities must have had their reasons for keeping the car's identity a secret. Who knows? Perhaps it had something to do with the vehicle being reinforced with bullet-proof armour plates. Maybe they feared some local villains would use it for no good.

Although Tony sold the car for only a minor profit while the old man was 'missing in action', Dad realised there was cash to be made in the car caper and he turned his mind to trying to scam some money from it. All he needed was time to find an angle and he stumbled upon an idea after reading the 'Cars Wanted' section of the local newspaper.

When Dad saw that some models were in far greater demand than others, he approached a dealer to test drive one. Then, after parking the vehicle outside my grandmother's house, he rang the people who had advertised for such a car until one of them bought it. He'd then return to the caryard and pay the manager cash for the vehicle and scurry off. On a good day Dad could make a quick fifty quid profit! It was one of Dad's more honest rorts and the money he made from it helped him buy a fleet of his own used cars to sell.

A lifetime later on our farm in sunny Australia, Dad viewed old cars as a way to help get some money together and I would accompany him to Bourke Street where he would bid small amounts on broken-down Holdens, smashed-up Volkswagens and banged-up Mini Minors. The real fun arrived when Dad had to tow the car back to Mangrove Mountain because even though I was only fourteen he'd get me to 'drive' the car he tied to the back of his vehicle with a two-metre chain.

Sometimes when we were on the highway he'd hit one hundred and forty kilometres an hour to overtake the slow-moving vehicles loaded with families on their way to a Central Coast holiday. While it was twenty-odd years ago, I can still vividly recall the look of horror on people's faces when they realised the driver of the second car flying past them was a kid who should have still been at school! But Dad didn't think anything of it, he just viewed my helping to transport the cars home as earning my keep.

And sometimes I really did earn it because there were occasions when I thought I'd die. Like the day when I had to slam on the brakes on the Sydney Harbour Bridge after Dad came to a sudden stop. I could smell the smoke coming off my tyres as they locked and I waited an eternity for my car to slam into Dad's. Thankfully it didn't happen. My car pulled up inches from his bumper bar and I reckon Dad must have realised he would have needed to do a lot of explaining to the police about the reasons why he had a kid in control of the second vehicle. I say that because when we returned to the farm he ruffled my hair and said, 'You did real well back there, Dean!' My chest puffed out and I felt ten feet tall. I'd done well. Dad was happy and it felt as if that was all that ever really mattered.

*

As a kid anything mechanical, like the old cars, would occupy my mind for hours. While I was miles from being the world's best reader or writer, Dad taught me there was a special form of poetry in the way machines and engines worked. They fascinated me and there were times when I would worry Dad by spending hours at the workbench trying to figure out why a fuel pump didn't work properly or why the tractor wouldn't kick over. 'Leave it be, Dean, come in and have something to eat – come in NOW!'

He thought I was obsessive, and he was spot-on. I enjoyed working with the machinery a heck of a lot better than doing what Tracey and Christine had to do. They would wake at the crack of dawn and spend hours grooming and hosing down the horses in the stables.

Dad fancied himself as a horse-trainer. He philosophised the same principles applied to horses as they did humans and they responded well to him. He guided one stead, Stately Gauntlet, to a great win at Wyong where it failed to break the course record by a miserable hundredth of a second! I won't go so far as to suggest he was a horse whisperer but Dad knew how to get the best out of broken-down horses who were destined for the knackery!

With hindsight, I think Dad must have read *Black Beauty* once too often because, while the likes of TJ Smith and Bart Cummings had hundreds of thousands of dollars to build their Melbourne Cup dreams upon, Ces Waters honestly believed he could make his millions by buying broken-down hacks with bad feet. He'd travel to the old Homebush abattoirs in Sydney with a couple of hundred bucks in his pocket and look for his dream-maker among horses which were condemned to end up in tins of dog meat.

Dad acquired what can only be described as an 'interesting'

stable of horses with names such as Gauntlet's Boy and Fear No Evil. While he enjoyed some minor success with them, the outlay for feed, vitamins, veterinary charges and racing fees far exceeded what they won at the track.

Unfortunately Dad's dream of riding to riches on the back of his perennial 100-1 long shot Fear No Evil was ruined the day it collapsed and died at the track. The poor bastard collapsed in full stride and I remember thinking the jockey was lucky not to be crushed under its weight when it hit the deck. The vet's autopsy report suggested the stallion died of atrial fibrillation (a condition which does not allow the heart's valve to open and close properly).

As the course tractor cleared Fear No Evil's corpse without ceremony, a racetrack desperate asked whether Dad needed the bridle anymore! The man's audacity sent my father into a rage, but worse was to follow when he tried to locate the horse's remains the following morning and found it had been chainsawed into four pieces at the local abattoir.

It was tragic: despite being a worthy competitor on the racetrack Fear No Evil could not escape his destiny to become canine tucker and Dad chucked a right wobbly! His eyes almost popped out of his head when he was told the news over the phone and he screamed at the manager down the line. But, at the end of the day, he realised his protests were as useful as the wind out of a monkey's arse so he slammed the receiver down and cursed the butchers.

To be honest, Dad's horse-racing aspirations were a pain in the butt for me, mainly because I had to accompany Dad and Christine as they drove all the way to Cessnock so the horses could do their trackwork. Don't get me wrong – I loved the horses and would have done anything to look after them, but I also liked to sleep in.

I loathed the trip to Cessnock. It was a one hundred and forty-kilometre, ball-breaking drive over a bumpy, winding dirt track and Dad, Christine, Guy, the horses and I felt every ruddy jolt as we lurched along. The trip on the old Wollombi Road certainly took its toll on our truck because, after two years of doing the kind of trip which would have even tested a Panzer Tank's durability, the chassis gave way.

It was frustrating to think that the Wyong track was much closer but that, because of a two-year waiting list, I was condemned to those early morning drives. Until one day Dad struck a 'gentleman's agreement' which allowed us to do our trackwork on a private racecourse. The course belonged to the famous caricaturist, Larry Pickering, and he liked Dad's proposal which meant we would be credited with a run each time Christine rode one of Pickering's animals at trackwork. It went smoothly until the morning when Pickering, for whatever reason, told Christine none of us were to ever step foot on his property again. Because we were owed quite a few rides, Dad was ropable, he was ready to explode like a volcano. My friend Robert Jamison and I accompanied Dad in the truck as he hot-footed it to Pickering's beautifully manicured estate. I could sense the pressure building up in Dad with each second and from what I knew of his hair-trigger temper I realised Pickering would not need to say much to make him blow his top.

I don't think poor old Larry knew what he let himself in for when he told Dad to piss off because he received a beautifully executed Liverpool kiss. Dad lifted his head back like a cobra ready to strike its prey and when his forehead connected with Pickering's it sounded like a thick piece of timber had cracked in half! And then, in a scene reminiscent of a Looney Toons cartoon, Pickering fell back onto his wall, his trademark cap tumbled off his head to reveal he was as bald as a badger on top, and he slid to the ground. And adding to his obvious nightmare was Dad's voice at fever pitch, yelling, 'Your son is a queer, Pickering, and we know where he gets that from, don't we?'

In his dazed state, Pickering foolishly picked himself up, dusted himself down and shaped up to Dad like a bare-knuckle fighter from the turn of the century! Had I not intervened and grabbed Dad in a tight bear hug, I'm certain the old man would have really injured Pickering. I restrained him for what must have been a whole minute and tried to calm him down by begging him to leave it be so we could get on our way before the police were summoned. When Dad finally complied with my request I released him from my grip to let him into the truck.

However, the instant I turned my back, he raced over and shaped up to the still-stunned Pickering again! He was like a vicious terrier wanting to maul a crippled doberman. While it was a savage assault, at the time I felt proud of Dad. Pickering had a reputation around Kulnura for being arrogant and I was glad to see him get knocked down a peg or two.

Dad couldn't contain his glee on the way home in the truck, saying: 'If ever I can't tolerate anything, Dean and Robert, it is a bludger who swears!'. We laughed all the way home as Dad relived the beating and poked fun at Pickering's lack of pugilistic ability.

I returned to Pickering's place with Christine a little while later to check on his condition and, while he seemed to have survived it okay, it was obvious he had been shaken by the assault. As he stood on his verandah I noticed he was having difficulty rolling a cigarette because his hands were still trembling. Pickering wasn't impressed by Dad's manners and I heard him say: 'Fancy that – him headbutting me on my own property!'.

The way Dad handled the problem – violently and swiftly – made a mighty impression on me. Before I went to bed that night I told Dad I was proud of the way in which he dealt with the cartoonist. I know my pride in him meant a lot to Dad because by the time I finished speaking he had straightened his back and thrown his shoulders back. A night or two later Dad, Troy, Guy and I saw how bad the assault had really been when Pickering appeared on a television game show – it might have been *Blankety Blanks* or *Celebrity Squares* – and we saw him hiding his blackened eyes behind dark sunglasses. We all laughed at him and I gave Dad a special cheer as he did a Cassius Clay-like victory jig in front of our old television set!

It was one of the few times we applauded Dad's violent streak and I can only hazard a guess that we were happy to do it because an outsider – and not one of us – had received the latest hiding.

THE LION TAMER

Chapter Six

'I know you better than you know yourself. I've taught you all you know, but I haven't taught you all I know . . .'

Ces Waters to his sons

The well-known Sydney media commentator Mike Gibson once joked Dad's trademark beanie gave him supernatural powers as a boxing trainer. Sometimes my father liked to joke he wore his beanie everywhere – even while he was having sex – and on other occasions he would say he adopted it as his head-dress because he was a great admirer of the British commandos who wore them on covert operations during the Second World War.

However, one day Dad told me the real reason why he wore it and it now makes me laugh because it displays just how mad the bloke really was: 'Just like a car needs to be warmed up to run smoothly, son, I wear a beanie because it helps keep my brain warm and that helps me think more clearly! And remember a warm brain works better than a cold one!'

Dad's thoughts were often about his 'greatness'. I well remember the day we were driving to Gosford and he took me into his confidence. It had been a rough time for me because I had only recently discovered Dad had forced my step-mother into prostitution to help pay the bills. Dad did not know I was aware of his and Christine's secret so when he told me he had something special to tell me, 'something I have never told anyone else before', I held my breath in anticipation. 'I am a true genius, Dean, a genius!'

While it was not the kind of revelation I expected to hear, my reaction was just to nod dumbly because I believed what Dad said was true. After all, he was the smartest man I knew.

These days I'm asked by strangers who are aware of my background how the heck a bear of a bloke like me could have been beaten into submission by an old coot half my size. It's a fair question, but it is very hard to explain the hold Dad had over me and the others. It was like a magnetic force, but I guess it is one of those things a person must live through to appreciate, although there is no way I would want anyone to endure the things we did at Dad's hands.

The best way to explain it is to ask how lion tamers subdue the king of the jungle. They beat them and they deprive them of their natural pride, that's how. And it was no different for Christine and us kids. Dad brow-beat us into submission over a number of years by preaching the gospel according to Cecil Waters over and over and, believe me, there wasn't much talk about loving your fellow man in my father's book.

For as long as I can remember Dad's lessons on life revolved around such things as 'Women are dirty, they're diseased ... I'm the *only* person who can protect you ... You're *nothing* without me ... I *gave* you your life and I can *take* it away from you ...'

It was brainwashing and because I heard it every day of my life until I was about twenty-seven, I swallowed it hook, line and sinker. I believed women were diseased and needed to be avoided at all costs. I believed Dad was my guardian angel. I relied upon Dad to look after me and, while I accepted Dad as the giver of my life, I knew he could take it away from me if he wanted to. If we ever doubted what he had to say, we felt his wrath – a well-aimed backhander or that bloody hose pipe! We copped it until we surrendered our will and embraced Dad's view, no matter how bizarre it might have been.

It eventually took its toll on my spirit because until I became the heavyweight boxing champion of Australia and the Orient Pacific Boxing Federation in 1986, I had no feeling of self-worth. The moods I felt – happiness, sadness, anger, despair, sorrow or even depression – depended on which string Dad pulled like a puppeteer.

Dad was amazing in the sense he could make a bald-faced lie sound like God's own truth. However, when an outsider displayed the slightest doubt about one of the old man's stories, he didn't hit them or scream like a lunatic. Instead, he would nag until they at least pretended they too saw things the Ces Waters way – even if it was as bizarre a thought as cars being outlawed because of the number of animals they kill! Or another of his favourite topics, which was to say the Nazis weren't as bad as history has portrayed them. He based this opinion, he said, on his experience sharing a prison cell during the Second World War with a German U-boat commander who was waiting to be transferred to a prisoner of war camp.

In one conversation the Nazi submariner told Dad he could not understand why the British press lampooned the Fuhrer by printing cartoons of him doing such degrading things as eating out of a garbage can. While Hitler, his henchmen and supporters had no qualms about ordering their Luftwaffe to reduce London and beyond to rubble during the Battle of Britain, the U-boat commander said the Germans would never dare belittle the British Prime Minister Winston Churchill because they had far too much respect for his position to do that.

I have no idea whether this alleged meeting really influenced Dad to sympathise with the Nazis but he would delight in telling people in later years that Goebbels wasn't that bad a bloke and he'd sometimes reinforce his support for Hitler and his ideas by revealing the roughly sketched SS symbol he had tattooed on the inside of his left arm. It would disgust most people, but few bothered to argue about the virtues of the Third Reich with the old man. While I have no doubt some were genuinely scared of him, I think the majority of people realised it was a waste of time to get into a debate with a madman.

While Dad could charm some people with the nicer of his stories and his appearance of concern for old people and animals, he did not bother much with teaching Tracey and us boys any social skills. While we were always polite and never smoked, drank alcohol or used bad language, we weren't taught how to use a knife or fork properly and Tracey had no idea of what a clothes iron was until she escaped when she was twenty-one.

We realised from an early age not to expect much of a fuss to be made over our birthdays or Christmas. I have a birthday card Dad gave me when I was about six and while it says 'Happy Birthday from Dad, Guy and Troy' my father left Christine and Tracey's name off it, as if they did not deserve to be on the card because they were women.

Such a mentality made it hard the year Christine bought me a birthday present when I was a teenager. I should have been bowled over by her kind gesture, but the truth is I didn't know how to react except to give her a clumsy peck on the cheek. It was awkward because Dad had made it clear Christine was forbidden to show us even the slightest hint of affection. Indeed, she risked a bashing if she displayed any motherly tenderness towards us, or we towards her. So there were never any hugs and kisses and the more I think of it, the more I realise we were emotionally crippled from an early age.

While I'm working hard on changing, I still have trouble expressing my true emotions and real feelings properly but you have to realise I was programmed as a boy to have none, except for my father. We were isolated from the outside world and Dad used fear to keep us on a tight leash. Because of the stories he told us – about murders, diseased women, homosexuals and rapes – there was little chance of us being drawn to the bright lights of Sydney, or even nearby Gosford, for that matter.

We were taught from an early age not to trust the police because they were supposedly out to get us, like they had Dad in England. We'd have our hands cut off if we were ever caught stealing. We risked death in a bus accident by going on school excursions. Our real mother, according to Dad, proved how bad women were by abandoning us when we were kids in London.

Dad's word was law and he would throw up stories – like the one about the Roman commander – to prove we were smart to listen to someone as wise as him.

Back in the Roman days, Dean, Caesar's troops were in North Africa and they were outnumbered in one particular battle by an enemy who had horse-drawn chariots. The situation was quite serious and the night before the battle the commander ordered his men to shine their shields and, as you'd imagine, they thought he was daft! Surely they should be sharpening their swords for the bloody encounter waiting to happen in a few hours' time? However, the General stood firm and he ordered the men to polish their shields until they could see their reflections in them.

The next morning when the chariots commenced their charge the commander ordered his troops not to assume battle stations but to instead raise their shields towards the rising sun! You see, the shine from the polished shields blinded the chariot drivers and they went crashing over a cliff, killing them all. The commander enjoyed a great victory without losing a single man and he was hailed a hero back in Rome. However, Dean, the moral of this story is very simple. Don't question those who know – and, son, I know plenty.

It should then be easy to understand why my head was a mess, and I now realise Dad wanted it that way. He wanted us to be vulnerable because it best suited his purpose. He'd stoke our fears by doing such things as driving past a house where a doctor had murdered his family and then turned the gun on himself. After telling us all the gruesome details, about the blood that would have painted the walls and the terror the kids must have felt before they died, Dad would shake his head thoughtfully and almost whisper, 'It must be a terrible thing to kill your family'.

The offhand way he said it made it sound as if it was a normal thing for a father to do. And Dad made it clear to us, especially me, that he had it in him to extinguish a life or mutilate someone's body if need be.

He would tell us of the time he went to prison in Britain after he killed a man during a street brawl. Apparently the victim hit his head on a gutter after Dad whacked him four times and he died as a result of injuries to his brain. On another occasion Dad claimed to have cut the breast off a woman who crossed him and, I can't remember it exactly, he either hurled the woman or the breast down a well to rot and decay.

We would be terrified by his tales, but, as was the case with many of Dad's fanciful claims about his life, they were proven to be yet more lies when his criminal record was revealed in our murder trial. About the most serious charges, outside of being nabbed for such things as stealing a bag of flour during the war years, were a few cases of assault. And while that was bad enough, it failed to weigh up against his claims of a life devoted to serious crime.

Nevertheless, he imposed the dark side of the world upon us by making us read such things as *Real Life Detective* magazines about rapes, bashings and murders. We read about such characters as a quiet-natured bloke who killed people at random and stored their bodies in the refrigerator so he could cannibalise them at his leisure – like living off the huge leg of ham for days after Christmas! When I read that sort of story it made me feel scared of the world beyond our front gate at Kulnura. And even though he battered us without fear or favour, it made me feel grateful to have Dad protect us from such evil people. How naive could I have been?

One of Dad's other methods of exercising mind control was to wake us from deep sleep to see if we were still breathing. I guess it was his way of making us think he looked out for us and it seemed as if he would either shake me or call out my name every night. 'I wanted to check you were still alive, Dean.'

The nights could be the most terrifying time of all for Tracey because Dad would sometimes go into her room and beat her as she lay in bed for something that may have happened earlier in the day. It was akin to hearing a baby seal get clubbed to death but we couldn't do anything except lie in our beds and listen as she screamed.

I wasn't allowed to lock my bedroom door until I was in my early twenties and I was extremely grateful I had fought a long and hard campaign for that right one night soon after when Dad and I had a blazing argument. It was heated stuff and I think I might have shaken him up because he screamed at me, 'If you *ever* raise your hand at me, Dean, I'll kill you – I'll *kill* you stone dead!'.

That stopped me in my tracks. However, as I rested that night I could see my door-handle turn quietly and slowly. My room was illuminated by the full moon and I remember feeling a sense of dread as I pictured the old man on the other side of the locked door. I'm certain had Dad been able to gain entry into my room that night he really would have caused me terrible harm. When Dad did bash me – from when I was a kid until I left the farm as an adult – my only defence was to cover up and pray for the best.

However, the crazy thing is a couple of hours after the assault Dad would appear very remorseful. He'd say he was so terribly sorry, but that didn't stop him the next time. Worse still, Dad did not know when to call it quits. It didn't matter if it was Tracey, Christine, Guy, Troy or me, we could be battered on and off for a couple of hours. If I was ever asked to sum up a few of my worst childhood memories these are what they'd be:

Degradation one: Being forced to attend nudist camps with Dad in Australia and England. He only went to satisfy his perversions by spying on the other people and taking photographs of them without their knowledge. He enjoyed the fact people would rub up against each other in the canteen line. Sometimes he'd participate in wife-swapping parties while we kids played outside. I *hated* going there. He'd make us trim our pubic regions and while I *detested* the whole scene it was easier to comply with his demands than risk being flogged for rebelling.

Degradation two: Having Dad hold my penis while I urinated into a bucket placed in the middle of our living-room (where we also slept) at Terrey Hills. It always felt as if Dad was doing the wrong thing when he held my little acorn. It would also embarrass me to see my step-mother and sister squat over the bucket to relieve themselves because Dad refused to allow them to use his toilet. To give them some privacy I would roll over on my side and pretend to be asleep whenever they needed to relieve themselves during the night. In another bid to humiliate the girls he refused to allow them to use pads or tampons at that time of the month when they bled. They had to use toilet paper and I think Dad did that to reinforce his belief that all women – even his wife and daughter – were worthless trash.

Humiliation: I pissed my pants when Dad beat me when I was about fourteen. I released my bladder through fear and I felt the urine burn my legs. It may as well have been acid. I felt so ashamed when Dad stopped belting me to point out the wet patch of urine dripping from my trousers. The shame I experienced far outweighed the pain of the beating. It took me a long time to forgive Dad for making me wet my pants. In later years, whenever I made a mistake, Dad would call me a 'six-foot idiot' so often I eventually accepted I was a big, dumb and useless being who had little, if any, worth.

Slavery: We worked our butts off on the farm. Guy and the girls spent hours a day tending to broken-down racehorses who had as much chance of winning a major race as I later did when I hit the scales at a whopping one hundred and thirty-two kilos! Dad made us his virtual slaves by making us do such things as massaging his feet and pull at his hair because it helped him to relax. I did my utmost to do it better than anyone else all because I wanted to please Dad the most. I sometimes had to pull it so hard he'd be lifted half a metre out of his bed and, as a result of the force I applied, clumps of white, greasy hair would come out of his scalp. On other occasions he'd use us as his televison's remote control – he'd tap on the wall with a tin cup to let us know when he wanted the channel to be changed – and Lord knows there would be hell to pay if one of us didn't run in immediately. Whenever Dad returned from a trip to Gosford he'd park the car outside the gate and no matter what the weather was like he would blast the horn until one of us ran the couple of hundred metres up the driveway to let him in.

Survival: I learnt to be quick on my feet from an early age to avoid being bashed. While I deeply regretted that time I blamed Guy for something he didn't do to save myself from being flogged, I had no qualms about lying when I was defeated in the shotput event of a crappy school championship. Dad was furious when I failed to win after my third and final throw. And because I remember how badly Tracey was flogged when we first arrived in Australia and she was beaten in a race I cried foul. I said the other boy had beaten me by a matter of centimetres because he cheated. While Dad wasn't happy with the result he at least accepted my excuse and we went back to the farm. I didn't like lying but I told myself it was better than being beaten with the dreaded hose pipe.

Dehumanisation: We were dragged up amid the stench, the shit and the urine of hundreds of dogs who used our house as their kennel. The sight, sound and smells would make us dry-retch but Dad wanted us to live among the filth for reasons best known to him. I can't say this with much confidence but I believe Dad wanted us to be brought up in the most barbaric of conditions because he thought that type of environment would make us better boxers. And it almost worked because Troy was recognised as one of the globe's best junior-middleweights, Guy won the World Boxing Federation light-heavyweight crown and I had a crack at the Commonwealth heavyweight belt. Though the end for Dad – realising his dream of having three champion boxers for sons – did not justify the means, not by a long shot.

Our upbringing has affected us all in different ways. When I look at my sister Tracey these days I feel an enormous sense of admiration because she has overcome so much and has developed into a beautiful person and a loving mother of two kids. I tell people she is a credit to herself because when Tracey lived on the farm she took the full brunt of the physical attacks. She copped more than any of us because she reminded Dad of our mother. Apart from the incessant beatings he would also knock on the wall every ten minutes for her to serve him a cup of tea or to fetch a glass of water or to fix him some lunch. She had to do that on top of a full day's work which started at 3 a.m. and finished at 9 p.m. How she survived it, I'll never know. Her timetable read like this:

3 a.m.:	Wake and get ready for the day
4–5 a.m.:	Three-mile run
5–6 a.m.:	Exercise on the farm
6.15–7 a.m.:	Prepare and make breakfast
7–9 a.m.:	Hose horses down, feed animals, clean stables out
9 a.m.:	Cook and clean
1 p.m.:	Hour off.
2–8 p.m.:	Cook and clean
9 p.m.:	Bed.

If anyone should ever want to write a novel on the triumph of the human spirit, my tip is go and see Tracey because she embodies that – and more.

It was Tracey who taught us to run from Dad whenever he lost it. He was laying into her for a trivial matter one day when Tracey broke free and bolted like a sure-footed deer into the bush – Dad could not catch her! After seeing her escape a flogging by doing that we boys also took to running and we would hide in the scrub and wait a few hours for him to cool down before returning home.

However, when Dad realised we were escaping our punishment too lightly he despatched the dogs to locate our hiding spots and followed them as they bounded through the bush barking and yapping towards us. I would hear them rustling among the twigs and leaves and I'd pray they would just piss off and chase a rabbit or something. But the dogs were similar to me in the sense they just wanted to please Dad and whenever he found us cowering behind a gum tree or lying in long grass the whacking would start all over again. In their ignorance, the dogs would wag their tails. They were happy because they had helped Dad; they'd get their pats later on.

Tracey ran away when she turned twenty-one and didn't stop running until her coach pulled into Perth on the other side of the continent. The last straw for her came when she asked for permission to attend a country and western concert with a local boy. He worked on one of the stud farms around Kulnura and it was to be nothing more than an innocent night out. However, Dad accused her of being the 'local bike that is being ridden by everyone' and refused to let her go. Even though Tracey accepted Dad's decision, because she made him feel bad by looking unhappy with his answer she was given the mother of all hidings with the hose pipe.

It was during a similar assault that she had her jaw broken by the kind of punch which have won such heavyweights as Mike Tyson and George Foreman their world title crowns. Dad's punch sent my sister reeling across the room and while it was obvious she had suffered a terrible injury – her frigging jaw was hanging like a busted gate – Dad refused to allow her to seek medical treatment. It didn't mend properly and the injury still gives her problems.

Despite the terrible hidings she was subjected to, Tracey clung to the notion that Dad had some semblance of decency. I say this because of her falling out with a homeless girl who had earned her keep on our farm by helping to tend to the horses. The girl had developed a sudden fear of Dad and even asked Tracey to shower with her for protection. Her request puzzled Tracey but when she heard the explanation she refused to believe our poor guest's story.

It turned out she woke one night to find my Dad with

his hand under the sheets fondling her private parts. Tracey wanted to believe that Dad wasn't *that* low and she gave the scared girl a terrible dressing-down. In time we have learnt a few of Dad's sexual secrets and now believe the girl was telling the truth.

Apart from the homosexual encounters in prison, the molestation of handicapped kids, having sex on his wedding night with the whore his father favoured, participating in threesomes and enjoying wife-swapping parties, he sent our step-mother out to work as a prostitute in Kings Cross. The thought of it makes me feel terribly sorry for Christine because I have no doubt she is a decent person who was trapped in a dreadful mess from which she couldn't escape.

Troy had discovered her secret the day he stumbled upon Dad's secret cache of pornographic magazines under his bed. She appeared in what can only be described as the 'For Sale' section of the publication and while a black bar masked her face for identification purposes we could tell it was Christine by looking at her body and reading the text under the photo which went something along the lines of: 'Non-smoking, non-drinking young woman available for good time.'

It turned out while we were training to fulfill Dad's aim of boasting three world champions for sons she was making the cash to finance the old bloke's dream by selling her body. However, up until his death Dad denied any knowledge of Christine's activities. To throw extra weight behind his denial he sent Tracey a tape which suggested he would have loved to have known Christine was on the game because it would have made his life a lot easier:

> *What bugs me and it really, really bugs me is Christine had many boyfriends, she had a diary of boyfriends. Christine was a nymphomaniac in every sense of the*

word, believe you me. As a sex athlete I was no match for Christine. That woman had a list of all the boyfriends who would take her out. Sometimes she would go out to the Post Office Tower [Dad had this mixed up, the Post Office Tower was in England] for lunch and then she'd come home and tell me what a good time she had. She'd work of a morning at the garden centre at Terrey Hills and of an afternoon she'd be off to the city to the flat there. She'd go out and have lunch and tell me where they'd been and what they'd got up to. That was all right, I didn't care about that. Sometimes they'd give her presents of money but she was not on the game.

I'm going to tell you something, I would have had no qualms at all if she had wanted to do that because I would have organised it in such a way that she would have made a lot of money and we'd have paid for that property in the first twelve months! But she was not on the game as she makes out she was because if she was on the game she was putting the money somewhere that I didn't know about and she was on the game for her own back and not me! No. She had her boyfriends but she was not on the game ...

The truth is Christine was as much a victim of Dad's madness as we kids were. She surrendered her will long before the SS *Australis* docked at Fremantle in 1972 and I have no doubt she did that because she, too, feared for her life. Whenever she tried to get off the game he would give her a hiding. On one occasion he belted her over the head with a glass cola bottle and the gash she received was so bad it needed stitches.

Whenever Dad felt in the mood to puff out his chest and feel good about himself he would tell us of the time he saved Christine's life when he found her collapsed on the floor of our lounge-room in Finsbury Park. She was lying in a deep pool of blood and Dad said it appeared as if her life had been drained from her. The doctors said she had lost a life-threatening amount of blood after suffering a miscarriage and they added she only survived the ordeal because of Dad's decision to drive her to the hospital rather than wait for the ambulance to arrive.

The great joke of that story is that Dad always forgot to mention the reason Christine was in such a precarious state was due to his bashing the tripe out of her! He had a selective memory, my Dad.

While we accepted the beatings as a part of our life with Dad, I hated seeing Christine cop it and I would beg for him to stop. On some occasions, when it was really bad, I would grab Dad around the waist and drag him away from her. I would sometimes get beaten for interfering while at other times he would settle down and tell me not to worry because everything would be fine. But as soon as I walked out of the room where Christine was being bashed he'd lock the door and start on her all over again.

I have not seen Christine since the original murder trial and I haven't bothered her because it was clear she did not want to see any of us, especially me. After all, I killed her lover. From what I can gather, my step-mother is trying to rebuild her life and I'm happy to leave her in peace because she deserves at least that much. And I know she has scars which haven't healed. I have heard even though Christine knows Dad is dead and buried, when she is out driving, she sometimes feels the need to look in her car's rear-view mirror to see if he's following her, and she can only get to sleep with the light on.

*

While Christine treated me as well as she could I lost my temper with her once, and it was dreadful. I was watching television when she asked me to do something and I dismissed her by saying I would do it later. That wasn't the response she wanted to hear because Dad was on her back, and in her panic and anger she hit my television off the bench and it smashed onto the ground.

I saw red. Like the motorbike, the television was one of my few escapes and she had tried to wreck it! Then, as if to rub salt into my wounds, Christine threw my phone to the ground and smashed it.

I still don't know what came over me but after she walked out of the room I started to cry and I ran after her into Dad's room where I called her such things as a 'fucking slut'! Dad was laying on his bed watching television and in my rage I knocked *his* set onto the floor! He only needed to take one look at me to realise I'd snapped and he screamed out to Guy and Troy to help pacify me.

With hindsight I realise Dad was terrified I was going to explode because he knew he wouldn't be able to control my rage. The response to my outburst was amazing – Dad walked on eggshells for a few hours, Guy couldn't forgive me for swearing while Christine was mortified. When I finally cooled down she asked why I called her a slut and I was overwhelmed by a sense of pity. I could tell she would be horrified to think I knew her secret. So I apologised and said it was just a silly term the neighbour's kids used whenever they were angry with one another. I could see the relief on her face.

Dad's response was extraordinary because he didn't appear to give a damn about my brutal behaviour towards Christine. He was more concerned about my foul language and asked, 'Where in God's name did you learn that filth?' He was astounded because he kept us on such a tight leash he could not believe I would be exposed to such language. However, I was still Dad's special boy and when I sensed how disappointed he was by my swearing I broke down and started to cry like a little kid. Instead of nagging at me, Dad gave me a hug and told me to be a 'good lad'.

Guy has always been a brooder. Ever since I can remember he was always the timid and sensitive one of us kids. Fate was especially cruel to Guy; he should have been born into a family which was into art or music. His nature could not cope with Dad's brutal ways. I think he survived by becoming withdrawn and hiding in a cocoon he built for himself in his mind. He also threw himself into his chores and he had the greatest affection for the animals of us three boys.

One of my great regrets about growing up on the farm is that I did not help make Guy's life any easier. I went through a stage where I became a mirror image of my Dad and bullied him and the others around. It was unfair and as a result Guy refused to talk to me for a few months as a form of protest. Believe me, that silence hit home much better than any punch he could have ever thrown at me.

Nowadays we're the closest of friends: we go fishing a lot and we enjoy plenty of laughs about such things as the time we hooked a shark off Newcastle and it went berserk in the boat! It was like a threshing machine and we could hear its mighty jaws snapping at us like rabbit traps! Its desperate attempt to escape forced Guy and I to climb over the side of the boat as we waited for this monster to die!

Guy bought the boat after his world title bout against Dennis Andries and our fishing expeditions are something I always look forward to. However, as the skipper of the craft, he has made it clear I am not allowed to swear any more. He finds it offensive and I know he's serious when he says he won't allow me on board if I don't abide by his wishes. I used to laugh at him and say 'Piss off, Guy' but I have started to toe the line lately out of a sense of respect.

As the old adage warns, the silent ones are often the most dangerous because it was the quiet Guy who, after years of cringing and cowering, openly defied Dad's authority when he fell in love with a lovely girl named Sharon. Despite Dad's constant demands for him to dump Sharon – 'and find someone better' – Guy fostered a deep and loving relationship with her and they're now married and happy parents.

When Dad realised he was losing his hold on Guy he didn't hide his contempt for Sharon by saying that she was lazy and she would bring him down because she did not understand the strict discipline which dictates an athlete's lifestyle. He even warned Guy not to have any children with Sharon. 'They'd turn out handicapped and deformed.'

However, the boy who looked so scared when Dad exploded and started swinging the hose pipe put the fear of God back into the old man the day it appeared as if he was ready to lash out at Sharon in one of his rages. Guy stepped forward in a challenging manner and the old man turned to water. Whenever I consider the fear Guy overcame even to appear as if he was standing up to our father I look upon it as one heck of a heroic stand.

My baby brother Troy has a right hand which can jolt world champions as if they have been struck by lightning but away from the boxing ring he has always treasured a collection of over a hundred stuffed animals such as teddy bears and dogs. I believe Troy looked upon them as a substitute for the love he did not receive from Dad when Mum fled from our flat in Finsbury Park for her own safety. Sure, we gained a step-mother, but Dad made it clear he would hammer her if she 'interfered' with his children by mollycoddling us. While I think Dad spared Troy from a lot of hidings compared to the rest of us, he did not get out of it too easily.

I remember the day he was given a terrible beating after a game of soccer because Troy allowed his skipper to yell at him during a passage of play. Dad thought Troy's compliance was a sign of weakness and he hammered Troy with the brass attachment at the end of the hose pipe until his skin broke and he started bleeding. He then threw Troy from wall to wall and he crashed through the plaster board – he would get stuck in one wall and Dad would drag him out and throw him into another. I can remember going into our homestead after the dust had settled and wondering what the hell had happened because it looked as if the place had been ransacked!

Despite the tough environment he was raised in, Troy has a soft side to him and I find it hilarious sometimes to catch him crying after a soppy movie. Actually, we're both pretty hopeless in that regard and I remember the time we had to hunch down in our seats at the end of the Sean Penn movie *Dead Man Walking* a few years ago.

Troy and I weren't very close when we were young. Perhaps it was an age thing but I bullied him around. However, over the last few years we've become the best of mates and I am chuffed to see how well he has done for himself through his boxing. While Troy might not yet have a world championship belt in his trophy cabinet I maintain he is among Australia's greatest ever fighters and I believe as time goes by he'll gain the recognition he has lacked from what can only be described as an unappreciative media.

The bloke has fought the world's best in his division including the Italian champ Gianfranco Rosi, America's 'Terrible' Terry Norris, Jamaica's Simon Brown and Puerto Rico's Felix Trinidad. While he might have been beaten by them he never lost his dignity in any fight. Troy's real riches have come outside of the ring in the sense he has a marvellous girl in Michelle, he has bought a house through fighting and he's remained a decent human being despite being ripped off by a long line of users and shysters. However, I don't find it all that great a surprise that he has survived a few setbacks because after surviving Ces Waters' kingdom of the damned on Mangrove mountain, we can all survive anything!

WARRIORS ALL

Chapter Seven

'People may say I'm crazy but I am what I am and it only takes a narrow bridge that separates a madman from a genius . . .'

Ces Waters on sanity

It was obvious from the moment Dad asked whether we were ready to box in 1980 that it was not to be treated as a mere hobby by either party. Dad said if we agreed to fight we would have to first agree to a ten-year pact to not only give boxing our all but to do it as a team. In time, when he realised we had fires burning in our bellies, Dad unveiled the Ces Waters blueprint for his sons' boxing careers. It should have made our heads spin because his aspirations knew no bounds!

While we had not even fought as novices his plans included our fighting for the state and national amateur titles, boxing at the 1984 Los Angeles Olympics, turning pro, contesting the Australian professional crowns, winning the Commonwealth belts and then taking out world titles in our respective divisions. In retrospect I know that day – the day he announced our destinies – was the moment Dad had planned for, ever since we were infants forced to run around Finsbury Park in all kinds of weather. We had been programmed to embrace his dream since our formative years and he did it in so many ways.

For instance, while most normal kids watched cartoons we grew up watching 16 mm films of great boxing bouts featuring the likes of Muhammad Ali, Randolph Turpin, Ezzard Charles and Sugar Ray Robinson. And when he wasn't talking to us about crime, rapes, robberies and bashings we were reared on Dad's stories about the warriors he rubbed shoulders with in a number of English boxing gyms. Dad's associates read as a 'who's who' of British boxing and his conversations were dotted with such names as Jock McAvoy, Dick and Randolph Turpin, Terry Downes and Henry Cooper. Because he had studied their techniques from close quarters, Dad swore he knew what it would take to make us three boys into legends of the ring – and we believed him.

He described the technique he intended to base our ring careers on as: 'the purist style; not that Rocky Balboa rubbish Sylvester Stallone made popular at the movies'. Dad made it clear life under his regime as our drill sergeant–trainer would not be easy. It would be tough and demanding, he said, but it would also be rewarding. 'It will be like conquering Mount Everest. We'll train hard. It will be early to bed and early to rise. You will have faith in me as your instructor and do as you're told.'

We shared Dad's enthusiasm – then – and even though we did not have boxing gloves or a punching bag for quite some time we threw ourselves into the preliminary stages of his dream – our dreams – by running, skipping and shadow-boxing. Initially, I felt awkward dancing around and would often trip over my own feet. However, Dad proved persistence can overcome even a lack of co-ordination because, like Troy and Guy, I was soon skipping, ducking and weaving as if I was born to do it. (Well, as it turned out, I was!)

Dad called boxing the noble art of self-defence and explained a boxer is like a Roman centurion in the sense he should fight from behind his shield or defence. I don't know if Dad read this in a textbook or if he was told it by some old codger with cauliflower ears in London, but he put boxing into perspective when he said the Roman soldiers 'hid' behind their shield while they jabbed out at Caesar's many armies of enemies with their swords or spears. 'And they conquered the world!'

It was an extension of the old theory that boxing is about hitting your opponent and not getting whacked. Dad said success in the boxing ring centred around a nice, tight defence and our 'shield' was to keep our fists nice and high to protect our faces. We were also taught to be patient and to pick our mark before unleashing a volley of blows and then it was what Dad called 'kill-time', when we threw everything into our punches.

We steeled our bodies for what was expected to be a decade's worth of combat by doing such things as throwing shotput because Dad said it would enable us to develop a swivel action which would allow us to throw dangerous punches from various angles. And we ran, God knows we ran. We ran cross-country, we did sprints, we embarked on tortuous road-runs and we even ran backwards so we could step away quickly when we had to avoid a punch.

Under Dad's guidance we built our own ring with some of those logs we had dragged like slaves from deep in the valley and we ran bits of wire covered in hose piping around them so we could learn to fight on the ropes. The ring had a dirt floor and Dad measured it so it was half the size of a normal boxing ring. He wanted us to learn how to fight aggressively in confined spaces and he reasoned there would be no stopping us when we went into a full-sized ring.

Before we were allowed to participate in our first bout we did twelve months worth of vigorous sparring, bag-work, neck- and stomach-strengthening exercises, weights, medicine-ball work and more running. I liked the idea of following the footsteps of George Foreman and Joe Frasier by fighting, and for the first few years, at least, I loved the training.

Dad ran it along the lines of a military training camp – when the first rays of the new day's sun rose over the horizon he played a rather ordinary rendition of reveille on a toy bugle. I soon learnt to hate it and as the years went by and I came to resent the fight game and Dad's fanaticism towards it, I would lie in bed with tears streaming down my face as he played that bloody ridiculous tune.

On a good morning, Dad would rouse me and the others out of bed by singing a silly military-style song which went, 'Wakey, wakey, rise and shine you might have broken your mother's heart, but you won't break mine! C'mon we train lions here! C'mon boys up and at 'em!'

On other occasions, when he would accuse me of being a slacker for wanting to lie in and not train, he would stand and repeatedly slam the bedroom door open and shut until I climbed out of the cot and reached for my training gear. But that was to come. In the initial years I trained hard and wanted to master the so-called sweet science. As our first fight approached Dad applied to the NSW Amateur Boxing Association to acknowledge the Kulnura Boxing Club as a bona fide body. However, as the proposed club had only three members and a trainer who had already been dismissed by some people in the fight game as a 'crackpot' and a 'nutter', they were reluctant to register us alongside the likes of the Newtown Police Boys Club whose boxing trainer, Johnny Lewis, looked after dozens of kids including Jeff Fenech, Jeff Harding and Peter Mitrevski. In the end, after Dad bombarded them with numerous phone calls they relented and accepted us as an honorary member of the association.

Actually, it wasn't the first sporting club Dad had started. A few years after we moved to Kulnura he set about starting a soccer club which involved kids from Peats Ridge, Mangrove Mountain and Kulnura to form P.M.K. United, of which Dad was the self-elected president for a short time. He resigned from office when the committee did not comply with his orders to smoke their cigarettes outside! 'After all the hard work I went through to get the club started they couldn't even give me the courtesy of smoking outside!'

I didn't like soccer, I'd much rather have played Rugby League or cricket, but Dad was dead against those two sports. He thought the cricket ball had the potential to cause serious injury, while he thought Rugby League was far too dangerous. 'You get tackled in a game of rugby, Dean, and you're at the mercy of an idiot coming in late at the knees or by being king-hit when you turn your back to pass the ball. Rugby. No way.'

It was a great pity because the one game of league I played at school was tremendous. I cleaned one kid up and the 'mad' nature of the sport appealed to me. As for cricket, I reckon we Waters boys were the first people to ever play night cricket – we'd play by the light of car headlights until

Dad called us in to go to bed. I loved the West Indies back then and whenever I batted I was always Viv Richards and I'd try to blast Troy and Guy's best deliveries for six.

Apart from boxing, the only sport Dad allowed us to participate in was soccer. Guy and Troy enjoyed it and Dad often said if they showed any flair in the sport Australians described back then as 'wog ball' he'd arrange for them to get an apprenticeship with one of the top English soccer clubs where he had contacts.

In time we just focussed on our boxing and our individual styles quickly took shape. I was the classic heavyweight – I'd take a couple of punches to unload a good one. Guy was awkward – he didn't like being hit so he quickly learned to dance and dodge. He developed a beautiful style and in time he was acknowledged by some critics as Australia's most skilful boxer. Troy was naturally aggressive with a pair of boxing gloves on. He had a strong left but in the formative years he needed to work hard on his right – 'It's as soft as marshmallow' – so Dad would tie Troy's left behind his back and make him punch with his right. He punched his way to being recognised as one of Australia's greatest fighters who, I believe, should be ranked alongside the likes of Les Darcy, Tony Mundine, Lionel Rose, Johnny Famechon and Jeff Fenech.

We began our ring careers in late 1981 when Troy and I won our first fights and Guy was defeated. We had tasted blood and I loved it. And the more fights we participated in the more media attention we gained. Journalists loved to tell the colourful story of three boxing brothers who were trained by their 'eccentric' father, lived on a vegetarian diet, loved animals and lived deep in Mangrove Mountain. And, they noted, we could fight.

Troy was hailed as the 'Central Coast Tornado' when, at just sixteen, he was trading punches with a twenty-three year old hard-head. Most of the people in the crowd thought the fight had ended when my youngest brother was sent reeling through the ropes by one of the older fighter's bombs. Troy rolled over the judges' table and landed in a crumpled heap on the floor. However, rather than concede defeat, he stepped back into the ring and knocked his opponent out with a savage right.

In the audience watching the fight was one of Australasia's all-time great boxing trainers, Ern McQuillan senior, and he liked what he saw. Old Ern, who had trained the likes of the great Tony Mundine, Vic Patrick and Jack Hassen, could see a real star quality in Troy and he offered to buy Troy's contract from Dad.

'I offered the young fellow $5,000 to come and train with me', Ern told *The Australian* in 1985. 'He's outstanding. He is good enough to go anywhere he wants.'

Another who was impressed by the 'Tornado's courage in that particular bout was the referee, Joe Darcy. Joe had not only refereed over four thousand amateur bouts but he was also the youngest brother of Les Darcy, the legend who most astute critics cite as Australia's greatest ever fighter.

The great Darcy's life and death at the age of twenty-one from blood poisoning is one of the most tragic tales in Australian boxing. Darcy has been described as having the face of an angel, the body of a Greek god and razor-sharp reflexes of a cobra. After defeating such highly rated American imports as Eddie McGoorty, Bill Murray and George Chipp, he was hailed as the world's unofficial middleweight champion. However, when he stowed away to America to set his family up before risking his life on one of the First World War's battlefields he was dismissed by the Australian public as a slacker and a coward.

The allegations dogged him in America and he was not issued with a licence to box until he joined the US Army in 1997. While he was in training for a fight with Len Rowlands, Darcy collapsed, complaining of sore teeth, stiff joints and a burning fever. A few days later he died in the arms of his sweetheart and his tragic end has been on boxing Australia's collective conscience ever since.

However, the name Les Darcy also summons the image of a tremendous fighter who was rated among the world's top ten middleweights by Nat Fleischer, founder of boxing's bible, the *Ring*. Anyway, Joe could see something special in Troy and one day when we were up at his house in Newcastle he saw a photo of his brother which, he told sports columnist Jeff Wells, 'was like looking at a picture of Troy . . . I was so taken by the resemblance that I asked some people who were talking about making a movie about Les if they would consider Troy. It wasn't just the boxing style, it was the same lovely smile that Les had.'

While Troy was the glamour boy and Guy the purist, I was 'Mean' Dean and I donned longer than normal trunks which had the names Foreman and Frasier stitched down the side of them. I loved to rumble. I was twenty-one years old, I weighed one hundred kilos, I liked to rip into my opponents from the first bell, hide behind my gloves for a spell and then unleash bombardment.

In my early days I learned a lot about human nature in the boxing ring. I locked horns with courageous fighters, scared men, blokes who could be cut easily and fellows who liked to be beaten up. The masochists were the worse opponents because no matter how badly you whacked them they enjoyed it; they'd stand up to take some more punishment. As fighters those blokes did not scare me in the slightest, but their attitude spooked me because they were the ones who you could seriously hurt if the referee didn't stop the bout.

Jake LaMotta, boxing's 'Raging Bull', was such a fighter. When he was a kid in the Great Depression, LaMotta would fight on a street corner in the Bronx area of New York City for pennies, but instead of merely fighting, LaMotta risked death. Old black men who knew such things said LaMotta fought as if he didn't deserve to live. And it does not matter at what level you fight, the chances are you will always come across a person who seems to have a death wish.

In 1983 Troy, Guy and I created Australian boxing history when we became the first three brothers to win state titles on the one night. It was brilliant and the fact we had fulfilled the first stage of Dad's grand plan increased our faith in him as a father and goal-setter. And it didn't hurt Dad's feelings to hear some people declare we could become the most famous Australian boxing family since the famous Sands brothers.

Despite our euphoria, each of us knew we had quite a way to go before we were entitled to such a great accolade. Though it felt good.

Guy was the hero, clinching the NSW amateur middleweight title after having had to fight three bouts at the tournament with a busted hand. He slept with his hand in a bucket of iced water and gritted his teeth to pass the doctor's inspection. 'He kept squeezing my hand, I just kept telling him it was all right – but it hurt like hell', he told a *Daily Telegraph* journalist.

Dad was over the moon, he hadn't forgotten how the NSW Amateur Boxing Association dismissed him as a fruitcake when he tried to have our three-man club registered. 'I had trainers come up to me crying. They were whinging they never had a fighter win a title in years of competition and I had three in one night!'

And a feature story in the *Australian* made it clear we had done something special when reporter David Brearley spoke of our million-dollar dreams on a pauper's allowance:

> *There never was a backyard operation with a greater goal or a tinier budget than the Kulnura Boxing Club. The club's entire membership is the Waters brothers – one heavyweight, one light-heavyweight and one light-middleweight – each a NSW champion in his respective division and each determined to be champion of the world. Dean, Guy and Troy Waters aim to turn the Rocky story into reality.*
>
> *Like Sylvester Stallone's famous screen character who pulled himself up from nowhere, like Jeff Fenech who pulled himself up out of Marrickville, the Waters brothers will take on the world. But unlike those two local-boys-made-good, the Waters don't even have a gymnasium to work out in. The Kulnura Boxing Club via Gosford on the NSW Central Coast is nothing more than a makeshift boxing ring in the middle of a paddock, and a few dumbbells and punching bags on a dusty old verandah . . .*

The newspapers and television stations homed in on us and among a number of headlines in Dad's well kept scrapbook were such headlines as 'Fists of Fury – Hearts of Gold', 'Boxing brothers go for hat-trick', 'Bush Battlers Aim to be the Best'. It was an exciting time and in my naivety I'd do silly things for the photo sessions like roll up a pair of socks and wear a pair of tight-fitting strides to make it appear as if there was a lot more to me than met the eye.

While the socks were my idea and not Dad's, he would brief us before a journalist arrived to do an interview. We would be told what to say, what tone to say it in, and to make sure we wrapped Dad up with comments like, 'I know my Dad is the best trainer in the world.'

One thing about my father was he knew how to promote himself and causes he believed in. There was that time he brought to the media's attention the terrible effects of the great London garbage strike by dumping a load of litter on the front steps of 10 Downing Street. In another crazy chapter of his life he went to great lengths to promote an average pub band by jumping into the Thames in the middle of winter!

Somehow he had become the manager of a small-time band in London (I can't remember their name) and Dad, being Dad, figured they could rival the Beatles! However, they needed a publicity drive and Dad decided he would make a hero out of the lead singer. He hatched a plan where he would jump in the Thames and the singer would follow him in, drag him to the side and resuscitate him. Dad was no dummy because, in an attempt to hedge his bets, he jumped not far from where the London water police were based! While the singer gained his headlines it soon became obvious the band wasn't going to go any further than playing in dives and at weddings. When Dad's band disbanded to get 'normal' jobs he went on his way and dreamt of having sons who would win world boxing titles.

These days, when I look at some of the newspaper clippings, I can remember answering a question from the *Australian*'s David Brearley on what it was like having Dad as our trainer. Brearley had not only observed that Dad 'runs his son's world challenges with an iron fist, and love' but that we followed Dad's every command with an 'almost blind faith'.

When he asked about Dad's approach to training my response was similar to that of a parrot who is trained to say 'Who's a pretty boy?'. 'Don't get me wrong, he's not a dictator,' I told Brearley. 'Dad's very strict, but you've got to be if you're going to get anywhere, especially in boxing, because it's a very, very hard sport.'

In another interview with the *Daily Telegraph*'s boxing writer I was asked how we could justify not eating meat because we abhorred the way animals were killed, yet think nothing of bashing an opponent's head in. Once again, my answer was straight from Dad's brief and I could see him nod with approval as I spoke into the reporter's microphone: 'People are always trying to find fault with our way of life – they think we're crazy that we can box and yet can't bear to see an animal suffer. But no-one makes a boxer get into a ring and he's got a chance to defend himself.'

A NOT SO INNOCENT ABROAD

Chapter Eight

'They'll think nothing of slitting your throat.'
Ces' advice to Troy and Dean on the dangers of Indonesia

One of the earliest rewards I received for excelling at boxing was being selected to represent Australia in the seventh President's Cup Boxing in Jakarta, Indonesia. It doubled as a trial for the Australian Olympic team but I was over the moon just to be picked for an international trip.

As the respective national amateur welterweight and heavyweight champions Troy and I were automatic selections for the team, and while we were thrilled to be travelling overseas, we were bitterly disappointed a broken knuckle meant Guy had to stay back on the farm and tend to his chores.

However, I felt nervous as I packed my bags because the trip to Jakarta would be the first time I had gone anywhere without Dad shadowing my every step. And when it became obvious he would not be able to accompany us on the trip because of a shortfall in funds he became very worried about Troy and me being in a foreign country without him to steer us out of harm's way. He spent hours drilling us on the many dangers we could face in the Indonesian capital, ranging from corrupt police trying to plant drugs on us to having our throats cut in a back alley by local thugs who considered westerners easy pickings.

Dad based his knowledge on the time he said he lived among some cut-throat Arabs in North Africa (I think it may have been Morocco) when he was on the run from the police in England. Dad soon learnt the law of the land and he was advised not to rob a bank even when the building was left wide open and unattended while the staff were out at lunch or praying to Allah. Dad's contacts warned him that under Islamic law it could mean death if he was caught stealing. And the other culture shock which rocked Dad on his heels was the nature of the brothels in the city's red light area. 'Son, they were full of young boys and not women!'

From listening to the seasoned fighters on the plane I knew the brothels in Jakarta were jam-packed with slim brown women willing to do anything for the price of a bottle of cola. Listening to the other blokes talk about the ladies of the night it appeared that getting laid was as much of an ambition for them as winning a gold medal – and that appealed to me! I was a twenty-two year old virgin champing at the bit for some action.

However, as for representing Australia I stuffed up big time on the flight over because I embarked on an eating and drinking (water and juice) splurge soon after we strapped on our seatbelts. I ate so much I should have waddled through the Indonesian customs hall. My bloated belly was as full as a drunken sailor's and the legacy of my pigout was plain for everyone to see at the weigh-in when the scales creaked under the strain of the extra pounds I'd piled on.

I was ruled ineligible to fight in the heavyweight division and, because there were no other super-heavyweights, I was left out in the cold. I had cost myself any chance of going to Los Angeles and if that wasn't bad enough I had to contend with the thought of Dad's reaction to my foolishness. (He didn't talk to me for hours after I returned and because I felt so guilty to have let him down I couldn't look him in the eye for quite a long time.)

However, it was a great relief for me not to have to mix it with the collection of American, Canadian, Algerian and Korean heavyweights because I did not think I would be able to do anything without Dad being with me. I was a nervous wreck without him, but I refused to let the setback of not being able to box ruin my time in Indonesia. I focussed instead on a different mission – losing my virginity.

I wasn't alone in my search for sex – a few of the other boys joined me as I walked the streets looking for a girl to 'dance' with. I remember Jakarta as an unbelievable mixture of sounds, sights and smells, a muggy pot pourri of spices, neon lights, exhaust fumes, sizzling stir fries, ringing bicycle bells, squawking chickens, stray dogs, and the sing-song voices of the Indonesians.

It was bedlam, but I didn't worry about that because I was a man on a frantic search and destroy mission. Guy's replacement, Brendon Cannon, and I climbed on the back of a rickshaw and paid the owner a few piddling rupiah to take us on a tour of the city's fleshpots.

The other blokes, like Brendon, couldn't believe my reaction. I must have seemed like a thirteen-year-old to them, but they could not have realised how I had been cocooned from society on a farm three hundred and eighty metres above sea level and a million miles from anywhere. My eyes were like dinner plates as I ogled sexily dressed prostitutes offering their services for 11,000 rupiah – a high-sounding figure which converted to a low US$2! My senses – well, one in particular – had been aroused and I could feel the excitement building up in me by the moment. I was like a top waiting to explode off a shaken bottle of fizzy drink.

Apart from the initial embarrassment of fronting up to the madam, it wasn't that hard to negotiate a price for a girl to return to my hotel.

Once there, I ordered Jeff Fenech and Shane Knox to get out and to let me get on with business. I was nervous, I was trembling with fear and excitement, and she was in control. My first few attempts to enter her were way off course, it was a bit like a game of pin the tail on the donkey! My feeble attempts frustrated her – after all, time is money – and she ended up guiding 'Percy' in.

When I think of the Asian hooker I paid small change to take my virginity it disgusts me. She had dyed red hair, a scrawny chicken-like neck and she stank like rotten fish. However, I was prepared to put up with that in my bid to, as they say in the classics, get a bolt away!

It was anything but a glorious debut. She slapped me on the hand when I tried to pash her – 'no touch tongue!' – and it only got worse when Fenech and Knox jumped from their hiding spot and laughed their heads off when they saw my backside bobbing up and down like a cork in the ocean. They hadn't left the room at all. My first shot at having sex degenerated into a carnival and they cheered me on by yelling such things as, 'Give it to her Deano, Mount Isa!'.

I was far from happy with the way things had gone but

my sex drive outweighed my humiliation. I was not going to allow them – or her, for that matter – ruin it. However, it was all over as quickly as it started and to tell you the truth, I felt pretty grubby. I bundled a wad of banknotes into the prostitute's hands and asked her to leave the room.

After she went I was left to think about what I had done and I felt like a right wally when it was pointed out by my teammates I should have slapped a condom on my old fellow. Fenech and Knox did nothing to allay my fears of receiving a dose of the pox, and started to talk about the possible sexually transmitted diseases I'd exposed myself to like HIV-AIDS, 'drippy dick', syphilis and gonorrhea. I felt terrible.

However, after a restless sleep I followed my erection the next night and hired a rickshaw to take me around the city. I was taken through a maze of streets and back alleys and it was one heck of an experience. However, the deeper we went into this hidden city where freshly cooked ducks hung in rows, kids crapped into the dirt gutter and transvestites wore brightly coloured clothes, the louder the alarm bells in my head rang. I could hear my father's voice warning me about cut-throats and blood-thirsty villains who lurked in shadows and the possible threat made the hairs on the back of my neck stand on end.

It only got worse when the rickshaw driver pedalled through a long tunnel where a colony of homosexuals and transvestites lived. I could see their silhouettes against the small fires which illuminated the way and I almost soiled my pants when one creature charged out of the shadows screaming 'Waaahhhhhhrrrrr!'. I didn't know if 'it' was running at me with an axe or meat cleaver and felt an enormous sense of relief when it did nothing more harmful than chuck a dirty brown-eye at me and scream again.

After that I ordered the driver to take me home but then asked to be set down when I was close to the hotel. I had seen a prostitute there the night before who had made suggestive actions at me with her tongue – she was like a demon – and her lack of shame excited me.

All of the previous night's concerns about sexual diseases disappeared with a hard-on when I saw her on top of the bridge. The woman saw me looking for her and she was soon down on her knees satisfying me in plain view of passers-by. I became self-conscious and asked her to go behind a bus shelter so we could at least have some privacy and she reluctantly complied. As a result of the humidity and the excitement of having a woman do what I had always dreamed about my head started to spin; however, my trance-like state was broken halfway through the act when she stopped and asked for payment. I convinced her to keep going and any pleasure I felt was brought to an abrupt halt a few seconds after I hit the vinegar stroke when I heard her hack phlegm from the back of her throat to help spit my 'seed' into the gutter.

Before I had time to even catch my breath the demon demanded payment for services rendered: 'You-pay-me-now!'. However, when I reached for my wallet I realised it was in my motel room! I didn't have any cash left on me and I explained my predicament to her. She was filthy – and rightly so – but in the end the woman realised I was a boxer and warned it would be at my own peril if I did not return with US$10 ASAP. 'If you no return I curse you! You die next time you fight.'

Needless to say, I didn't return. However, ten months later and on the eve of my debut as a professional fighter her words returned to haunt me and I was terrified I would pay for what I had done to that woman. I was terrified and even made a silent promise to return to Jakarta to track her down and hand over the money, with interest, if I didn't die in the ring. However, I survived *that* curse and she's still waiting for the ten greenbacks.

Now that I have experienced a lot more of life I look back on that trip to Jakarta and shake my head in disgust at my behaviour – it was pathetic with a capital P. However, because of the way I was raised on the farm it was inevitable that I would go for broke the first chance I had to get my hands – and more – on a woman. But it is nothing to boast about.

Sometimes I hear blokes carry on as if they're Errol Flynn because they've bedded hookers in Manila, Bangkok, Jakarta, Saigon, Hong Kong and Pattaya, but it isn't a conquest. It's just a cheap holiday in a Third World nightmare. The women are desperate and the reason they're selling their dignity daily is because their family is dirt-poor. They become the family's breadwinner by sleeping with wealthy Arabs, Japanese and westerners – and wealthy is interpreted as anyone with a spare twenty dollars to throw around! And since the HIV-AIDS time-bomb detonated and sent its shrapnel throughout Asia and the rest of the world millions of people have been affected.

One of the great ironies is once the girls are struck down with the virus they are often not allowed to even step into the houses their sweat, sex and money allowed the families to buy. It stems back to the Asian belief of karma and it is very sad. In Thailand, for instance, they think it will bring bad luck to the entire family if a 'cursed' daughter enters their dwelling. Instead, the family's generosity extends to allowing the unfortunate girl, the two-dollar hooker, to live in an old shack in the backyard until the wicked virus claims her.

These days, I deeply regret my actions all those years ago, because by participating in the flesh trade I encouraged a couple of girls to see that as a way to make a living. In a small way, however, I paid for my stupidity by sweating like a madman as I waited for the results of my blood test for a cocktail of diseases to return from a Gosford pathologist. I breathed a huge sigh of relief when the results returned with 'negative' stamped over them.

In the Jakarta boxing ring Troy boxed well, really well, and I have no doubt whatsoever that he was cheated out of a place in the finals when he fought the Algerian contestant.

Troy was awarded the bout but the international judiciary overturned the decision and gave it to the European. The same thing happened to Jeff Fenech at the 1984 Los Angeles Olympics and brought howls of protests from Australia, but Troy was the first fighter to ever suffer such a fate.

I was devastated for Troy's sake. He was heart-broken, and it was cold comfort for my little brother and me to watch on as the Algerian won the silver and not the gold. Unfortunately it was the first of a litany of 'if only's' to dog Troy's career. He has had beatable world champions like America's Darrin Van Horn and Canada's Matthew Hilton dodge him when he was the International Boxing Federation's number one junior middleweight contender in 1989, and then he had his jaw broken in a serious car crash weeks before he was set to fight American John David Jackson for the World Boxing Organization title.

However, perhaps the major setback Troy experienced as an amateur came in 1984 when, having been measured up for his uniform to wear at the Los Angeles Olympics, he was inexplicably dumped. It upset a number of people, especially the other boxers because, apart from proving himself in international tournaments in Taiwan and Santa Domingo in the Caribbean, he was also a popular team man.

He was always up to his armpits in trouble, like the time in Taiwan when a taxi driver tried to fight Troy and two other boxers with a samurai sword. A few of the blokes had frozen oranges in their hotel room's refrigerator then hurled them down onto the streets below to 'bomb' cars. It was stupid and they made a bad mistake to hit home on this particular taxi driver's vehicle because he wanted blood. Fortunately for the blokes concerned, Troy was able to pacify the man and convince him he was barking up the wrong tree.

Nevertheless, despite his popularity and talent, he was dropped from the Olympic squad after the president of the Australian Amateur Boxing Association, Arthur Tunstall, and Dad clashed heatedly over the Aussie team's compulsory trip to Ireland as part of their Olympic program. Dad thought Troy would be a sitting target for an IRA bullet because of our English bloodline but Tunstall said the old man was 'crackers' and he made it crystal clear Troy could forget his Olympic dreams if he did not go to Ireland with the rest of the squad.

Well, true to form, Dad gave it to Tunstall with both barrels. In the process he also shot down Troy's chances of fighting for a possible gold medal because his name was struck off the list. On an official level Tunstall told the press that Troy Waters, Wilf Jensen and Dale Artango had all been scratched from the eight-man squad because Australia could only send five competitors to the Olympics in light of the number of medals we had won in international competition. In Troy's case – who was said to have been selected for the squad even before Jeff Fenech – this seemed like absolute crap. He missed out because Dad had a falling out with Arthur Tunstall.

While the situation highlights how stupid Dad could be, it also intensified our disregard for the boss of amateur boxing in Australia. Indeed, Tunstall's name had long been mud at our farm because he had been on two international juries which had overturned decisions, to go against Troy. 'He voted against one of his own countrymen!' Dad would tell people.

And fourteen years on, Tunstall has done very little to improve the way we view him because since dropping Troy he has lurched from one blunder to another with ridiculous comments about Aborigines. Not only do they outrage the Aborigines but his jokes upset all fair-minded Australians.

Dirty about Troy having been dropped from the Olympic squad, Dad went into overdrive and contacted the organisers of the 'Alternative Games' in Cuba. The games had been arranged for the Eastern Bloc nations who had boycotted LA in retaliation for the Americans snubbing Moscow in 1980. When they heard about a couple of Australian boxers wanting to participate they welcomed us with open arms.

I don't know if the Australian government would have approved our visit because it could quite easily have developed into an international incident but, at the end of the day, finances made it impossible for the fighting Waters clan to take on the best of Cuba, East Germany and the Soviet Union. 'It will show them up if you can win gold against the countries who have won the most Olympic medals, lads,' said Dad before he realised we could not raise the small fortune needed to jet into Havana. While we could not get under Tunstall's skin by competing against the communists, we ultimately told him and his cronies to get stuffed by turning professional.

THE CRYING GAME

Chapter Nine

'I teach my sons that if they are to be the gladiators they must fight the best. That way they can do themselves and Australia proud if they win. And if they lose there is nothing to be ashamed of.'

Ces Waters

After the drama involving Troy, Dad, Arthur Tunstall and the Olympic team, we were conscripted into the professional ranks by the old man, which meant we trained even harder. It was a chore, but I knew Dad was spot-on when he said the professional boxing ring was a totally different prospect to the amateur circuit. He described it as the cruellest and the most unforgiving of all sporting arenas and the fact that three hundred-odd boxers have died in the ring since the bareknuckle days one hundred years ago supported his theory.

As a father myself these days, I cannot understand why Dad was so keen to pitchfork us into it. I won't encourage my boys to be fighters because it is a mug's sport. A fighter is seen as nothing more than a brainless slab of meat and he's easy prey for heartless managers, corrupt officials and the drunken hordes of people who turn out to the fights to see blood shed in the name of entertainment.

I've heard people describe such sports as Rugby League and ice hockey as being tough on the body and brain, but apart from bull-fighting, I can't think of another sport in which the prime purpose is to render an opponent helpless and then knock his block off! So, armed with the knowledge we could end up in a hospital bed if we weren't properly prepared for the professional ring, we trained to ensure we'd have more than enough stamina needed to fight for twelve punishing rounds. It was no picnic. Under Dad's fanatical regime we lived, breathed and ate boxing.

Our training started at sunrise with the sounding of that stupid toy bugle and it ended three hours later after we had thrown hundreds of punches, skipped, run and sometimes sparred against each other. I often wondered what I had put myself in for by agreeing to Dad's plan to become the heavyweight champion of the world; apart from Sundays there was no respite from the fight game. It pervaded our every moment and sometimes when I'd be watching a show on television Dad would barge into my bedroom and ignore my protests as he whacked yet another boxing video into the VHS machine. Even though I pleaded to be left alone for a while I would end up watching the fighting styles of Foreman, Ali, Frasier and the new boy on the block, Mike Tyson.

While Guy and I didn't particularly enjoy our spartan lifestyle, Troy thrived on it. He plastered his bedroom wall with posters of his boxing heroes and sometimes he'd be awake long before Guy and me, out training for the world title belt he was so keen to win.

Dad based his training regime on that of a drill sergeant in the British army and he knew himself there were times when we hated him for it. Indeed, as he pointed out in the *Sunday Telegraph*, that was exactly what he wanted. 'It is hard for me. I want them to love me as a father, but when we are training they must hate me, no, despise me!' he said. 'The day they stop snapping during a training session is the day I have failed them.'

Bearing that in mind, he didn't fail us too often. In later years, when we split from Dad after the great family fall out in 1989, Guy told the *Daily Telegraph*'s Ray Chesterton of our daily grind. 'It was like an army camp. It was boxing for breakfast, boxing for dinner.'

I doubt whether too many modern-day warriors have followed the daily training timetable we were forced to. I'm certain it would have tested even the toughest person's resolve and it eventually burnt me out. I'm sure our training was just as responsible for killing our love for boxing as Dad's relentless drive.

We would wake at 5.30 a.m. to start our chores – I fed the dogs, Guy helped tend the horses (after Tracey ran away) while Troy milked our cow, Mary Too – and then we'd start training. We could run anywhere between two and ten miles a morning and then we would learn all about being gladiators in our home-made gymnasium.

I didn't like the sparring much because sometimes it only needed one punch to be delivered that little bit too hard to start a wild brawl. While the exchange of blows might have only lasted a few seconds it was more than enough time to create an enormous amount of ill-feeling between us brothers for a couples of days, if not weeks. It was especially terrible for Guy because there were times when he finished our sparring sessions with migraines which lasted for days –

the pain was sometimes so severe he could not lift his head off the pillow. While Dad did not object to swallowing handfuls of pain-killers when he needed them, he forbade us from taking any ourselves. Instead, we were told to be gladiators and that meant Guy would have to overcome the headaches to spar some more.

Another time when the old man should have shown Guy some mercy was when he had made the mistake of wearing a new pair of boxing boots into the ring. As a result his feet were terribly blistered – the bubbles were so bad I'd have sworn he had bathed his 'plates of meat' in an acid bath! However, as part of our radical recovery program, Dad would make us rise the morning after a bout and go for a road-run. It was barbaric at the best of times, but on this particular occasion when Guy had trouble walking it bordered on sadism to send him out. He should have been allowed to rest, but the drill sergeant thought that was being soft and to this day I can still see the look of agony etched on Guy's face as he tried to run the two miles.

Apart from holding some bizarre beliefs such as the post-bout run, my father was, I still believe, one of Australia's best boxing trainers. He had a great knowledge of the sport and, just as importantly, he knew how to get his message through to even the most dim-witted novice who would occasionally come to our farm determined to learn about the noble art. Most of them dropped out once they realised how hard a life boxing was, but at least they took with them a few tips from my Dad such as, 'The quickest direction between two points is straight ahead, so when you punch, lad, punch straight!'

However, Dad had one glaring fault as a trainer and that was he would panic before – and during – a fight. The bigger the fight the worse his negative energy would be and it affected us during a bout. I remember his negativity became so bad during Troy's IBF world title bout against Gianfranco Rosi, Troy actually told him before the last round to 'shut up and get back to the dressing room!' (Though I should stress the outburst only occurred after the shooting and Dad had lost his hold over us.)

And while Dad was recognised by some critics as the best boxing trainer in Australia, he had no idea of such things as nutrition. Because we were committed vegetarians – which happened when Christine said it was hypocritical that we called ourselves animal lovers yet we thought nothing of eating them – our main source of energy was baked beans, potatoes, cheese, eggs and the stale, mouldy bread Dad bought cheaply from a bakery in Wyong.

Once Tracey left, Dad was the cook and his meals could never be described as appetising. At best they could be regarded as colourful because his standard tucker was to mix a few tins of baked beans with cheese and eggs in a glass dish and plonk the concoction in the oven for twenty minutes. I don't know how or why it happened but the eggs would not only turn out green in colour, but they would also be crunchy when you bit into them! It was dreadful stuff and it sat in our guts like the ballast in the belly of an old sailing ship. However, we knew never to complain. Not only did we not want to risk a beating, we knew we would go hungry if we turned our noses up at Dad's meals.

Our only treat was the occasional chocolate and biscuit, and to make it into our pantry they could not contain animal products! If we ever ventured to a McDonald's restaurant we'd eat hamburgers without the meat patties! My favourite day of the week was Friday because that was the night we went to the movies at Wyong and hoed into a vegetarian pizza and garlic bread at a little Italian restaurant.

Even though we were all in our twenties Dad sometimes chaperoned us on those outings to ensure we kept an arm's length from people he dismissed as 'glory-hunters' and 'gold-diggers'. He said they were a low breed who would try to attach themselves to us because of the fame we were achieving through the media.

There was plenty of attention, with respected journalists, like Jeff Wells, portraying us as three happy, wholesome boys: 'You would probably have to sneak into a Vienna Boys Choir practice to find a larger aggregation of well-mannered, patriotic, animal-loving and comprehensively pleasant lads under one roof than the Waters boys, even if their chosen profession is transmitting violence to mandibles and ribcages ...'

However, away from the headlines and the television cameras, life on the farm was still a nightmare. While we were being touted as future world boxing champions in the press we lived in constant fear of being bashed by Dad. Adding further drama to my mental state was the fact my life had taken a confusing twist because I had fallen for a girl named Kelly Baker.

Our relationship went against the grain with Dad who said women were dangerous creatures who could bring a fighter down because of the time and attention they required. When he realised my feelings for Kelly were much deeper than a fleeting friendship, Dad did his best to destroy everything by constantly bad-mouthing her, arranging for me to go on dates with other girls and homing in on any faults he found in her. He said Kelly would have a bad influence over me because he had heard her parents drank alcohol, smoked cigarettes and used bad language. However, not even his worst comments could deter me from seeing her at every possible opportunity and I could tell he was worried he was losing his grip on me.

Through it all, boxing was still the beacon we boys blindly followed but our early bouts, which Dad promoted, didn't make us much money. It was frustrating because we would see the people jammed into the auditorium but by the time Dad had paid out the bills to the referees, the preliminary fighters, our opponents and the bloke who put up the ring, there was very little cash left for us.

I now realise the reason for that was because Dad was out of his depth when it came to handling money. While he knew he had a marketable commodity in the three of us, he made some terrible blunders like the night he promoted our triple state title bouts at the Central Coast Leagues Club.

The auditorium was packed to the rafters and the mob cheered the place down when we wrote a new chapter in the history book of Australian boxing by each winning professional titles on the same night. I defended my belt when I beat the experienced Tongan Malie Haumono, Troy defeated tough-as-teak Tony Campbell while Guy beat Johnny Bogolin in a violent stoush. Guy's battle went down so well with the punters that they showered the ring with $200 in coins, and, as it turned out, that was just as well because it was all the money we made that night!

Dad explained we couldn't be paid because the club management had demanded he cough up extra cash for the lighting man, the sound-recording bloke and the fee for the hall. He said the management's demands cleaned out our coffers. However, he told us, money wasn't everything and we should be happy to have at least won our titles. I was not happy about the lack of cash for fighting Haumono, but I was over the moon to think my retaining the NSW belt at least gave me the right to fight Victoria's world-rated Dave Russell for his Australian and Orient Pacific Boxing Federation crown!

Dave Russell was a tough-looking dude who sported a shaved head, an art gallery's worth of tattoos on his body and a punishing punch which had put many contenders to sleep. When I signed on to fight Russell he was bound for a crack at the World Boxing Council's cruiserweight title and many high-profile commentators, such as former international Rugby League and Rugby Union player Rex Mossop, gave me no hope at all. It didn't bother me in the slightest. Even though I had only taken part in three professional fights I had more than enough faith in my own ability.

The funny thing about boxing is while I have grown to loathe most of what the sport stands for, I did not hate any of my opponents. However, I resented Russell because of the fact he made his living as a slaughterman in an abattoir. It riled me and an important part of my pre-fight psych-up was to imagine the fear the animals must have felt as they waited to be butchered by Russell and his work-mates. Apparently the cattle know they're about to die as they wait in line and they make terrible, blood-curdling noises; the image of my opponent slaying them in cold blood fuelled my anger like coal does fire! It helped me maintain the rage even after I hurt my right hand a fortnight before the bout and needed to have cortisone injections pumped into it to allow me just to clench my fist.

As it panned out, I was also informed I would be making the journey to Swan Hill on the banks of the Murray River without the old man in my corner. Dad had secured Troy a crack at In Chul Baek's OPBF belt in Korea the very night I was signed to rumble with Russell! Dad, it seemed, was at his cunning best against the Koreans because he fed them wrong information regarding Troy's style by saying such things as he was a southpaw who lacked a genuine KO punch.

The old man left, saying it was up to me to avenge each of the animals Russell had killed over the years. 'As an animal-lover, Dean, you can't possibly let this murderer win!' I vowed I wouldn't. After all, I was the bloke who went into a mad panic the time we were being interviewed for a newspaper article and it appeared as if Dad was about to step on a spider! I yelled for Dad to look out and I then carefully cradled the insect to a safer spot away from his feet. The reporter noted my behaviour and described me in his yarn as being 'emotionally fragile'. Looking back on my life then I don't think even he could have realised how close to the mark he really was.

Guy was an important part of my entourage when I fought Russell at Swan Hill's Oasis Hotel. It seemed a decent enough pub, but at the end of the night it was a bloodhouse. There must have been a full moon because it was a crazy old night. Russell had a lot of bikers cheering him on. They made it obvious the thought of me taking his belt and claim to a world title bout did not appeal to them at all.

However, we proved to be just as wild because one of my group, Robert Jamison, had a mohawk cut especially for the fight, wild tattoos on his biceps and last, but not least, a samurai sword attached to his belt! He looked one hell of a mean dude and as I sized up the hostile crowd baying for my hide I was glad to have him in my corner.

There was something about this fight which was

completely different to all my others and as I waited for my date with fate I realised it was a relief not to have Dad ranting and raving like a madman. Instead, Guy took control of the situation and, unlike Dad, he instilled great confidence in me. He told me I looked like a champion: he said he knew I had worked hard to lose weight and tone up and he maintained I deserved success and that he believed I would win the fight.

It was by far the biggest bout of my life and as I waited for the referee to finish giving his instructions, a line from my favourite ACDC song ran through my brain: 'If you want blood, you got it!'. I made that my motto for the night!

As for blood there was buckets of it by the tenth round because the Victorian slaughterman bled like a stuck pig when I opened him up above his eye in the first three minutes. The fight should have been stopped but the referee ordered us to continue. Who knows why. With the number of irate bikers on hand he might have feared there would be a riot.

It was a bitter and bloody contest and I was quite happy in the tenth round when I uncorked a big right which, while it may have iced Russell, sent his army of supporters into a frenzy. They were devastated to see their hero counted out and their response to the result was to threaten to rip me limb from limb.

I should have been over the moon at being the new national heavyweight champion, instead I feared for my safety. The mob howled down the result and I felt a sense of relief when five police officers arrived to escort me back to the dressing room. When I looked down from the ring as I waited to accept my belt I saw a woman crying into her hands and when I recognised her as Russell's girlfriend

I felt so bad and I opened my hands as if to say sorry. However, rather than acknowledge my gesture with a nod of her head – or even a smile – the woman gave me the finger and told me to get fucked! While I was floored by her response the only thing that mattered to me that night, apart from winning the Australian heavyweight and OPBF titles, was when Guy hugged me and said he loved me. It was special because, as I have already mentioned, there were times when our relationship was Antarctic icy, but after that amazing night at Swan Hill we've been inseparable and I want it to stay that way forever.

The trip home was brilliant. I was on such a natural high by the time we returned to Sydney I could quite easily have floated all the way to Kulnura, but we caught the train back to Wyong all the same. It was an incredible journey and I was skylarking so much a few transit police officers moved towards me to have a quiet word. However, they changed their tune once they heard I was the new national heavyweight champion and instead of threatening to fine me or put me off at the next station, they shook my hand and offered their heartiest congratulations.

It was a great moment and in my mind I have no doubt Dean Waters came to life the night he won those belts. Sadly, the same bloke 'died' just a few short years later.

However, for now I was alive. I think a bantamweight who fought in the early 1980s named 'Sparrow' Freeman summed up the way I felt, when he said from the ring:

> *Before I became a professional boxer I was nothing; didn't even know about self-esteem let alone having any. The same with confidence. I never thought I'd ever be able to achieve anything ... that I'd just drudge along each day heading nowhere.*

I might have lost more bouts than I won, but each of them added to the value of my life. I had been rescued from complete obscurity. Only I will ever know what it meant to me hearing people call my name and knowing I was capable of being recognised. When the people cheered me it was like being lifted high in the air where I could feel I'd never again have to think of myself as worthless...

While Guy, my entourage and I celebrated my victory in fine style, Troy endured a bastard of a time in South Korea. Dad might have thought he was a crafty bugger, but, by the time Troy entered the ring, the Asian fight promoters had taught them both a lesson or two about deviousness.

First, the fight was not staged in Seoul as Dad had expected. It was instead scheduled for an outpost close to the North Korean border called Knangdiong. It was a five-hour drive from Seoul and the conditions Troy faced were abysmal – apart from being plonked in a village where the temperature was five below zero he could also hear cannon fire roaring from the 42nd parallel!

The hotel they were based in sounded like Korea's answer to Fawlty Towers. In addition to having to sleep on a lumpy mattress, there were no sheets, no towels, no hot water and a group of guests – who Dad believed were paid by the promoters – who partied hard until 4 a.m. If that wasn't bad enough the promoters had arranged for a 6 a.m. weigh-in so two hours after the party had finished the fight officials banged on Troy's door and demanded he jump on the scales.

It was a tough slog and it was little wonder the Koreans didn't believe Troy would survive the opening round against their man who was rated number five in the WBC and number six in the WBA. In Chul Baek's record – thirty-five knockouts from thirty-six bouts – suggested it was always going to be a battle for Troy to win; however, the Koreans ensured they had the cards stacked in their favour by appointing two local judges on the three-man panel, which was made possible by the WBC's representative from Thailand failing to appear on time. According to the Australian judge, Denzil Creed, it was no wonder the Thai did not leave Bangkok – he was only notified about the fight the previous day!

However, out of the fires of torment are forged men of steel and Troy distinguished himself in a hostile environment. After spending his pre-fight warmup shivering over a tiny kerosene heater with the preliminary boys, my brother gave In Chul Baek a hell of a time, a point Jeff Wells proudly recorded in the *National Times*:

> *When the fight began Troy proceeded to give In Chul Baek a lesson, boxing his way inside, the way Ces had taught him, and nailing him with good combinations. The Korean, sensing he was in trouble, resorted to low blows.*
>
> *'He was blatantly hitting Troy in the testicles and kidneys but the referee would not even issue a caution. I kept screaming foul but nobody was listening,' said Ces.*
>
> *At one stage In Chul Baek hit Troy so hard below the belt that the cup flew out of his protector and spun on to the mat. The referee did not stop the fight to have it replaced but, as if to remind the world that South Korea had qualified for the World Cup, neatly soccer-kicked it out of the ring.*
>
> *'Troy was fouled so badly he was peeing blood after the fight,' said (Denzil) Creed. But Troy Waters showed true world class by fighting back and in the ninth of the twelve rounds had In Chul Baek in such trouble that the Korean couldn't throw a punch . . .*

Unfortunately for Troy's sake the local judges did not share Denzil's view and awarded the fight to the home-town hero. Rubbing further salt into Troy's wounds was the fact that after the fight he and Dad were placed straight on a local bus crammed with Koreans and such cargo as clucking chickens in bamboo cages. It must have been a terrible trip and I don't think Troy's being propositioned to be some Korean bloke's boyfriend helped make the ride any more pleasant. Poor Troy, he was ripped off by shady judges, pissing blood and trapped on a creaking old bus in hostile territory and all for the princely sum of US$1,500! But, hey, that's boxing – and that is why I call it the crying game.

KELLY

Chapter Ten

'Women are a bad invention . . .'

Ces on women

Apart from the time Eve wandered about the apple orchard in the Garden of Eden, I can not think of too many instances where a woman has rocked a place to its foundations quite like Kelly Baker did at Kulnura. Kelly shook Dad's little kingdom by opening my eyes to the ways of the outside world and he despised her for it.

He saw her as a threat and devoted plenty of time to trying to nip our relationship in the bud. However, Kelly wasn't the only person rattling the shackles because Dad also had another 'outsider' on the farm, a horse-breaker he invited to work there, named Allan Hall. He was a shady character but in time he and Christine commenced what would become a very dangerous liaison.

It didn't end there because others started to visit the property and with each different person, what Dad had long feared began to happen. We developed an interest in the outside world. It helped shift our attention away from boxing and Guy and I, at least, pined for the chance to explore other places. I had Kelly, and when Guy met her friend Sharon, Dad could not fathom why he enjoyed her company more than training or looking after the horses!

When Guy and Sharon first started going out they didn't hold hands or show any signs of affection because Guy was terrified of being caught out by Dad. He knew the old man wouldn't approve because he was always on about the kind of women who brought champion athletes down. He warned us that women made unfair demands on a man's time and he made it clear none of us should become involved in a serious relationship until we hung our gloves up.

While Dad did not like Kelly, he actively loathed Sharon and he tried to force Guy into abandoning their relationship by saying such things as she was 'tapped' (mad) and by making Christine tell Guy he could do much better for himself. The most hurtful comment of all, however, was when he advised Guy not to have any kids with Sharon because, he said, 'Your offspring will be born spastic.' While Guy and I flew in the face of Dad's demands concerning women, Troy remained focussed on boxing. As a world-ranked junior middleweight he was in line for Commonwealth and world title fights and nothing, not even being nominated heart-throb material by an army of girls, could distract him. While Dad at least had one genuine gladiator who was prepared to devote his life to the fight game, he was infuriated to sense the first cracks, which would eventually form a huge rift, developing.

He did not respond to the situation very well and tried to crush my interest in Kelly by saying she wasn't good enough for me. In his mind Dad thought we should mate with athletes, or, at least, athletic-looking women. He wanted us to breed a dynasty of boxers for him. In later years Jodie Brockwell, a local journalist who had followed our careers, told a court that Dad had tried to convince her to leave her husband and marry Troy to become the mother of Australia's boxing future! (Though I'm sure Troy would have also bucked at that.)

Before I met Kelly, Jodie was the closest we three boys had come to talking to a girl in a relaxed manner and I would ask her the dumbest questions about girls and the way they thought. To her credit Jodie was kind and understanding. She said there was a child-like innocence in my manner.

Dad said because Jodie had the same body frame as our mother back in England, she would more than likely have the genes to sire a future generation of world champions. When Jodie said her husband would probably have other ideas about Dad's plan, the old man is alleged to have said he could take care of that problem. Obviously she declined and Dad ranted she was turning up the opportunity to be the queen of Kulnura, because he was the king of the mountain!

When she still refused to entertain his plan Dad reacted by phoning the Brockwells around the clock with threatening calls. Jodie wisely ceased coming to the farm after that experience and Dad concentrated on destroying Guy's and my relationships with our first girlfriends.

Dad was wasting his time in trying to convince me to forget Kelly because from the moment I was introduced to her through a boy who trained at our farm I was captivated by her. Apart from her resemblance to the American actress Meryl Streep, I instantly fell for her obvious love for life. In the short space of time we spoke I could sense she had a real energy and I wanted an opportunity to share it.

By the end of our first conversation Kelly invited me to a party and while I really wanted to attend it, my response – that I first had to get my father's permission – must have taken her aback! After all, I was a man of twenty-three, but to her credit she just asked for me to do my best to get there.

I spent the entire trip home from the fights trying to work out the best way to get Dad's blessing to attend the party. No matter how hard I thought about it I knew he would turn me down. After all, it was a party, a place where there'd be copious amounts of alcohol and cigarette smoke, and that didn't fit in well with Dad's plans to have three healthy sons. However, being able to spend more time with a vision named Kelly was the prize in this battle, and I intended to somehow win it.

I had fought – and lost – a similar battle to do weights at a local gymnasium a few months earlier. With hindsight, I realise there was never any chance of me winning that one because Dad was always paranoid that by training somewhere else I would give a so-called 'glory hunter' the opportunity to crow they had played a role in my success. I accepted that decision but this time, with the party, I took a leaf out of his book and nagged and nagged and nagged until I finally eroded his will. Though every time I challenged Dad's authority with a hurt look and demanded to know why I couldn't go and enjoy myself I half expected to receive a backhander!

The moment I laid eyes on Kelly at the party made every minute of the many hours I spent begging and arguing with Dad well worth my while. She looked beautiful and I made an immediate beeline to stand by her side for the entire night. While I was like a puppy dog, eager to please Kelly in whatever way I possibly could, I was also like a doberman, doing everything but growl at any male who dared to speak to her.

I had been out alone on a few Friday nights but only on the strict understanding I was to keep a tight midnight curfew. That was fine early on but the more I went out and experienced many of the things I had been sheltered from, the longer I wanted to stay out. I would dread it when the clock neared 11.30 p.m. because that marked the time I had to leave for my half-hour drive from Gosford back to Kulnura.

The more I went out the easier it became to convince myself that I could make it home on time even if I left at 11.45 p.m. and then it became 11.50 p.m. Hell, I so wanted to make the most of every second I was out one night, I actually believed I could still make Dad's curfew when I left at 11.57 p.m.!

It was crazy, however, nothing came close to the night I attended Kelly's party and I stayed until the last dance. While I was horrified to see the time was 3.30 a.m. I did not care.

At the risk of sounding like a Mills and Boon novelist the reasons were dead simple: I wanted to spend as much time with her as I possibly could because she was such a beautiful girl and I hoped there was a possibility that she could offer me a warmth I had never really experienced before. I wondered how I could win her over and make her my girlfriend.

However, all those powerful feelings vanished on the rushed trip home along the winding road which led through Mangrove Mountain, the Yarramalong Valley and to our shack. The image of Kelly's smiling face was replaced by the fear of knowing how angry Dad would be because I had disobeyed him. A terrible sense of panic overwhelmed me because I knew how he would react – violently.

One time when I was late home from the car racing, Dad battered me so badly I could hardly walk the next day. He said I copped what I deserved being insolent. After that, when I returned at 12.15 a.m. or even 12.30 a.m. he was content just to give me an earbashing and after he'd finished blasting me for a lack of discipline, I would meekly tread over the puddles of animal mess and go into my room. While I did not like making Dad mad, more often than not on those occasions I would lie in bed and smile at the memory of the night's activities.

However, on this night, the party night, I feared I would *really* cop it. And my terror was justified when I saw Dad waiting at the gate for me! Because I expected to be flogged I drove past Dad and stopped when I reached what I hoped would be a safe distance from him. My heart was pounding like a drum when he walked towards me, so I wound down my window and asked as innocently as possible, 'What's wrong, Dad?' in a desperate attempt to defuse the situation.

Well, he exploded! 'You're no good,' he screamed, voice at fever pitch. 'Your bags will be packed – you can get out!'

I knew what was to follow so I put my car in reverse and parked in a neighbour's driveway. I lay there waiting for him to calm down and when he approached the car I braced myself for a fierce hiding. However, rather than bash me Dad just motioned his head for me to follow him.

It was amazing because what followed was our first real father–son chat. He told me I had done the wrong thing and I should realise my boxing and training took priority over all things. I was so relieved not to be beaten I nodded my head like a chastened schoolboy, yet at the same time I felt grateful to Dad. Grateful that he not only spared me from a hiding but that he spoke to me like a person, almost like an adult. God knows, I loved him even more for it.

As the weeks went by I began to look forward to my Friday nights because they were when I saw Kelly. The anticipation of seeing her was always exciting and saying goodbye always tore at my heart. If there was any comfort to be found in our farewells it was the fact she, too, felt the same. Not being allowed to see Kelly at that stage of my life hurt me much more than any punch Dave Russell or Kevin Barry ever landed on my chin, and I told Dad how it felt. Well, he showed no sympathy. He told me to wake up to myself. It wasn't the response I wanted and the heartlessness of it sowed the seeds of rebellion in me. I shouted if I wasn't allowed to see her on a more frequent basis then I would leave the farm; it was an ultimatum which shocked me even as I said it. However, it did not faze Dad, who snarled: 'Go then, go! Get out because you're no good, Dean. Mark my words, though, you'll come crawling back on your hands and knees!'

Well, I was finally granted the freedom I had long wanted but I was terrified because I had no money, no place to go and I felt a dreadful guilt that Dad and I had parted on such bitter terms. I wanted to cry but there was no time for that.

I went to the only place possible, and that was to Kelly's parents' house. Mr and Mrs Baker were great to me – they opened their house and allowed me to stay for a few nights as I tried to come to grips with what had happened between Dad and mc. Wc had fought – really fought – and I feared life could never be the same. However, just when I thought we might never speak again Dad phoned the Bakers one day, crying like a baby. He told me he wanted me to return to Kulnura because he could not cope without me.

I told Dad there was no way I could – or would – return unless he accepted Kelly as my girlfriend. He consented to my demands but his words belied his feelings because not long after he regained his position of power over me and I moved back to live amid the stench of the animal waste, he started to run Kelly into the ground again. We fought but Dad won.

He forced me to ring Kelly and demand to speak to her brother. When he answered the phone I said something along the lines of: 'Can you tell Kelly that I'm not going to ever see her again? Would you tell her I'm not allowed to see her again?'

By the time I slammed the telephone receiver back into its cradle my heart had broken into a million little pieces and my will was all but exhausted. Dad then followed up on the telephone call by dictating a letter for Christine to write to Kelly as if it were from me. I have forgotten how it went but the message was ruthless and without sentiment.

It said my training and boxing came first and no girlfriend was going to alter that. They weren't my thoughts but I knew I'd be beaten if I did not sign the letter or if I put up any hint of a fight. I thought of Kelly and I cried. I wondered how all the crap must have affected her. I had unwittingly dragged her into a nightmare and I felt lousy for it.

Ultimately, Kelly and I got back together and at Easter, 1985, she moved out of her parents' home to live on the farm. The first time I took her to the property for a visit a few weeks earlier it dawned upon me how bad the place must look to an outsider. When she asked to visit the 'little girls' room' I felt so ashamed I hid her eyes with my hand

and turned off the lights before I guided her up the hallway because I didn't want her to see the animal waste. I'm certain Kelly sensed my embarrassment because she did not ask questions, nor did she comment on the brown stains left on the wall where the dogs had rubbed their worm-infested backsides.

However, she was prepared to put up with all of that when we were (begrudgingly) given the opportunity to live together. Dad was still dead against our relationship, and in an attempt to scuttle it, he arranged for us three boys to go out with some local girls to the movies. Poor Kelly was left alone on the farm with Dad and he didn't miss the opportunity to try and start trouble between us. As she watched the television, Dad would walk into the lounge-room and shake his head in mock disbelief, asking, 'How could they do this to you? How could Dean leave you here?'

I wasn't having much fun in Gosford because all I could think about during the meal was Kelly and how she was doing back at the farm. I wanted to leave, but I knew that would only cause trouble. When I returned home Kelly and I went to my room and I did the usual ritual before she bunked down on the thin foam mattress she used for a bed. I rolled a towel up and covered the gap between my closed door and the floor to stop a stream of dog's urine from entering the room and waking Kelly up in one of the most unpleasant manners you would ever want to imagine.

However, our life took a turn for the better when Christine bought us a caravan to live in after Stately Gauntlet won a race at Newcastle. (I think that was the day Dad's advice to the jockey was to pretend he was a cowboy being chased by a bunch of Red Indians!) Anyway, the caravan was Christine's way of thanking Kelly for helping her with the chores. Needless to say, we appreciated the gesture because it gave us some privacy.

While Kelly had long realised mine was far from a normal upbringing she gained an insight into how tough our lives had really been the day she heard a scream and saw Dad throw Christine against a wall. My step-mother fell to the floor and lay as if she had been knocked out. However, worse was to come when Dad booted her in the stomach and demanded she get to her feet. Christine climbed to her feet all right, and bolted through the kitchen with Dad in hot pursuit. When he caught her near the tractor shed, Dad grabbed her and started to hit her all over again.

In a bid to save Christine, Kelly ran to the kitchen where Troy was cooking eggs. She demanded to know what he was going to do to stop the bashing, but she didn't understand – and how could she? – we were used to such scenes. I'm certain she condemned Troy when he simply shrugged his shoulders in an uninterested manner and kept stirring his eggs on the stove. Once she realised Troy would do nothing, she screamed for Guy and I to help but we were already on the scene, trying to pacify Dad.

From that day on Kelly and Sharon were given an unabridged insight into Dad's cruel ways. One of the worst examples he gave them was the time Kelly's dog, Suzie, mauled a chook and left it half dead. Rather than mourn the chicken's demise Dad looked both girls in the eyes and snapped its neck – hhhrrrkkk – before walking off with the bird's limp carcass in his hand. In a voice as cold as an Arctic gale Dad said: 'That's all you have to do . . .'

Kelly quickly learned to recognise the warning signs before Dad exploded into one of his rages and lost control of his actions and she would get out of the way. One day when she saw Dad start to lose control she bolted like a scared rabbit towards the caravan. Believe me, she moved even faster when she realised Dad was running after her with a knife in his hands! She locked herself in the van and hid behind a table as Dad screamed all sorts of blood-curdling threats at her.

Some people would say Kelly should have left and ended the relationship then and there, but we were in love, and she was prepared to endure anything Dad threw her way if it meant we could stay together. Like the time she and Sharon accompanied us to Hobart for one of our triple title bouts at the Wrest Point Casino. Dad made them eat at separate tables and keep away from us in the lead-up to the bout, ostracising them from our group. It was demeaning but love conquers most things.

The breaking point for Kelly and the farm came when Christine ran off with Hall. It threw Dad's life into a turmoil because apart from everything else he was short-handed and needed help with the animals. He conscripted Kelly to fill the void and the old coot worked her into the ground. She hated it, she hated the lifestyle and she hated Dad's hold over me. Kelly was sick of hearing me answer every request she made with the same line of: 'I'd better ask Dad.'

And she despised Dad the day he made me hold Christine's dog Foxy (six weeks before she escaped with Hall), as he took to it with a metal bracket. I was struck with a few full-blooded blows as the terrified creature tried to break free and when I couldn't take its yelps anymore I let go of my hold on the dog so it could bolt.

It was an act of compassion but Dad took to me with the bracket for letting him down. While each blow felt like an electrical jolt there was nothing I could do. I just cowered and waited for him to stop. God knows, it hurt and I knew

Kelly was right when she said we had to leave after that. Apart from the assaults, it wasn't fair for Kelly to be exposed to such a life.

When I told Dad I was leaving he went ballistic.

'Ha! You won't even be able to get out of bed to train – your career is over. You'll come crawling back to me, wait and see.'

I didn't. I continued training on the farm, partly because I didn't want to give Dad the satisfaction of describing me to my brothers as a lost cause. I would set my alarm for 5 a.m. and hot-foot it from our place at Berkeley Vale to the farm. I trained hard, I continued to do my chores and I returned home to Kelly.

Life fell into a decent enough routine and everything was fine until one morning at 2 a.m. when Dad phoned. He was crying and he sounded very distant. The tone of his voice spooked me and my sixth sense told me to expect some bad news.

'I've dreamt of my second wife, Dean, Doreen, you know, she committed suicide?' he said. 'She has asked me to come with her. She wants me to follow her.'

A criminal psychiatrist was later to describe that call as 'psyche manipulation', explaining that Dad had tried to make me do what he wanted by making me fear he was ready to neck himself. I was in a real bind and when I told Kelly we had to move back to the farm she bawled long and hard; I may as well have told her we were going to prison. When I saw her reaction, her fear, I realised there could be no going back. I had to somehow sort things out with Dad. Though he had other problems to contend with, namely Christine and Allan Hall.

A FATAL ATTRACTION

Chapter Eleven

'I can't understand how you could have an affair with such an object . . .'

Ces Waters to Christine on her relationship with Allan Hall

I didn't like Allan Hall much, but I didn't hate him either. He was just an average-looking bloke who came across as a bit of a rough and ready type. Unfortunately for me, and Hall, he became entwined in the Waters story the day he met Dad in a supermarket queue in Wyong.

By the time the traffic jam of shopping trolleys had cleared and the pair bought their groceries, Hall had just about spilt his entire life's story to my old man. He had obviously followed our careers because he spoke in great detail to Dad about some of our fights and his enthusiasm struck a chord with the old man.

As it turned out thirty-eight year old Hall was himself a veteran of forty-odd professional boxing bouts, though he lost more than he won. However, what really appealed to

Dad was the fact Hall not only broke in horses but he had learned the trade from J.D. Wilton, a legend in the equine industry. Dad seized upon the opportunity to capitalise on Hall's adulation for the fighting Waters clan and he invited him around to our farm to work with Christine on a few of our horses. It was a terrible mistake for a man who had built up an invisible barrier to isolate us from the outside world. Indeed, it turned out to be a fateful decision because it would eventually destroy just about everything he had worked for.

Hall fitted in well with our way of life and quickly went about teaching Christine some different techniques of caring for horses. Looking back on that time I guess there was a chemistry between the pair: even though Christine didn't like the look of Allan when they first met, they certainly worked well together in the stables. They always seemed to be laughing and carrying on. While I initially tried to befriend Hall because he had a good sense of humour and I liked to swap jokes with him, I became very uncomfortable in his presence when I realised he and Christine were having a sexual relationship.

Despite Hall's seemingly cheery disposition Dad developed an intense dislike for just about everything to do with him. He resented Allan's mere presence and some of the things Allan did – such as dumping hordes of malnutritioned mutts on us – drove my father to fury. 'Allan's given us more hungry mouths to feed,' he'd moan.

However, rather than explode, Dad was keener on having me spar a few rounds with the horse-breaker. I was reluctant because Hall was far too small to fight a bloke my size and the thought of roughing him up made me feel like a bully. As a result Dad sent him in against Troy, and even though he pulled his punches my little brother still had enough sting to knock Allan around.

I have no doubt Dad wanted me to box with Hall because he wanted *me* to punish him for his relationship with Christine – and Christine with him. The pair spent plenty of time together on Hall's farm, though, based on what Christine told the courtroom a few years later their affair was engineered by the old man as a means to satisfy his twisted mind.

Christine swore on the Bible that Dad had encouraged her to pursue a sexual relationship with the younger man because he figured she needed to be cured of her so-called 'frigidity'.

'I want you to have more sex with younger men because you're too frigid. You are not compatible with me or what I require – I suggest you start with Allan Hall.'

In a throwback to the days when he was a snotty-nosed kid who spied on the whores in the brothels of Manchester, Dad would get off by watching Christine and Allan have sex. Initially, Christine was a reluctant participant in Dad's plan because she did not like the look of Hall – he was overweight and, if the truth be known, he was a bit of a slob. However, bearing Dad's previous form in mind, I have no doubt Christine told the truth. After all, Dad had her sell her body for thirteen years to make enough money to finance his dream to raise three world champs.

Nevertheless, the more Allan hung around our farm the more we learned about his shadowy past and Dad didn't like it. We heard he had a criminal record six feet long and it was crammed with such offences as homosexual assault and drug-dealing. He was credited with destroying the marriage of a mentally retarded bloke on the Central Coast and I had it on good authority from a friend who had worked with him at a local abattoir that he wasn't to be trusted. Apparently Hall would borrow cash from his workmates in the slaughteryard and offal room and would challenge them to a punch-up when they dared ask for their cash to be repaid.

He was a bad egg, but I didn't hate him for it, though I could quite easily have smacked him about later on after Dad convinced me Hall was a child molester. I was wary around him and I watched him carefully.

When Christine told Dad her interest in Hall was more than just for casual sex – it was love – his ego was crushed. He warned Hall to stay away from our property and ordered my step-mother to steer clear of him. Dad reasoned that, because we boys had started to gain a public persona, the last thing we needed was for the family name to be dragged into the mud by the sort of scandal a person of Hall's character would most certainly bring to the farm. Tragically, they were to be prophetic words.

Dad's hatred of Hall reached fever pitch when we returned from our triple title bill in Hobart and found Christine had packed her bags and disappeared. She had left us to live with Hall on his property at nearby Warnervale and I remember feeling very empty inside. To the best of her ability Christine was the closest thing to a mother figure we boys had ever known. While I knew the Waters clan had more than its fair share of problems, I always believed we were no different from any other family. I thought ours was the way other families behaved, but now our mother had left and each of us took it to heart.

Troy was withdrawn, Guy brooded and I blew off steam. I couldn't believe what had happened, and I wasn't happy with Hall. Dad was also far from impressed with the development and ordered Christine to terminate the relationship immediately or to be responsible for Hall coming to an ugly end.

'I will have to have Allan Hall mutilated or killed in order to break the relationship. Most of all, you will not allow me to take part in the relationship. I feel as though there is too much affection between you and not just sex as I indicated. If you want to save his life you will have to stop seeing him.'

When Christine defied Dad's wishes he tried kindness and even suggested they both go on a holiday to Fiji to spend some quality time together. He was adamant they could work things out if they left the home front and basked in the sunshine. When that did not get the desired reaction Dad started a harassment campaign against the lovers which was straight out of a psycho thriller.

Christine told the court of one instance when Dad went to Hall's house determined to cause trouble. When Christine tried to snatch the keys from the ignition of his car Dad punched her in the face and then tried to strangle her.

'I was trying to get the keys out when my former husband reached through the door and punched my face,' she said under cross-examination. 'He tried to strangle me, started to put his arms around my neck. He let go when I bit him on the forearm.'

In other ugly episodes Dad made threats such as 'You'll both go together' and 'You've got a shock coming . . .'

The more Dad dwelled on the Hall problem, the more wild his mind became. He sat down one night and wrote an unsigned letter for Hall's attention. While Dad spent most of his life as an illiterate, he was sharp enough to write the letter in such a way it could not be interpreted by the police, or even a court of law, as a death threat!

It said: 'No wonder you fail as a human being, as you did a boxer . . . People like you who have fed dope to the young and who use alcohol to excuse their gutless attitude to life, can only expect the worst from life . . . You are a loser for life and much more is to come. It is only a pity that poor soul has got to be a part of your self-destruction. You are scum with no respect for anything or anybody.'

In another letter, this time to the Wyong police, Dad complained Hall was observed drugged to the eyeballs and firing a .22 rifle he didn't have a licence for. Dad signed the letter, 'Concerned', and added he was terrified Hall would one day kill someone with his wayward behaviour.

The truth is Dad was desperate to end Christine's liaison and he even staged a meeting with a man who I believe was a wharfie from the Newcastle docks. Dad did not beat around the bush as he made his request. 'I want Allan Hall's right hand hacked off and I then want him to be castrated.'

The wharfie was shocked; I think he expected to make some quick money by simply bashing Hall in a dark alley and maybe perhaps slapping Christine about in Allan's house. However, once he absorbed what Dad had requested he nodded his head and said it would take a 'special' person to perform such a crime. However, when Dad could not pay an upfront deposit the wharfie left and we never heard from him again.

Christine had boxed Dad into a tight corner when she demanded payment for her stake in the farm. While we didn't have any liquid assets, the property was worth quite a lot of cash and Dad did not want to be placed in a position where he had to sell the farm, his crumbling kingdom, to pay her off. Instead, he had to destroy the relationship and he looked at me to be the wrecking ball.

Initially I was used as the go-between, running letters

and messages to and from our place and Hall's. It was an emotionally draining time and Dad planted poison seeds in my head to take drastic measures by saying terrible things about the pair such as, 'Hall is a child molester . . . Christine is a creep . . . she's a hobo, look at what she has done to us . . . Hall is a druggie.' It was like a broken record and I listened to it because Dad wanted me to.

Just as our step-mother left us to live with Hall, Tracey returned from her six-year exile in Western Australia with her husband Marc Erbsleben. I was as pleased as Punch to have resumed contact with her, after Kelly had jotted down Tracey's telephone number from a Christmas card she sent to Kulnura.

It took me a few days to build up enough courage to phone her because I was terrified of the punishment Dad would dispense if he caught me; in his mind, Tracey had betrayed him and he would often say even if she came to him dying of thirst he wouldn't even give her a glass of water.

While my fingers trembled with fear and trepidation as I dialled my long-lost sister's number in Perth, I figured the risk of being bashed was well worth the while when I spoke to her for the first time in six years. She cried as we tried to swap as much news as we could in a few frantic minutes. The important thing was my big sister was safe.

A few months later she returned to the Coast and we'd meet during my nights off from the farm and training and seeing her again was as if I had located a missing part of me. Our meetings were always arranged in secret because we were both terrified of feeling the wrath of Dad if he caught us out.

I had a panic attack one night when Dad's voice came

over the CB in my little blue Datsun while Tracey and Marc were in the car. He demanded: 'Where are you, Dean? You should be home by now.' In my mad panic I immediately stopped the car and all but kicked them out into the cold night air even though I was a fair distance from their place. However, Tracey understood where I was coming from. She knew I would soon be hitting one hundred and twenty kilometres an hour in a bid to try and save myself from being belted with Dad's 'magic wand', the rubber hose she was so familiar with.

I spent as much time as I could with Tracey and Marc and I enjoyed their company immensely. In time my trust in Marc, a martial arts expert, was so great I even approached him about bashing Hall when Dad stressed it was up to me to ruin his and Christine's relationship. Marc, however, was wise enough to keep a wide berth from the family problems and declined. But the more it appeared as though Christine was going to drive Dad to financial ruin the more desperate he became to do something, *anything*. In time Dad unveiled his grand plan and it made me feel sick to my guts. I was to kill Kulnura's answer to Romeo and Juliet.

FINDING GLORIA

Chapter Twelve

'I am still a renegade to the boxing people of Australia. But I can handle that and we will be back.'
Ces Waters after Dean's Commonwealth title defeat

I wasn't even in good enough shape to box chocolates when I received an offer to fly to England and fight for the Commonwealth heavyweight title. I was hopelessly out of nick and my mind was a complete mess.

Since Christine left the farm to live with Hall my main purpose in life was to run messages to her from Dad and it was as emotionally draining as it was mentally. Dad had already planted the seeds in my head that I had to do something about the situation and, while I did my best to resist his mad demand, it was a relentless campaign. To make me fall into line, Dad emotionally blackmailed me by targeting my sense of loyalty and devotion to him.

I tried to escape it on a few occasions by not turning up to the farm, yet Dad couldn't be thrown that easily. I used to take the phone off the hook to try and keep him at bay but the constant engaged signal would send him into a rage and he'd drive the thirty-odd kilometres from the farm to Kelly's and my place like a man possessed. I always knew when he arrived because the car would screech to a halt and he'd slam the door. A few moments later he'd bang on the door and berate me for being lazy and for being no good.

Dad had a great motivation for keeping me on a tighter leash than normal; he wanted me to obey his orders to kill Hall and after his efforts to win Christine back failed she too became a target. He'd tell me in a hushed tone how I was letting him down, that I had no choice but to kill them because of what they had done to the Waters clan and our 'great' name. It had to be done and I was to do it because I was Dad's 'special boy'.

I couldn't escape it; it became a nightmare from which there was no relief. My brothers wondered why I would bellow 'Leave me alone!' whenever Dad bailed me up during training and whispered his evil intentions in my ear. I didn't tell them the reason for my outbursts but Dad was *always* on my case and I dreaded hearing him say such things as 'You know what has to be done, Dean! It has to be done', in between training rounds.

I was in turmoil. Apart from the Hall problem I was also trying to convince Dad to accept Kelly as someone who was very important to me, but that was a lost cause. He had disliked her from the outset and, no matter how bright a light I painted her in, he could not be convinced to change his attitude.

It was a tough time all round and I received the offer to fight British bruiser Horace Notice with mixed emotions. I was in no condition to fight him – I was soft around the middle and my mind was in a constant spin – however, it was Dad's call. At that stage of my life I still trusted his opinion totally and I felt guilty when he expressed his disappointment in my lack of enthusiasm.

He described it as a 'career-making' opportunity because at around this time Dad had spoken to the handlers of the then-world champion, Mike Tyson, about a possible match-up. Apparently the response from New York was they would be happy to talk turkey once I broke into the world top 10 rankings. After all, I was white and one of the great clichés of boxing is the world wants another great white hope.

So, there was a lot at stake and Dad dismissed my misgivings about fighting Notice with a wave of his hand. 'You're strong, son, you have heart. You know you can do this.'

With hindsight, as my trainer and, more importantly, as my father, Dad should never have accepted the bout. He *must* have known I risked serious injury by entering the same ring as the WBC's number thirteen heavyweight in my sad state.

The *Sydney Morning Herald*'s Peter Bills made it clear the fight wasn't one to take lightly, describing Notice as an intimidating black bruiser who had put plenty of opponents to sleep. Bills warned that my opponent was blessed with a punch which could short-circuit a man's neurosystem. Few people in Britain thought I would last the distance against him and Bills noted their sentiments when he wrote I was 'very much the unfancied outsider brought across the world to provide cannon fodder for another of Britain's aspiring young heavyweights'.

While my back was well and truly to the wall I should stress no matter how grim some things have looked throughout my life I've always backed myself in any contest which came down to a matter of ticker, and I always will. After all, I won the Australian and OPBF belt after only three bouts and I backed that up by going punch for punch with world-rated Tony Fulilangi on the undercard of a Jeff Fenech world title bout.

Fulilangi, a tough Tongan, was the world's number nine cruiserweight at the time and Dad was adamant Fenech's promoter, 'Break-even' Bill Mordey, had matched me with him to not only teach me a lesson but to also quieten down my all-consuming campaign to fight 'Aussie' Joe Bugner anywhere, any time.

I was young and angry and viewed the man who'd gone at the great Muhammad Ali as a way to short-track my path to greater things. I did everything to shame him into fighting me; one time I even handed him a white chicken feather (the ancient sign of cowardice) on national television. When that didn't work, I said wild things such as that I was the Aussie champ and there was no room on my turf for a one-time Hungarian, one-time Pom and a Johnny-come-lately Australian.

It was a big call, especially coming from an immigrant, but it was nothing more than meaningless fight talk. Indeed, even though I scrawled 'BUGNER MUST FALL' on my punching bag I didn't feel any real malice towards him. I've seen Joe's record and he has my total respect – it is punctuated with some of the business's greatest names. Indeed, at the time of my writing this book 'Aussie' Joe was still going strong at forty-eight. Indeed, he had even beaten 'Bonecrusher' Smith for the WBF heavyweight title. While Fulilangi beat me on points in what the media described as a disgraceful decision, I certainly did a lot better than the three rounds Break-even Bill and his buddies expected me to last. Notice was to prove an entirely different proposition.

When it became obvious to me there would be no escaping the bout I tried to find as many positives as I possibly could. I hoped the trip to England would give me some respite from Dad's deadly plan for Hall and Christine and I figured it would allow me to find out some more things about my real mother, Gloria Newman.

Apart from being told by Dad how she abandoned us when Troy was still in nappies, we were also brought up to believe she was dead. However, as a kid I always imagined Mum was still alive and well because it sometimes helped to think that she remembered me on my birthday and hoped I was happy and healthy. Most of all, I day-dreamed Mum would one day hug me and say she had missed me.

Sometimes I would listen to what Dad said about her and I'd get angry that she walked out on me and the others. Dad always offered his slanted version of events and he painted her as a wicked woman who didn't give a hoot for her offspring. Sometimes I wondered how I would react if I ever did meet my mother and my emotions ranged from hugging her tightly to screaming, 'Why?'. However, I considered these to be wasted thoughts. Dad had told us many times she was dead and buried on the other side of the world.

While I call Australia home, I could not help but feel a sense of belonging as we walked about London. While I didn't quite hum the old tune, 'Maybe it's because I'm a Londoner', I felt happy to walk around the streets of my childhood with my dad. The place was a blur of noise, colour and history and I'll never forget some of the people we saw: would-be reggae singers, punk rockers, bobbies, crims and businessmen.

Dad lapped it all up. While he loved the solitude of Kulnura he was clearly happy to be in his old environment. It was obvious to me from the moment we hopped into a London cab to take us from Heathrow Airport to our hotel in Wembley that London was *his* town. There was a sparkle in his eyes as he pointed out such places from his past as Nags Head Corner in North London and the old cafe where he met Mum.

It recently struck me that Dad was extra happy because my fighting for the heavyweight title of the British Commonwealth represented his triumphant return to England after leaving with the backside out of his pants and a criminal record a kilometre long! He'd made his mark and I noticed how he puffed his chest out proudly whenever we bumped into characters from his rogue days. A few days before my battle with Horace Notice, Dad took me on a sentimental journey around Finsbury Park and showed me the house I was brought up in: the place where I saw that 'geezer' who died after he lost his grip on the bus one Christmas, the place where Mum left us when she could no longer take Dad's abusive treatment, and the place where Dad taught a woman never to steal from him.

We shared the old building I grew up in with a lot of 'battlers' because the rent was affordable. One of them, an old Irish bird, annoyed Dad because she was forever stealing coal from our bin in the cellar. When Dad asked her to stop it she was offended to have her honesty questioned by a man of Dad's disposition. Nevertheless, the coal continued to disappear and when Dad had enough he took matters into his own hands. He drilled a hole into a large lump of coal and packed the dust around a bunger-style firecracker in it. We didn't think any more about it until later that night when we heard an almighty 'BANG' from across the hall! And when Dad heard the old lady screaming like a banshee he laughed himself silly. 'That will teach her not to thieve from me!'

After we visited the school I attended before we emigrated down under Dad pointed to a block of council units in the distance. While the block looked like a butter box, the flat with a blue door had a special significance for me because that was the place where my mother grew up. He then decided to see if my grandparents still lived there.

Our welcome from the old lady who answered the door was very strange. When she laid her eyes on my father she called for her husband to 'come quick' and I'll never forget the old bloke's reaction: it was as if he had been struck by a lightning bolt. His jaw dropped and he gasped: 'My God, it's Ces Waters!'

The meeting, as brief as it may have been, was a revelation because I learned my mother was still alive and she went by the name of Joy Murphy. What's more she worked as a London bus driver. Dad looked guilty because he had always maintained she was dead! However, he covered his tracks quickly by saying he had read that news in the paper ... but it was a lie, he was lying through his teeth! I didn't think much about it then because I was desperate to meet her. I wanted to meet my mum so much I could have burst in my nan's lounge-room!

My grandparents were reluctant to give us her address. It seemed as if they were protecting her from something and, with hindsight, I know what it was: the beanie-wearing goblin sitting next to me on their couch. While I was disappointed by their not telling me where I could find my mother, at least they took our hotel's telephone number down and promised to pass it on to her, which meant everything to me.

As I sat willing what the Cockneys call the 'dog and bone' to ring, all my problems – the fight, Dad's deadly plan for Christine and Allan, my battle to have the old fella realise Kelly was my girlfriend – seemed insignificant. They were pushed to the back of my mind because all that mattered was hearing this stranger from my past ring and say: 'Hello, Dean, this is your mother.' And as I sat there, it dawned on me they were the words I had longed to hear all my life.

The phone *did* ring after I went to bed and I thought it was Kelly calling to see if I was all right. However, when I heard the girl at the other end of the blower had a Cockney accent I figured it was a local bird Dad had tried to line me up with, so I said impatiently: 'Oh, is that you Donna?'. The reply, however, almost caused me to drop the telephone because the 'voice' said, 'Don't you know who I am? It's your Mum!'.

It was a magic moment and when Mum said she would see me the next day my mind went into overdrive. I wanted to look nice for her so I spent hours in the bathroom and combed my hair, smothered myself in aftershave and even brushed my pearly whites. With that done I tried to come to terms with the magnitude of my impending encounter. This was Mum, the woman who had long been a mystery figure to me. She was that ghost who drifted out of our life when we kids needed her most.

My thought process was interrupted by the shrill ring of the phone. Mum was in the foyer. When the elevator doors opened I saw a tall, beautiful woman standing before me. My long-wondered question about how I'd react to meeting

A priceless family photo of my mother, Gloria, holding Troy and Guy in her arms as Tracey and I stand at attention. This shot was taken about 18 months before my mother was forced to flee for her own safety after constant beatings from Dad.

Would-be tough guy Ces Waters trying to look mean and hard in London.

Publicly my father liked to make out we were the perfect, happy family . . .

Guy, Troy, me, Tracey and our step-mother Christine absorbing some rare English summer sun before migrating Down Under.

The Australia-bound Waters clan in Cape Town, South Africa. The old man actually thought of dropping anchor here.

We lived like our gipsy ancestors as we crossed the Nullabor Plain in 1972.

A tragically prophetic Christmas photograph. Dad encourages me to 'take aim' with a toy pistol at the camera.

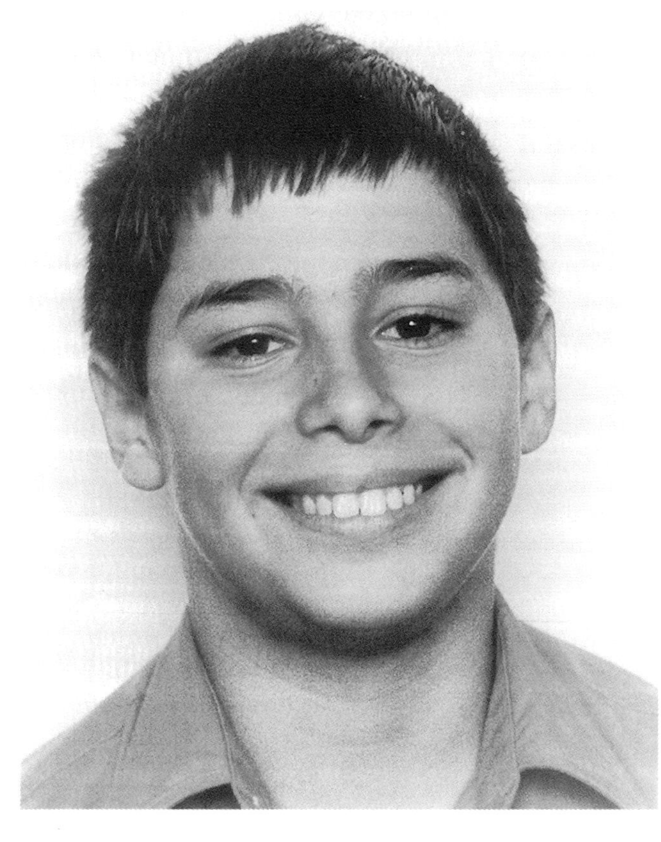

An angelic looking schoolboy. My toothy smile hid the terrible fear which gripped me whenever I was away from my dad.

Dad often bragged about his acting career and he'd delight in telling anyone who listened how we were related to John Wayne.

Before boxing became the focus of his attention Dad dreamt Guy and Troy would return to England as soccer stars.

The dogs Tracey is nursing had a much better life than any of us at our farm in Kulnura.

The Waters brothers on their way to becoming household names for their fistic ability. The view from our homemade boxing ring was beautiful.

As a young man I had a mad streak which got me into plenty of strife.

My first wife Kelly's uncanny resemblance to the American actress Meryl Streep captivated me from the moment I laid eyes on her.

'Mean' Dean Waters, heavyweight champion of Australia and the Orient Pacific. *Photograph courtesy of Fairfax Photo Library.*

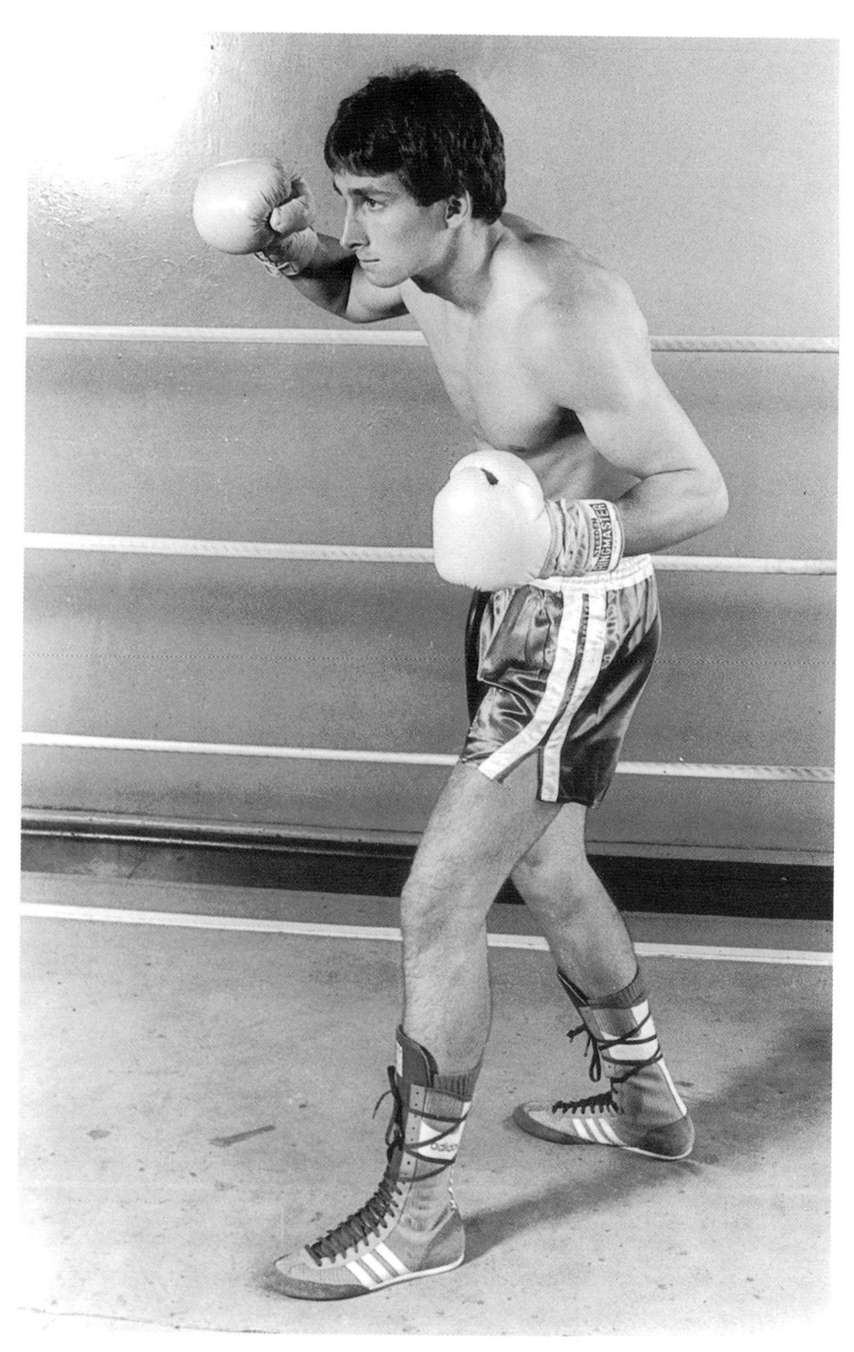

My brother Guy might be a former world champion but he's also close to being an angel.

My reunion with my natural mother meant more to me than the Commonwealth title shot which took me back to England. (Note the body language . . . she wants to be nowhere near Dad.)

Despite Dad's best efforts to foil my meeting with Mum we still found plenty to laugh about.

Our home at Wilberforce Road at Finsbury Park was rough and ready by any standards, but it was a palace compared to our ramshackle farm at Kulnura.

I'm pictured with former World Heavyweight champion Greg Page after our sparring session.

The Glamour with the Hammer, Troy Waters meets 'Hitman' Tommy Hearns in Las Vegas.

My failed comeback against American import Jack Johnson is best remembered for my dad passing on tips to Johnson's camp!
Photograph courtesy of Ern McQuillan.

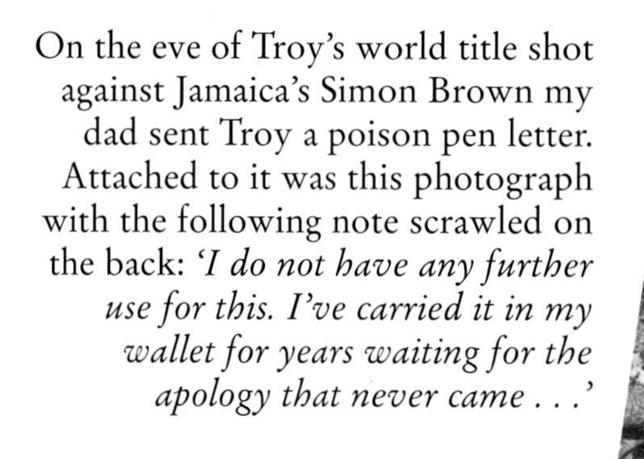

On the eve of Troy's world title shot against Jamaica's Simon Brown my dad sent Troy a poison pen letter. Attached to it was this photograph with the following note scrawled on the back: '*I do not have any further use for this. I've carried it in my wallet for years waiting for the apology that never came . . .*'

While Dad did his best to cover his tracks after Allan Hall he didn't mind advertising the time he was wrongly accused of my mother's death back in London.

With Joe and Doug on the door of Melbourne's Pulse nightclub. I had some of my wildest times in the Victorian capital.

The most special person in my life . . . Renee.

This photograph with my beautiful children was taken before the judge handed down his historic decision in 1997. The strain is obvious on my face because I didn't think I would see them again for a long, long time.

My two beautiful daughters Rebekka and Courtney.

With my sister Tracey in 1997. Tracey has put aside a tragic upbringing to blossom into a beautiful woman and I'm proud of her.

her was answered in an instant: there was no shouting – it was hugs all round.

Gloria embraced me and it felt as though she would never let go. She kissed me on the cheeks and told me over and over I was 'so big ... so beautiful'. Inside my head I was experiencing a number of strange emotions and, apart from knowing at least to return her hug, I didn't know how to handle them. Even though she was my mother, Gloria was a complete stranger. However, that feeling quickly vanished: this was my mum and I needed to get to know her.

Unfortunately Dad ruined the moment. He returned from a shopping expedition soon after Mum arrived and refused to leave us alone for more than a few moments.

While Mum was to wait a long time before she told me how horrific her life with Ces Waters had been I gained a small insight into what it must have been like for her one time when I was clowning around in the motel room before the bout. I shaped up to her and while I have tried, I can't forget the look of horror which overcame her. She was terrified!

'Dean,' she gasped. 'You should never, ever raise your hands to a woman – never!'

Mum's rebuke took me aback; after all, it had only been a harmless joke. Actually, it shocked me to the boots and I almost started to cry because I was so upset by her reaction. In time I learnt her reaction was the end result of the violent life she endured with Dad. When she came to visit Troy, Tracey, Guy and me in Australia, I learned that my father not only battered her on a regular basis but also forced her into prostitution. And when I heard Mum tell her terrible stories, it brought back a few dim memories from my childhood in England of such things as the woman whose face was masked in blood after Dad attacked her with a bottle. However, that was to come later. I put the so-called fight of my life on the back burner and instead basked in the warm glow of finding my Mum, the London bus driver!

I enjoyed myself so much in England I actually toyed with the idea of basing myself there if I won the Commonwealth belt. However, I knew the stoush was going to be an uphill battle because Notice was being hyped as a future world title contender, and it seemed as if every cabbie and bobbie was keen to point out he remained undefeated after fifteen professional bouts.

When the press asked for my thoughts on the fight, I simply promised to give it my all. I said: 'I don't profess to be the best in the world but what I do say is I will fight the best I can and I am not scared of anyone.'

Birmingham-based Notice entered the ring to a thunderous round of applause. The muscular fighter was the shining light in a nation that craved a world heavyweight champion. Their search to fill the void was a desperate one, though I'm sure the crowd felt as though they were a step closer to having their dreams answered when they saw my soft belly. They jeered and yelled such insults as 'Christmas turkey'.

I must have looked ordinary and I'm certain the brave few who placed a few lazy pounds on me, creating an upset, ran to the betting shop, Ladbrokes, to try and somehow salvage their cash. While I didn't want to take the fight in the first place there was no turning back once I climbed through the ropes. And as I stood eyeball to eyeball with the finely chiselled Notice I could feel every gram of my one hundred kilos hanging from my frame.

Nothing clicked for me: I was flat-footed and I lacked speed. Hopelessly outclassed, I did my best to survive the onslaught. While I kept pressing forward I had no answer to Notice and his opening salvo went virtually unchallenged: I took enough punches early in the bout to know there was only going to be one result.

However, I refused to wave the white flag. Even in my dazed and dreadful state I vowed Notice would have to finish the job! As a kid I was raised on Dad's songs and stories of brave feats and perhaps the tale which made the biggest impression on me was of an American captain whose ship was hit by a German torpedo during the Second World War.

As his crew jumped overboard, the skipper stayed behind, destroying important documents in the communications room. As he went about his business he heard the U-boat commander's voice over the crackle on the radio demand: 'Do you surrender?' Rather than concede defeat, the US officer replied: 'I have not yet begun to fight!'

And that was how it was for me against Notice. My body may have been spent but I had no intention of surrendering my spirit. Unfortunately, any hope I had of bringing some boxing glory to Australia was shattered the instant a big right hand exploded on my temple! My head spun, my knees buckled and for the first time in my fight career I was beaten on a TKO. And while my pride hurt like hell I was glad it was over and I could spend time with Mum.

Needless to say, my father was not happy with the outcome and while he vented his spleen, others, like fight scribe Peter Bliss, saw my stand as something to be proud of. He wrote: 'By accommodating such blows Waters showed courage and bravery. He stuck it out as long as he could, only delaying the inevitable. The savagery of Notice's blows to the head and body would have put some men down earlier.'

However, Dad was not prepared to pump me up at all. When I tried to say something to the crowd Dad snapped. He said I had embarrassed him enough and I should be ashamed of myself. My face was swollen, my head buzzed and I wanted to cry but Dad said his pride was hurt more. He figured all of his old associates from his past were crammed around television sets from Manchester to London and he was angry they did not see a Ces Waters victory through me. He added to my hollow feeling of failure by criticising me to the press when it could have been just as easy for him to put his hand on my shoulder and say, 'You did your best, son.'

Instead, the drill sergeant side of his character seized the opportunity to lambast my decision to leave the farm and move in with Kelly. He said: 'Dean was lackadaisical tonight. He didn't seem to get going at all. He can throw good punches but he wasn't doing anything. Now he has to double his work rate. It is either go all out or forget it.'

On a personal note, Dad took time out to fire a shot at his rivals in the Johnny Lewis-run Newtown Police Boys Club when he sneered: 'This loss will please a lot of people in Australia like Bugner and Fenech. They will be rejoicing and glad to see one of my boys lose . . .'

While Dad cursed the fight as a lost opportunity, I did not give a stuff about what my critics thought of me. I had given my all. While the Commonwealth heavyweight title belt remained on Notice's waist I returned to Australia with something of much greater value to me – my lost mother's love – and that felt a lot better than any boxing title.

LOST LAMBS
Chapter Thirteen

'They wouldn't be boxing if I had my way . . .'
Gloria Newman on our spartan life

Thanks to Dad, the media was out in force to capture our tearful reunion with our mother at Sydney airport. He had phoned just about every news editor in the city to tip them off on a big story concerning the 'famous' Waters boys. He sold himself well and the press turned out in their droves, which was a great shame because it meant Troy, Tracey and Guy's first meeting with our mum in twenty years was an awkward, self-conscious experience.

Nevertheless, despite having their most private moment turned into a public event it was obvious my siblings were just as happy as I had been to hug the woman they had long believed to be dead.

Her visit started off well, very well, but it deteriorated quickly when Mum told me things about Dad, like the way he treated her. It caused problems. For the first time in my life I dared to question Dad's ways and I listened intently when Mum said she thought Dad had too great a hold over me and the other boys. Gloria thought we lived too spartan a life and she was far from impressed by the fact we were professional fighters. She said we would never have stepped into a boxing ring if she had had her way.

Dad, a true survivor, could smell the familiar whiff of trouble in the air and he set about trying to nip it in the bud. He knew Kelly had already planted the seeds of rebellion in my brain and the last thing he wanted was for Gloria to nurture them. The old man's response to the threat was to work overtime to win back my favour and it didn't take long for me to fall under his spell. He won me over by saying such things as I was his favourite, I meant a lot to him and he didn't want *anyone* to get in the way of our relationship. Not even my mother.

Gloria stayed with Tracey and Marc and it didn't take much prompting for them to swap their many horror stories, and compare war wounds, from their life with Ces. However, Dad punched his way off the ropes and put Gloria on the spot by asking her such things as why didn't she ever contact us kids after she left us? Why did she desert us? What happened to the ring which belonged to his mother? Dad's questions went on and on until Mum had the same hunted and haunted look I could sometimes feel on myself.

It was a heart-wrenching time for me because, while I wanted to get to know my mother after two lost decades, I also had to be a good soldier and follow through Dad's orders to send Gloria packing on the first plane back to London. It was tough and when I told her over the phone she had to go home because she was causing too much trouble between Dad and me, her voice broke.

Mum could not understand my actions, or the coldness

in my voice, and she cried. I didn't like doing it. I was just following Dad's orders to the letter because I still wanted to please him, be the loyal son and, to tell you the truth, I have regretted it with all my heart ever since.

An article which appeared in *New Idea* magazine a month after Mum left still torments me. I was quoted saying how bad Mum was because she thought our lifestyle was unnatural and that we were all under our father's control. I told journalist John Burfitt:

> *She should have been trying to make things up instead of judging us by the way we live. It has been twenty years and we have been doing all right. Then we brought her over here and she started judging us. She was judging us because we didn't smoke, drink or eat meat, and she thought that was really weird. She also thought Dad had too much influence on our lives. We thought she would be happy with the way Dad brought us up and how we turned out. I don't know if she was bitter because Dad had stuck by us, which she didn't.*

Talk about words to choke on! While I was being the good son yet again, the motivation for me talking to Burfitt was fear. Dad often placed words in our mouths. For instance, whenever we won a fight he would tell us to make sure we acknowledged him as Australia's best boxing trainer. When the press came he would instruct us to tell the journalist such things as Dad bordered on being a genius and that we couldn't get by without him.

Another time when the journalist Steve Crawley wrote something which infuriated Dad – he said we pigged out on hamburgers and Coca-Cola when Dad's back was turned – I was ordered to take him to task the next time he came to the farm for an interview. When judgement day arrived Dad said 'Give him a good fright, Son' and I went out huffing and puffing like a bear with a sore head.

However, rather than berate Crawley and threaten the physical harm Dad had ordered, I told him I had to put on a show for the old man because he was looking through the window. I waved my hands around and told him if he ever wrote another story like that again there'd be hell to pay. Crawley, who I consider to be a decent bloke, just nodded and I watched as his car disappeared in a cloud of dust. Dad's plan worked of course because he never wrote another bad thing about us. Actually, come to think of it, I don't think he ever wrote another line about us again!

I spoke to my mother a month after shooting Hall to say I loved her very much and I was truly sorry for sending her home. I told her it was one of my great regrets and we both cried. Gloria was well aware I had been charged with murder and she begged to know if everything was all right. I told her not to worry because I had not done anything wrong. There were more tears and we finished our conversation saying we would always love each other, no matter what.

The significance of those words hit home a few weeks later when I heard from Tracey that Mum had been hospitalised with a cerebral haemorrhage as she hung the phone up after our conversation. On learning of Mum's poor state I told Dad I was going to England to be with her. That notion went down like a lead balloon: he exploded and he started bad-mouthing Mum again. 'She's no good, Dean; she abandoned you when you were a baby! Anyway she's better off dead because she can't cause trouble for anyone now.'

Dad's words about Mum abandoning us had long since lost their sting because I was well aware she fled because of his brutal temper. My relationship with him had nose-dived since I killed Hall. He behaved as if it was just another chore and that attitude made me resent him. The spell Dad had over me had broken and nothing could piece it back together. We constantly argued.

However, few of our fights were as fever-pitched as the one which followed his callous comment about my mother's misfortune. I erupted and for that split second I really hated him. I saw him for what he was – a little man with no compassion – and it began the start of a bitter feud which would eventually tear Dad's world apart.

A TICKET TO HELL

Chapter Fourteen

'Good lad . . .'

Ces Waters' compliment to Dean on a job well done

Christine caused the old man some serious grief when she wrote a letter to his solicitor ordering him either to sell the farm or face the prospect of her blabbing many hurtful stories to the press about 'Waters' World'. After two decades of being told she was nothing, Christine finally had Dad where she wanted him. She had the upper hand because she knew he would not dare risk having the public profile we had developed as boxing's so-called 'savage innocents' being tarnished by stories of how he made her work as a hooker or how he battered us.

Dad slammed Christine's letter down on the table in disgust and screamed he was being blackmailed by a bitter woman. If that wasn't bad enough, Dad was sent reeling a few days later when a second letter said Christine expected to receive seventy-five per cent of the proceeds from the sale of the property. That hurt Dad and Christine should probably have known better. After twenty turbulent years with Dad, she should have realised she was playing with a dangerous fire.

Compounding the drama associated with Christine's demands other financial pressures began to mount as a series of outstanding bills rolled in. And they were steep: $4,000 for animal feed, a $5,000 vet bill and, the granddaddy of them all, a whopping $100,000 bill from the Australian Taxation Office! While Dad blamed Christine for not submitting the income tax forms he signed for our agent every year he definitely felt under siege. The tax office threatened serious action while the creditors screamed they would repossess Dad's belongings unless he coughed up some cash – and quick-smart!

It was a tough time and with each demand Dad's hatred of Christine and Allan Hall grew even deeper and I felt the full brunt of it whenever I trained at the farm. 'You have to do something, Son, you have to fix this problem!' I was at a loss and in my wish to please Dad I sometimes allowed my imagination to run dangerously wild.

I needed to scare Hall so I sought out Tracey's husband Marc – he'd fought for a NSW kickboxing title – to teach Allan a good lesson. I gave Marc Dad's old spiel about Hall being a dirty 'druggo' who had caused my family many problems. Hall, I said, deserved a thrashing because, after ruining my father's marriage, he rubbed salt into Dad's wounds by walking hand in hand with my step-mother at the local shopping centre.

While I waited to hear of Hall's being set upon in a dark alley I was to learn much later on – in a courtroom – that Marc had no intention of acting on my request and he forgot about our conversation until he was called upon to give evidence against me in the murder case.

As each day went by Dad demanded that I prove my worth as his special boy: it was up to me to sort the mess out. He had me on my knees, so to speak, and with the old man's urging I set about trying to put the fear of God in the hearts of Allan Hall and Christine.

The campaign started innocuously enough the night Dad and I stopped outside Allan and Christine's place and I fired a cap gun two times and we sped off into the darkness when we saw them rush to investigate the noise.

My next visit to their property, however, was a lot more serious because Dad and I had been to Hall's place a few nights before on a recon mission to see how accessible the place was by driving past it a few times ... we considered it to be a soft target and a few nights later my mate Damon Cooper and I were sent to burn the place down.

We parked a kilometre up the road and ran towards their house with a tin of dieseline on our shoulders. It was real commando stuff: whenever we heard a car hurtling down the road towards us we hid in the bushes and waited until they were out of view before we pressed on.

As soon as I'd ascertained Christine and Hall were out, we seemed to go into auto-pilot. Damon kicked the door open and I removed the animals locked inside. They were barking like crazy when Damon entered the place but they calmed down quickly when they saw me; after all, I used to feed most of them back at Kulnura. As I doused the place in fuel Damon opened the windows to let the air in and help feed the fire. We then shooed the dogs away because I knew it wasn't going to take long for the house to be engulfed in flames.

Once we were certain everything was under control Damon and I fled the scene and when we drove past I was glad the place was an inferno because I was certain I had done the right thing for Dad. My father was adamant Christine would crawl back to him if she had nothing and I actually looked forward to an end to the months of badgering I had been subjected to.

While I was confident I'd left nothing to chance I was distressed later to learn that Foxy, the dog I had been forced to hold when Dad beat it with a metal bracket, jumped back into the house through an open window and was incinerated in the inferno. However, though her dog was dead and her home was a pile of ashes, Christine did not return to Kulnura as Dad had expected. Instead she defied the old man by staying with Hall and that sent him to a different level of madness.

He became even more forceful in his demands for me to kill her and Allan. Dad described her lover as a rotten child-molester, a drug-pusher and a brute who bashed women. My step-mother he described as a woman of low morals who deserved to be punished. A typical spiel went something like this:

> *She's a whore putting it out for everyone. She is shaming us, Dean, and she is shaming me. Christine is destroying our good name, a name we have worked so hard to build into something. We have to do something, son, you have to be the good soldier and kill them. I'm looking at you, Son, because you're my special boy and I can count on you. Hall is a druggo who abuses children and bashes women. I want you to stop him, Dean. They're evil and they're laughing at us. I want you to shoot them. I can count on you. It will be so easy. I'm counting on you . . .'*

That was the kind of assault on my ears and mind and sense of loyalty I had to contend with every day. God knows I tried to resist it, but you have to understand the hold Dad had over me. He had broken me.

In the end I endured one nagging session too many and it was the straw which broke the camel's back. Dad had finally won. I surrendered my will because I was emotionally spent and mentally fatigued. There was no fight left in me and my triumphant father set about putting his plan into practice.

When he figured I was ripe to kill for him, he took me for a drive deep into the Ourimbah State Forest. As he pulled up I was instructed to get the two shovels out of the car and to follow him into the woods. I did not think to ask what was going on, I just followed him blindly. As we dug a hole I stopped midway and asked Dad what we were doing. His words chilled me. 'Son, this is where your mother is going to be when she is dead.'

I tried to think of a way out of my terrible predicament and could find none. I eventually downed tools and begged Dad to think of another way to deal with the problem, I cried I could not do it, I even threw down my shovel and walked off. I could visualise Christine dead in the hole and I wanted to escape, but Dad was snapping at my heels and his words buzzed around in my head until I felt dizzy. 'Dean, you're being a coward you're being yellow and no good. You aren't doing the right thing – she has to go!' I don't remember anything after that. My mind switched off and everything is a blank. I was so exhausted by that stage I could not compete with his madness. Indeed, I can't even remember a thing about the trip back to Kulnura after we dug the graves.

The second time Dad took me into the forest I thought it was a father–son outing. He suggested the two of us should go out shooting which appealed to me because I loved any opportunity to blast away with the twelve-gauge pump-action shotgun Christine had purchased on my behalf a few years before.

It started off as a tremendous day. Dad egged me on as I shot at trees, tins and cans and even an old washing-machine which had been dumped by a litter bug. But then it started. With each blast he told me Christine and Hall had to be finished off. Who knows, it may have been a form of hypnosis. Dad understood that type of thing.

He read books about how to manipulate people's minds and Troy has often told the story of how Dad convinced a boxer who visited the farm for a training session that he could have a serious heart problem because of the way he breathed. The bloke was as fit as a bull but Dad wanted to prove to Troy how he could make people doubt themselves. 'Your breathing doesn't sound right: is there a history of heart trouble in your family? I don't like the sound of it at all!' The boxer, who was the portrait of health and fitness, looked so terrified Troy reckoned he rushed straight to his doctor after the session finished!

Despite Dad's immense power of persuasion, the thought of my step-mother lying in a bush grave made me feel nauseous and very bloody scared. The mere idea of *hurting* her sickened me. After all, Christine was the woman who screamed out for me to *help* her while she was being battered by Dad.

However, Dad did not allow me to wallow in my misery. He instead kept at me, saying it was right to kill Christine and Hall because they were evil: they were debauched and they had shamed my family. I don't think Dad had much faith in my completing the deed because without my knowledge he invested many months in convincing one of my best mates, Damon Cooper, to help me see his plan through.

Cooper, who trained on our farm, was also brow-beaten into submission by Dad. He could not do anything without having his every step shadowed by the old man. Dad would have him dragged from out of his workplace to be told Hall and Christine didn't deserve to live, he would phone Damon at home at all hours of the night with the same message, and he was always in Cooper's ear, like a blood-sucking tick, whenever he visited the farm.

I was present on one of the occasions when Dad took Damon into the forest and handed him his weapon – a .22 rifle – and encouraged him to open fire. Whenever my mate peeled off a round, Dad patted him on the back and encouraged him. He built Damon up by saying such things as he was a wonderful shot and would be a wonderful bloke to have in a tight situation. He then told him over and over again how Allan Hall was a child-molester and drug-pusher. Make no bones about it, Cooper was brainwashed into believing he was doing the right thing and the day before the killing he and Dad shot at targets on our property. A neighbour apparently phoned the police to complain about the target practice and more than one person who has studied the case has wondered whether Dad would have shelved his deadly desire had a squad car been despatched from Wyong to investigate the call.

While I know the date 29 June 1988 will live with me until the day I die, I don't remember too much about it. Troy, Guy and I spent the day at the Parklea prison in Sydney's Western Suburbs, where we sparred with some of the inmates. It was Dad's idea of a goodwill visit aimed at gaining us some positive publicity and I believe it was also his way of letting the inmates know he, as a former con himself, hadn't forgotten what it was like to be locked up.

I boxed against a heavyweight who showed a bit of form, however, I think Dad's idea of grabbing the bruiser once he was granted his freedom were dashed when the bloke killed two police officers!

The day was an eye-opener and after we finished I drove home to find Kelly had prepared a nice meal for me. I wasn't hungry. Instead I was agitated and in no mood to talk. We argued and when I stormed out of the house I told Kelly I was going to watch some old fight videos back on the farm with Dad.

Minutes before I stormed out of our front door to kill a man she had told me we could expect our first child. She was pregnant, and she was over the moon, but my mind was such a mess I could not acknowledge what she said. I was on a different plane and at a much later date, in court, Kelly said my eyes were in the same trance-like stare I had before a fight.

I don't remember picking Damon up from a Wyong pub. It's one of the many blanks I have from that dreadful night. I can't even recall *why* I decided that would be the night to end Dad's problems. It just happened. My mind was all over the place. I went from the idea of killing him to shooting him in the legs dozens of times. I tried desperately to sift my way through his mighty problem but my main concern was to please Dad. I felt I had no choice. I had to be the good soldier. I wanted to stay his special son because I loved him in a way no-one will ever understand. Right and wrong was not an issue. I had to do as Dad instructed – it was mapped out for me.

We drove past Allan and Christine's home a few times and when I thought it was time to do the deed we reversed the car into the bush at the end of the street, put on some white cotton gloves we bought from a Wyong pharmacy and then cleaned the ammunition of our finger prints. The house was set away from the road and we had to walk along a dirt track to take our positions. The ground was damp from recent rain and I could feel the cold rising from the mud and slush as I lay down.

It was all too terrifyingly real. There were flashes of lightning going through my head as I tried to come to terms with what I was about to do and I could hear Damon's breathing, loud and laboured. He had his doubts. I could feel the cold from the ground against my body and it made me shiver, as did my fear.

Suddenly Damon lost his nerve and in his fright he ran back towards the car. With hindsight it was probably the right move but at that time I was in hell: the instant Damon bolted, I knew what had to be done. Hall could not live and it was up to Damon and me to finish him off.

'We have to do this,' I gasped. 'It is what Dad wants.'

We trudged back to our spot and settled on our line of fire.

Hall and Christine were watching the Clint Eastwood movie *Tightrope* when Hall walked outside to see why his dogs were causing such a commotion. Suddenly there was a rapid-fire *crack crack* in the air. My immediate reaction was to think Hall had fired his rifle (it was actually his stockman's whip) and my fear intensified.

That was it, that was my signal. Kill-time. I raised my shot gun at the silhouette, closed my eyes and *bang*, *bang*, *bang* I fired. There was a muzzle blast and I heard a heavy thud.

For a split second or two time stood still. The smell of gunpowder hung in the air and Allan Hall was dead on the ground a few metres away from me. I was to learn later he died instantly.

I couldn't go through with the second killing, of Christine. While I lay there struggling with the idea of shooting my Mum I decided I could not hurt Christine. She was my Mum . . . I loved her . . . I did not want to hurt her. Indeed, my last clear thought, before my abhorrence of killing someone set in, was to hope Dad would forgive me for sparing my step-mother's life.

As I fled the scene I was amazed to hear what I thought was Hall's whip cracking. 'Fuck! He must have survived!' However, I later learned it was Damon discharging his rifle.

As we roared off into the darkness the realisation of what I had done hit me like an electric shock and I started to shiver. I had blood on my hands and all I could think over and over again was, 'Oh God, what have I done?'

It was dreadful and I prayed it was nothing more than a dream. 'Please God, make this a dream!'

Unfortunately it wasn't. Hall was as dead as a doornail and all the praying in the world could not bring him back to life.

Once reality kicked in my mind went into overdrive. While Damon and I were not criminal masterminds, I guess there was some degrees of 'cleverness' in the way we went about covering our tracks – like cleaning the ammunition before we loaded it in our weapons. The other tactic we employed to throw any police investigations off our trail was to vacuum the car out after the shooting and to throw soil from a different area over the carpet.

I thought we were smart then, but as I drove off, the realisation that Hall was dead in the driveway of his house crushed me inside. I felt as if I had handed my soul to the Devil on a silver platter, though the devil I knew wasn't happy when he heard the next day that Christine was still alive.

Dad wanted to know *every* detail and he went into a mouth-frothing rage when I told him my step-mother had survived. He berated me as if I was the six-foot idiot he often ridiculed. He maintained I should have run into the house and shot Christine dead and then done the same to Damon!

Dad's outburst left me feeling stunned. I had killed in the name of my father, yet it wasn't good enough. Not only did I feel so empty but I was also confused. I was lost and had nowhere to go. Why would he want Damon killed? I had thought everything would be all right once Hall was off the scene, but I could not have been further off the mark. All that happened was a part of me had died.

My innocence vanished that terrible night and for a great number of years I free-fell from one disaster to another as I tried to come to grips with the enormity of the crime I had committed. I have never been the same person since that night and I could not cope with the aftermath of my actions so I punished myself and those around me.

The first few days were all right because once my father composed himself he reinforced the message Hall was a scumbag who had only ever caused the people he came across loads of trouble and heartache.

When those words eventually lost their impact I sought out an old bloke who lived on a remote riding school on Mangrove Mountain. He was a feeble man with mental problems but Dad told me Hall had wrecked the poor coot's life by having an affair with his wife. By that time I had heard enough of Dad's stories and decided to speak to the man by myself to see what he really thought of Hall.

I have no doubt the man realised I was the one who had gunned Hall down – hell, he could have seen that by looking into my eyes – but rather than condemn me with a hard look, he did his best to ease my troubled conscience by saying the person who killed Allan Hall had done society a great favour. They were the words I needed to hear and I drove from his homestead feeling a little bit better.

But it was only temporary relief. I was soon struggling in the depths of despair and, apart from being choked with guilt, the cops were onto us. In time, I faced life behind bars for murder and I feared I would not be able to survive.

ON THE ROPES

Chapter Fifteen

'The only thing I am guilty of is being married to the de facto of the murdered man. I am not a violent man. The death of any human saddens me – even the death of an animal makes me sad . . .'

Ces Waters on being suspected of Allan Hall's murder

Wyong police received a phone call at 10.38 p.m. to report the murder of Allan Hall at his Warnervale property.

Poor Christine made the call – after she heard the shotgun blasts she had run out to see what the hell had happened.

When she saw Hall lying on the ground she thought he was playing a practical joke on her. Even when she saw what appeared to be blood splattered all over the place she figured he had somehow taken a bottle of tomato sauce from the kitchen and poured it over himself to make his 'death' look more convincing.

It was no joke and the cops were soon on the scene.

They retrieved two spent Bruno brand cartridges and found shoe print impressions in the soft mud.

They didn't need to bring Sherlock Holmes in to point the finger of blame in Dad's direction. They were well aware of the problems between Dad and Christine and they swung straight into action. The law realised they could reach our property much quicker than Dad – if he was the gunman – and some officers who lived in the Kulnura area were contacted by central command to set a road block at either end of Springs Road to prevent anyone arriving at or departing our farm undetected.

At about 2 a.m. the police raided our property. They cut through the chain around our gate with bolt-cutters and then a convoy of vehicles made their way down the bumpy driveway until they came to a stop outside the old concrete-block house. Their lights went straight through the windows and illuminated the entire house. Dad's pack of dogs, who were locked inside, were spooked by the strange goings-on and made a terrible racket.

A detective armed with a search warrant informed Dad Allan Hall had been shot dead and they were searching for the murder weapons. Even though the shotgun and Dad's .22 were stored safely in a drain on Damon's parents farm, he told the police to come back in the morning. However, as the police started turning the place over, Dad saw a live .22 round lying on the floor! It would have been a nail in both our coffins but, rather than panic, Dad's criminal mind took over and, when they weren't looking at him, he bent down and calmly placed the bullet under his tongue. He later bragged; 'It was just as well I had to keep my mouth shut otherwise I'd have laughed loudly at their incompetence!'

The police were given a first-hand experience of what

living conditions were like at our property – many of them slipped in the dog messes which dotted the floor like a minefield. I learned one young constable copper ran out of the house gagging because the stench was that bad, and Dad loved it. 'It pleased me no end to see them get manure over their shoes, Dean.'

The police had nothing to go on but they asked Guy and Troy to accompany them to Wyong all the same. My brothers went, against Dad's wishes, and spent the next five hours being grilled about everything and anything concerning Dad's stormy relationships with Allan and Christine.

The next morning, when I returned to the farm to train, a police helicopter hovered over the property as I washed Dad's car. The officers must have thought I was trying to wash away some evidence because within minutes about sixty coppers swarmed over the farm trying to find something concrete to link Dad with the murder. The scientific squad was on hand and skindivers trawled along the floors of our dams to see if we threw the weapons there.

They found nothing. Dad adopted the strategy that attack was the best form of defence and, just like the time when he was accused of my natural mother's murder in England, he pleaded his innocence to the press. He claimed he was a man more sinned against than sinning and he took comfort in the fact a Detective Senior Constable Peter Ryan conceded Hall was a well known petty criminal, and lady's man, who probably had many enemies.

Dad swore he and his children had no role in the man's murder and told an army of journalists how we had trained at Parklea prison the day Hall died. He said we were too tired to have done anything but sleep.

'There is no way I could have been running around like Ned Kelly in the bush, which is how the police have described it,' he told the *Sun-Herald*. 'I was the one who introduced Hall to the family. I gave him a job breaking horses and that's how he and my wife first met. I always found him to be a fairly quiet bloke – I certainly had no feeling of animosity towards him and neither did any of my family.'

Dad also complained how the police frogmen had contaminated our drinking water by splashing about in it during their search for nonexistent weapons.

While Dad seemed to be enjoying himself I soon came into the police investigation team's calculations as the killer. When they realised Dad did not pull the trigger, their forensic science team established there were two men at the scene and they pegged me as being one of them. I was beside myself with fear, guilt and grief. When the police knocked on my door I was overwhelmed by a sense of relief because I thought I heard Dad's voice and figured he was on hand to sort things out for me. I was dead wrong. It was a team of detectives who were there to search the premises. I was in a cold sweat because the shoes I wore that night, the ones with the tell-tale footprint the forensic squad had taken from the crime scene, were on my bathroom floor.

It was a close call because the bathroom door was open and my mud-covered shoes were lying in plain view. I was gripped by an all-consuming fear and I waited for one of them to realise the evidence they needed to convict me was right in front of them. However, the officers became sidetracked when they found a piece of paper on my table which had scrawled on it, *A Time to Kill*. It was a movie I had been told to get out on video, but the police figured they had stumbled upon something which could solve a murder case and they were ecstatic. While they fussed over the piece of paper I discreetly closed the bathroom door and then accompanied them to the station. On my return home, however, I threw the shoes in the bush and it was just as well that I did because the crack police investigation unit arrived at my front door and they went over the place with a fine-tooth comb. It was during that investigation when I heard a detective shout out from my kitchen to his mates to: 'Better take a look at this'. He had discovered my cache of ammunition – five thousand rounds I had bought in bulk from a gunsmith – and it led to all sorts of questions.

A grief-stricken Christine finally fulfilled her threat to go to the media with all sorts of claims about Dad and she conscripted the help of Jennifer Byrne from Channel Nine's *Sixty Minutes* to tell her shocking tale.

A year earlier Jennifer had spent time up on the farm to tell a story of an eccentric family of boxing hillbillies. That was the story in which I broke down when she asked how could I survive if Dad was not around. The funny thing about her question was it was not one Dad had thought to coach us about, it went past the obvious ones of whether Dad was a good father and a good trainer. While it now embarrasses me to see myself start crying, the truth is I pictured Dad in his coffin and I could not hold back. It had never struck me before that Dad might not always be around to guide and love me.

That was the same program in which Dad stunned even the seemingly unflappable Byrne when he asked whether the people who dined on seafood ever stopped to think that fish eat sewage! He also admitted in that interview that he was a tyrant, a sergeant major, a lunatic and a madman but it was all seemingly innocent. At worst, he came across as a crackpot wanting to guide his sons to boxing greatness.

However, the second time Jennifer turned up to our farm

it was far more serious – they were investigating a murder. The *Sixty Minutes* minutes crew arrived at our property on the basis they wanted to get Dad's side of the Allan Hall killing and how it felt to have the place raided by the police. However, once the cameras were rolling, Jennifer aired a number of Christine's allegations including the claims that Dad had forced her into prostitution, that he bashed her, and that he had made threats.

Tracey told of her own battles with Dad and I'm certain she shocked thousands of viewers when she revealed she had scars on her breasts and arms because she ran through a barbed wire fence rather than face another beating from my father. And she told of the time when Dad bashed her with a broomstick until it snapped in half. Rather than stop Dad held the sharpened end up against Tracey's throat and told her he had killed better people than her.

As for Dad, he did a convincing job of maintaining his innocence until he denied writing a letter to Christine and Hall. It turned out Jennifer had a copy of it in her possession and she showed it to him on national television. He was later advised by our legal counsel to admit he had lied about that.

The thing which most preyed on my mind was when Dad said he could not push himself to kill a person. This was to later gnaw away at me because it was true, Dad could not push himself to kill – he had me do the job for him.

The program affected me and my two brothers, and our attitude towards Dad changed quite dramatically. He had lost his grip on us and there wasn't much he could do except make threats. Though he had me over the barrel for a while. Whenever he thought I was slackening off at training he would tell me in hushed tones that he would have no qualms in showing the police where the murder weapons were hidden. Because I believed Dad was crazy enough to do that I buried them in a different spot. It's funny but I was so brainwashed I didn't even stop to think that Dad would implicate himself if he put me in. I'll never forget the panic which gripped me as Dad and I took the guns which were stored at Damon's parents place and moved them to the grave we had dug for Christine because Dad and I were certain we were being tailed by the police. While it was a risk it had to be done quickly before the police started really nosing about. While being scared of the police was bad enough, what really spooked us, Dad especially, was when the boot opened of its own accord as we drove along the dirt track which led to the grave site.

Not long after the program was aired, the police arrested Dad for conspiracy to the murder of Allan Hall. When I visited my old man at the station to see if he was all right I was charged with the same crime.

I was placed in a cell next to Dad and it was a terrible ordeal. While Dad was in control and told me not to worry, I sobbed to myself. Sleep on the cheap foam mattress was impossible: police cars would pull up and there seemed always to be some sort of racket going on outside. Thankfully a good friend of mine named John Hark provided the $100,000 needed for bail and I will always remember the cop who grunted: 'It must be good to have friends with money' as I signed the necessary forms.

There was an incredible number of media people waiting outside the station and they chased Kelly and me as we tried to make our escape to a friend's farm. I felt like a scared rabbit as the camera lights shone on my face and reporters yelled out their questions. I was hot news and, while a friend on a motor bike harassed the reporters as they tried to pursue us, I later learned we were tailed by a television station's chopper as we made our way to the refuge.

I couldn't watch any of the news reports on television because it brought the shooting back, it made it all too real. Though there was never any escaping it and my heart sank when I saw the 31 October 1988 edition of the *Daily Mirror* which screamed: 'DEAN WATERS MURDER CHARGE – Police claim fresh evidence'.

As I struggled to come to terms with the murder charge, Dad was driven to East Maitland prison and he didn't take long to establish himself as some sort of hero among the inmates. He had them doing push ups and other exercises and he told a lot of them they'd be boxing champions when they were released and he could train them.

Prison is a small world because in Maitland Dad met another prisoner who had crossed paths with Hall. Indeed, one of the charges which landed him in the clink had been belting his drug supplier, Allan Hall!

Four days later Dad was transferred to Long Bay in Sydney and his bail was set by the High Court at $100,000. It looked as if Dad was set to stay in prison until our criminal proceedings took place in March 1989 because we could not raise the money needed to free him. However, another faithful family friend, named Ces Perkins, put the money up because he respected what Dad had done for Australian boxing.

While Dad was in prison we decided to send some of the dogs to the pound because we feared if the old man could not raise bail we would not be able to look after the animals on our own. It was very tough; I felt sorry for the dogs as they were loaded in the van because I knew most of them would be destroyed before the day was out. However, my whole life had been turned upside down in so many terrible ways. I was withdrawn, Kelly and I always fought, friends turned their backs on me, Kelly was sacked from her job and I was forced to apply for the dole after it became obvious no-one was willing to employ an accused killer.

Amid that raging sea of chaos and disorder Kelly and I announced our engagement. As she'd announced on the night of Hall's death, she was pregnant. In my heart of hearts I feared my child would grow up as I rotted in a stinking cell. That thought scared me, but what really preyed on my tormented mind was knowing I killed Hall.

I was blessed in the sense I never (and haven't yet) dreamed about the shooting because I'm certain it would have sent me over the edge. However, I could never stop thinking about that night. It was like a video which kept replaying the one scene until the viewer suffered a headache and then a migraine.

I could not live with myself and at the lowest point, I held my pistol in my mouth and thought of how ending it all would be so bloody easy. At that dark point of my life I couldn't win. If I spoke to the police I was condemned, if I stayed silent I was damned for all eternity. I was trapped in a corner – the most dangerous place a boxer can be stuck during a fight. Redemption, I thought, was impossible. As far as I was concerned I was destined to spend all eternity in hell and that thought terrified me more than any other as I prepared to end my life by blowing my brains out.

As I bit down hard on the pistol's barrel I hoped death would come quickly – and painlessly – and for 30 long seconds I tried to summon the 'strength' to complete the final act of my insanity. I believe God works in mysterious ways because as my finger curled around the trigger I caught sight of my reflection in the mirror from the corner of my eye and the image crushed me inside. And that split second it took my focus away from the job I thought *had* to be done.

In the mirror I saw a portrait of tragedy with a gun sticking in his mouth. And then, when I realised how badly I'd ruined everything for the sake of a father who didn't really care for my feelings, I bawled long and hard. When I finally realised I didn't have it in me to kill myself I cried even harder because by throwing my pistol down on the bed I knew I'd sentenced myself to an unknown number of years worth of mental torment. No matter how hard I ran – even after a jury found me not guilty of a horrendous crime – I knew there'd be no escaping that dreadful night.

Dad was at me all the time to train because I was scheduled to defend my Australian heavyweight title against the very tough Kevin Barry in Adelaide. It had the makings of a disaster because I wasn't mentally right for another battle. I'm grateful fate intervened – I was spared what could very well have been a thrashing when I fractured my right hand during training. However, Barry and I did cross swords a few months later in Canberra.

I felt some trepidation when I entered the ring weighing ten heavy kilos above my ideal fight weight to face a man who had chased me hard. Boxing was the last thing I wanted in my life at that stage, nothing seemed to matter, and I think I was lucky to finish what was shaping up to be a wild brawl when I KO-ed him in the fourth round.

It was another successful night for the Waters clan because, apart from my victory, Troy and Guy hammered two high-profile American imports. While Troy won accolades for the way in which he disposed of Ricky

Stackhouse, he also suffered a broken jaw and burst eardrum in the fifth round of his ten-round bout.

It annoyed me to think Dad was more preoccupied with our boxing careers than the need to defend ourselves from the murder charges. To Dad it was another tilt at authority and life went on. He seemed oblivious to the pain I was feeling and that made it hard for me to accept anything he spoke about.

And all his rules about our boxing went out the window – I broke them all. I did such things as sleep with Kelly before my last fight. I ate the wrong foods and when Dad ordered me to hit the heavy bag or skip rope I worked on a broken-down Holden in the farmyard. It angered Dad, who saw his great dream of siring three world champions crumbling before his eyes.

Guy also became rebellious and he found it hard to hear strangers tell him how great our Dad was. They were only trying to be friendly but, like me, Guy saw them as ignorant fools.

Troy slogged on. He was in line to fight for the International Boxing Federation's world title and he wasn't going to let anything stand in his way. He remained focussed and listened to Dad when he said things like, 'I didn't bring you up to be ordinary.'

Kelly and I married in a garden setting and what should have been a beautiful day was tinged with the sadness of knowing I could soon be going to prison for a very long time. However, I wanted to make it a special day for Kelly and smiled like a Cheshire cat for the army of media photographers when I could just as easily have cried.

It was such a terrible mess. What really spooked me were the stickers Dad said were on the doors of his cell which gave me an ugly insight into what could await me.

'It amazed me, Dean, because the stickers warned inmates to always use a condom when they had homosexual encounters and to only use a needle once to prevent the spread of HIV and AIDS. And there must be a bit of it going on because what surprised me was the fact there are only two prisoners per cell. In England it is three in a room to make homosexuality more awkward.'

On hearing that kind of talk, all I hoped was the bloke charged with defending me, Chris Murphy, was as good as his supporters suggested.

THE FIGHT OF OUR LIVES

Chapter Sixteen

'You have no idea of what it has been like, I have had to change my underwear twice at night because I become soaked through perspiration through nerves . . .'

Ces Waters on the court battle

A friend of my father's had suggested we employ Chris Murphy's services because he was regarded by many as the best defence lawyer in the business. While Chris – known in legal circles as the 'celebrity lawyer' – was happy to take on the case, he made it painfully clear he was not a charity and we could expect to shell out $30,000 for his services.

It was a lot of money for two blokes on limited funds. Dad was facing bankruptcy and I was forced to register for the dole when the police refused to grant me a security guard's licence. To ensure we had some hope of fighting for our freedom, Dad sold ten per cent of his twenty-five per cent stake in Troy's future earnings. By the way my little brother was being built up in the press, that stood to be a substantial amount of money. Troy was being billed as the great white hope and the common belief was that once he had won a world title he could write his own ticket to fame and fortune, because he had the look and the image companies kill for. Anyway, Dad sold part of his share to the former singer-turned-fight-promoter, Marty Rhone, and, along with some cash he borrowed from a friend, he appointed Murphy to represent me while another top barrister, Patrick Costello, looked after Dad.

Murphy inspired plenty of confidence. He pepped us up by saying such things as he had a good record for murder cases and didn't intend to hurt his average with me. It helped revive my flagging spirits. Kelly had given birth to our first child just weeks before my court appearance – beautiful little Rebekka – and I was terrified of going to prison.

While I was twenty-five in terms of years on the planet, I was still a kid in regard to life's experiences. I was certain I would die in prison and that thought terrified me – it kept me awake at night and haunted me every day.

After doing his research, Murphy ascertained that the police believed Dad and I were guilty but that they had nothing to pin on us except the plaster-cast of a size twelve shoeprint and the fact I had owned a shotgun which I told them I had sold months before.

When we attended the pre-trial murder committal proceedings, Chris made it clear to the court that Allan Hall was a person who had made many enemies during his life as a petty crim. The computer print-out detailing Hall's crimes since the late 1960s seemed to stretch for miles and included, among other things, drug-dealing, drug-cultivation, homosexual assault and violence alongside break and entry. Murphy also revealed information which had been kept from the public like the stabbing murder of another local drug-pusher a few days after Allan's death. And there was also a newspaper report of an aeroplane landing at Warnervale airfield with no lights on the night Hall was killed – did it ferry the murderers?

Costello asked whether the Crown had any evidence which connected Dad with the crime and when the reply was 'no', he demanded the case be dropped immediately. However, the answer was it would continue.

Christine was the main witness against us and she filled plenty of inches in newspapers around the country with claims that Dad had paid a deposit to have Hall castrated, that he had beaten her on regular occasions, that he forced her into prostitution, that he raped her and also forced her to take lovers to cure her 'frigidity'. It was a scandal and the public lapped up every sordid detail.

Chris had Christine stuttering and by the end of his cross-examination she came across as a poor witness, a liar. Murphy played up to the court and he would finish his questioning by looking at her and saying, 'I'll tell you one thing, Mrs Hicks. You're one cool woman.'

According to Murphy, the most damning evidence against Christine's claims was the fact she had stayed with Dad for twenty years. That comment sounded convincing to many people in the room but I knew: I knew she was speaking the truth when she said she could not leave Dad because she was scared of the repercussions. However, I just sat there.

It was just like on the farm, it was a case of every man for himself. I was fighting for my freedom and Christine was on her own.

Murphy called her a liar and described her as a bad witness. However, it tugged at my heartstrings when I heard my step-mother tell the court that, despite my being accused of the shotgun murder of her lover, she bore me no malice. She told them we still enjoyed a loving friendship and that she enjoyed nothing more than being with my baby girl.

My brother-in-law Marc was called to the stand to tell of my request to have Hall bashed several months before the shooting. It was strange to hear my sister's husband try and put my neck in the noose; it took me quite some time to get over what I saw as a case of betrayal. I was angry with him and Tracey because she had intended to tell the court Dad and I were cursed with violent streaks but she was not called upon.

While I felt sorry for Christine when she was being torn to pieces by the whip-like tongue of Chris Murphy, I felt nothing for Marc when he copped a verbal pummelling. I had told Murphy of the time Marc grabbed me on the penis! – he was a wild bloke back then and wanted to see how big it was – and Chris threw the incident straight in his face in the witness box. He ripped in like Mike Tyson and asked Marc why the hell he had grabbed my old fella. It embarrassed him no end.

Later on, my brother-in-law played into Chris' hands when he stammered he couldn't remember the incident and that was Murphy's cue to let fly. It also made an impression on the magistrate because he scoffed in a theatrical way 'anyone who grabs the heavyweight champion by the penis is not likely to forget the incident'.

In time the anger I felt subsided. Tracey, Marc and I are now close and I dismiss that court experience as something which must be forgotten. We have to get on with our lives as a family.

However, Marc's crumbling in the witness stand was the first brick in the wall and it soon came tumbling down.

Kelly's brother said I showed him my shotgun two days before the killing but he was howled down on the basis I had supposedly sold it months before Hall's murder.

The pre-trial committal proceedings ran out of time to review the mountains of evidence and reach a conclusion. Chris applied to have the prosecution drop the case but they refused his request. Instead committal proceedings were adjourned until October 1989, and while it seemed a lifetime away, Chris was confident we'd then be free.

While I had long since stowed my boxing gloves away, there was plenty happening with my brothers in the ring. Troy and Guy created history when they became the first brothers to hold two Commonwealth titles simultaneously. While Guy broke into the world light-heavyweight ratings, Troy fulfilled his dream of getting to fight for a world title when the IBF president Robert Lee ordered Italy's Gianfranco Rosi to defend his title against the young Aussie by October 1989.

The fact Lee had to force the fight to go ahead demonstrates how scared the world's best junior middleweights were of Troy. He had to sit and watch as the likes of Canada's Matthew Hilton and the USA's Darrin Van Horn and Robert Hines ducked and dodged the prospect of having to defend their title against the number one boy from down under. Hearing that news was the best tonic for me, I prayed I would be a free man by the time Troy was ready to jet out to Italy for his date with destiny.

In between hearings I became a born-again Christian. I embraced the love of Jesus and the Holy Father because I realised it was my only salvation from the darkness which had surrounded me.

I was blessed to meet with a family friend who we had not seen for a long time, Tara Stanley. Tara had become a born-again Christian and I wanted to hear all about it. The more I heard, the more I wanted to devote my life to the Lord. I had thought I was beyond all forgiveness for my terrible crime but when Tara told me God forgives all sinners it gave me great heart. For the first time in my life I really knew God was there for me and He was more important than anything else.

I started going to church but I sat up the back because people had started to recognise me as the bloke on a murder charge and they stared at me. However, my lack of trust eventually disappeared when many of the congregation prayed for me and that moved me. These people who did not know me, apart from the stories they had read in the newspapers, displayed much greater compassion than many of my so-called friends, who turned their back on me when I needed them most of all.

And the more I heard the word of God, the more it touched me. Sometimes, when I read the Bible I cried because it seemed at that stage of my life the word of God was speaking to my heart.

By becoming born again, I regained a reason to live. My terrible crime was not the death sentence I had made it to be in my mind. It was terrible, and I will still have to answer to God for my actions, but I learned from reading about God that I did not have to punish myself. I was actually allowed to forgive myself, though I must admit it took a great number of years and sleepless nights for me to let go.

While I found God, Damon found drugs. We had drifted apart since that night and in his drug induced psychosis he even believed the police had shot a laser beam at him from outer-space while he was in the shower. The beam terrified him and he looked frightened as he told me of the way he tried to escape it by running and diving through his house naked. When I tried to tell Damon he had been taking too many drugs he broke down. He started crying and said the police were trying to send him mad in order to finger him for his role in Allan Hall's death.

In his closing statement to the court in October, Chris Murphy said he did not believe I had it in my make up to be a murderer when he stated: 'The evidence is of a quiet, simple fellow who doesn't give any vent whatsoever to the type of passion that might activate some people to commit the type of crime we have here.'

The magistrate, Bill Pierce, finished our fifteen-month legal battle in just ten minutes when he said of Dad: 'There is evidence he didn't like the man and made some threats. There is no evidence he aided, abetted, inspired a murder or anything else. There is no point relying on motive to say he did it.'

Of me, his honour said I appeared to be a mild-mannered Clark Kent – well, at least outside of the boxing ring! He said there was insufficient evidence to place us before a jury and he ended it all when he said: 'Case dismissed!'

I may have thought to myself at the time: 'Free at last, thank God, I'm free at last'. But I wasn't. I was still a prisoner to my conscience and I would have to face many more demons before I did the right thing and stepped forward.

My greatest moment of relief was when I saw Kelly outside the court clutching my beautiful Rebekka. We both cried as we embraced each other, though, despite my freedom, she was to later realise I wasn't the boy who had fallen in love with her a lifetime ago. She later hit the nail right on the head when she said the ordeal had 'bloody ruined us'.

The press swamped us and Dad held court saying we were framed and the police knew all along we were innocent.

'There is a dirty story of intrigue and conspiracy by people I will not mention now, who will be mentioned at some time in the future, who were responsible for me being arrested and for my son being arrested. They knew perfectly well we did not do this.'

I called Chris the 'heavyweight champion of the legal profession' and for a number of years rang Murphy's office regularly to thank him for gaining me my freedom. However, I took aim at the two-faced people who had betrayed me at a time when I needed moral support, by telling the *Daily Mirror*'s Adam Connolly: 'When I needed them they weren't there, but now I'm on top of the world they are crawling out of the woodwork. I guess that's life.'

Troy was at Sydney airport waiting to leave for Europe when the news of our freedom came through. He said it was the result he needed to help put him in the frame of mind needed to defeat the experienced Rosi. He even joked, 'One down, one to go', in relation to the court case and his tilt at a world title. Guy and I told Troy we would meet him in St Vincent, Italy before the fight but we were going under our own steam and not as slaves to Ces. Our eyes had been opened wide and neither of us wanted anything to do with him. And by the time Troy's battle with Rosi was fought and finished our clan had broken up and the scars would never heal.

FALL OF THE ROMAN EMPIRE

Chapter Seventeen

Originally my boys only went out on Friday nights. What's happened is they have gone down to the bright lights of Gosford and met all the back-slappers . . .

Ces Waters on the fall of his empire

I know I'll never fight for the world title I once dreamed of, but I came close to trading blows with an ex-world champion the night before Troy's world title shot at the St Vincent Sports Palace. The American hero Darrin Van Horn was the focus of my angry attention: it appeared to me as if the fighter known as 'The Schoolboy' was doing his utmost to upset Troy's sleeping pattern by having his television on full blast in the early hours of the morning.

Gianfranco Rosi had become the IBF world champion after the Yank ducked Troy's constant calls for a showdown, in preference for a supposedly 'easy' defence against the ageing Italian. It was a terrible blunder because Rosi carved him up and Van Horn had now travelled to Italy to challenge the winner. Van Horn was a real pain in the backside – it seemed as if he was intent on sticking his nose in whenever there was a television camera around or a press conference in progress.

Somehow 'The Schoolboy' managed to obtain the room next door to Troy's and made the mistake of testing my patience well after midnight. I was very tired and extremely cranky after having been posted on sentry duty, a measure we had taken after a high-profile international boxing official warned us the Italians could try anything to unsettle Troy's sleep in a bid to upset his preparation. The official said they could do anything from banging on his door at 3 a.m. to throwing a brick through his plate-glass window. We had already expected the worst prior to his warning, because two nights before the fight we received calls at 4 a.m. but whenever we picked the phone up there was silence at the other end of the line. I didn't want Troy's chance at setting himself up for life ruined by a bad night's sleep so when Van Horn turned the volume of a rock 'n' roll video show up I saw red and banged on his door. Rather than pussyfoot around I vowed Van Horn and his roommate would be thrown headfirst from the fourth storey window if he even snored too loudly! My threat must have hit home because I did not hear another peep from his room and Troy slept as well as could be expected.

St Vincent is a peaceful place. It is situated high in the Italian Alps and I loved looking at the snow-capped mountains and the nearby Roman ruins because after surviving a tough court case – a case I should not have won – I appreciated the simple fact I was free to enjoy such sights.

However, we disturbed the tranquillity of the small casino

town with a stormy pre-fight press conference. At one stage I thought it was going to erupt into a pub-like brawl after an Australian journalist asked why Rosi had requested ten-ounce gloves instead of the normal eight-ouncers used in the junior middleweight division. Was he scared of Troy's punching power?

When Rosi scoffed he did not fear Troy the old man yelled: 'Troy Waters will fight in bare fists if that's what you want!'

The place went berserk after Rosi said money was not everything to him, just moments after he had admitted he attempted to fight a Swiss challenger (before the IBF intervened and insisted he fight my brother) for 'financial reasons'. His contradiction instigated a ferocious ding-dong slanging match which stunned the Italian press.

Dad brought it all to a head in his own unique way when he hit his palm and shouted 'Finito Rosi!' (Rosi is finished) which sparked a violent reaction from the crowd. Rosi's wife screamed for Dad to 'Shut up!' and his followers made the 'Devil's salute' at Troy and us.

When the heat started to rise Rosi pushed his chair away from the table and walked out of the room with his hands raised in mock triumph – however, he looked far from being a confident man. As he left, Troy's entourage and I chanted '*Finito Rosi, finito Rosi, finito Rosi*' like men possessed. And Troy let fly with a vicious verbal salvo at the champion when he screamed such things as, 'I'm going to end your career!' and 'If Gianfranco Rosi thinks he is going to end my career he should wake up and apologise!'

It helped to raise the blood pressure and, when the dust finally settled, an Italian television reporter asked Troy whether he was just putting on a brave face to camouflage his fear for Rosi. Now, my brother has never feared any opponent, and I knew where he was coming from when he held up his two fists and sneered: 'These are my brave face.'

Rosi did not take Troy's insults on the chin and in another part of the hotel he promised to spank his backside for his insolence.

'He's unpleasant and rude. It will give me an additional reason to beat him,' he said. 'The Australian is trying to make me nervous but he has only increased my will to win.'

It was serious stuff and away from the press conference I heard Troy tell an Aussie reporter how much the fight meant to him. I could tell by his voice that he would give his all in what was certain to be a hostile environment.

'Sometimes I think about it (the fear of failure) so much I could cry,' he said. 'The fear of defeat is a good psych-up for me. I have spent nine years of my life for this one night. And it really is the night which determines my future. I do not hate Rosi but he is in my way and he will have to pay.'

While Troy remained in his room for most of his stay on the Italian-Swiss border, Guy and I roamed about the Alps and enjoyed the hospitality of the people. Wherever we went the name Troy Waters appeared to be on everyone's lips. The locals were captivated by the boy from the other side of the world, who lived with kangaroos, because he had a reputation for being able to knock a man cold. The fight promoter plastered posters everywhere in the township – in expensive shop windows or on ancient stone walls – to promote the world title fight.

Troy's reputation was so good no-one in the famous casino town was prepared to place any of their hard-earned *lire* on the local hero.

However, despite our team's tough talk, we respected Rosi. The thirty-two-year-old was a cagey customer who had tangled with some of the best in the business including Lloyd Honeyghan, Chris Pyatt, Lupe Aquino, Duane Thomas and Don Curry. Rosi not only boasted forty-nine professional bouts for forty-six wins (compared with Troy's skinny fourteen for one) but he also had a reputation for not being scared to employ underhand tactics in tight situations, an elbow here, a head-butt there or a low blow where it really hurt.

The first act of my emancipation once I arrived in Italy was to have a long and bitter argument about nothing with my father. It was the first of many blues because Guy and I had chosen this country, not unfamiliar with dictators, to launch a full-scale rebellion and it felt liberating. It was the first time I had openly defied my father without the slightest fear of retribution.

My devil-may-care attitude gave me a power Dad could not handle. I did everything I could to get under his skin, and looking back on that time, it was all quite childish. For instance because my father deplored foul language I swore at every opportunity; he did not like it one bit, but what could he do? This time Dad had to sit and take whatever was dished up to him.

In between fighting with Dad I tried to make friends with the locals. Whenever I walked past a beautiful woman – and there were plenty – I would test the old Kulnura charm and offer a lusty '*Bello, ragazzo*!' to make an impression. However, I went beetroot red when a cafe-owner pointed out I was actually saying: 'Beautiful boy!' (He pointed out I should have been saying *bella ragazza* or *bella donna* for the girls.)

As it turned out we managed to befriend a few *belle donne* from the casino who had taken an interest in the fight, and three of the four were absolute stunners. We took them to Troy's room one night to try and break the monotony of his waiting for the fight he had long dreamed of. The girls were happy to meet the bloke who they had heard so much about and we couldn't help but laugh when one said something about him being an 'angel'.

Ever keen to return the compliment, one of Troy's entourage pointed out individual beauty aspects about the guests. 'You have beautiful hair, it is golden like the sun,' he said to one. 'Your face would inspire an artist,' he said to the second, and to the third he said: 'Your body would make a goddess jealous.' However, to the fourth – the ugly duckling of the group – he had to think long and hard before he decided to praise her intellect by saying: 'You have a great mind, love.'

Well, it brought the house down except the only problem was the brainy one was the translator! She stormed out in a huff and the others eventually wandered out because of the language barrier: it was like talking to Martians.

I loved to entertain myself by driving the sponsor's car – a hotted up BMW – deep into the mountains. I would take the narrow bends like Peter Brock at Bathurst and it was a great escape from the dark clouds which, despite being found not guilty, had not dispersed from my mind.

I spent one day stopping off at remote coffee shops to talk to the few people who could speak English and I met some wonderful people. They could tell I was involved with Troy because the car had his name painted on the side and they were more than happy to have a chat.

Other times I thought long and hard about my life and where I was headed but at that point it was as great a mystery as not knowing what was around the next bend of the winding mountain road I sped along.

*

I will never, ever understand how my little brother lost the fight of his life. Rosi won with an overwhelming points majority, but it was not against the Troy Waters I had seen box before. Before the bout Dad had tried to pep Troy up by saying stupid things like: 'When the British fought the Italians in North Africa in the Second World War the prisoners took two days to march into the prisoner of war camps. You can beat this man. He refused to come out and fight [former world champion] Don Curry because he is weak!'

And to the disbelief of the partisan crowd Dad, who believed all Italians were superstitious, tried to put a hex on Rosi by holding a gold pendant up to his face while the referee gave his orders. It was a real stand-off. Neither Troy or Rosi would look at one another and they refused to shake hands as a hangover from the fiery press conference. In the stands the Italians were chanting, '*Rosi, Rosi, Rosi, Rosi, Rosi*' and it sounded like rolling thunder building up to one heck of a storm.

Even before the first punch was thrown Guy told me above the noise that something just didn't feel right, and he was spot on. There seemed to be a spark missing from Troy's approach to the fight and I wondered whether the fifteen months of hell which followed the Hall shooting had been too much for Troy's mind.

However, it was too late for theories and worries because he was centre stage and ready to rumble with a cagey world champion determined to keep the home crowd happy. Rosi upset Troy: he did things like throw a punch when the referee called 'break', he head-butted him and ran every time my brother landed a clean shot. From where I sat Troy lacked the sharp skills Australian fans had long admired and I screamed myself hoarse to try and help him hammer the 'go' button.

It took an extraordinarily long time for him to get going

and Dad did not help matters by panicking when the fight started to slip away from our corner. He screamed at Troy in between rounds and it got so bad towards the end of the fight Troy actually told him to leave him alone and to go back to the dressing-room!

Rosi was only troubled once and that was when Troy knocked him off balance with a powerful left hook at the beginning of the last round. I thought it was going to be a last-minute miracle but Troy did not follow up on it and the Italian survived the fight. It was devastating: I don't think I have ever felt as low after a fight as when the judges ruled Rosi had enjoyed a clear-cut superiority over my brother. Both Troy's eyes were cut from where he and Rosi had clashed heads and rubbing salt into his wounds, the hometown hero sneered, 'I have proven to you that I am the strongest!'

With that, Rosi was lifted onto the shoulders of his hangers-on and he punched the air as the crowd saluted their champion.

Our farewell from the Sports Palace was a bitter affair because we needed a police escort of about thirty officers to keep our contingent from the mad mob who wanted to tear Troy limb from limb. A fat police officer who tried to souvenir our Australian flag from one of the gang was sent reeling into a sea of empty chairs while the crowd – which contained some of the people who had shaken hands with Troy in the lead-up to the bout – spat upon us and chanted '*fanculo*' (which when translated meant to get fucked).

It was a relief to barricade ourselves in the dressing-room as we tried to come to grips with the result. To his credit Troy refused to make any excuses for the loss except to say he did not perform well enough. When someone tried to attribute his demise to the crowd's hostility Troy just shook his head and said he stuffed up.

'The crowd might have been loud but they did not throw any punches,' he said. 'I just couldn't get going. I fought badly, I was never able to press on him to hit him hard. Certainly he did all he could to avoid fighting. But I must blame myself for defeat.'

The pain of a wasted chance was too much for Troy in the end because he shed quite a few tears when he was left alone to think of what should have been. He was only twenty-four and it must have seemed the end of the world to him. However, we told him he could hold his head up high. And our sentiments were reinforced by the fight doctor who said Rosi came out of the bout looking a lot worse than Troy. He was also given a message from the champ which said: 'Gianfranco said to tell Waters he will be a world champion one day.'

It would have been best to leave it at that but, on his arrival back in Australia, Dad complained Troy's water may have been contaminated by the Italians in order to ensure the Aussie fighter did not perform to the best of his ability. Most people dismissed that claim as nothing more than a case of sour grapes and the lousiest of excuses.

Perhaps the most interesting postscript to the misery of St Vincent was we had thought it was strange Rosi refused to submit a urine test after the bout. It came as no surprise to me when he was eventually stripped of his title a few months later after testing positive to using amphetamines. Believe me, the way that cat jumped around during his fight against Troy was unnatural.

Our return home was far from the triumphant march we had anticipated. We had lost more than just a world title bout: our family had also been torn apart.

The courtroom drama, our boxing burnout, my incessant

arguing with Dad and his failure to accept and respect Kelly and Sharon finally took their toll and swamped us like a tidal wave. I severed my ties with Dad on our return to Australia. Guy soon followed and Troy left the farm to live with his friends the Wills family by the beach at Copacabana. Our family's fallout dominated the tabloids for a number of weeks and the headlines ranged from 'Stubbornness Clouds the View from Kulnura Mountains' to 'Waters' dream shattered'.

All we boys had ever wanted in our adult life was some concessions and Guy and Troy finally bucked when Dad continued to deny them basic rights like being allowed a night out on the town. I struggled with my decision to turn my back on Dad because I had recently embraced Christianity and I was haunted by the commandment which orders us to honour our parents.

I tried to soften the impact by telling the press such things as, 'As a father my Dad has given us one hundred and ten per cent', however, at the back of my mind I was angry with him and we crossed swords whenever we met. Some of these were fiery encounters which touched on everything from my new-found feelings for God to Dad's crazy theories on life – like wearing a beanie to keep his brain warm so he could think more clearly!

I now realise the root of my problems with Dad was that he was not in tune with me mentally. It seemed as if Hall's death did not matter to him any more because we had been cleared by the court, as though Dad believed the slate had been wiped clean of a terrible, terrible thing because a magistrate had cleared us.

I was consumed by guilt. My marriage was falling apart, I loathed myself and I had even contemplated suicide. Dad could not understand my anger and he lost me along the way. Guy and Troy rebelled because they did not want to keep eating boxing for breakfast, lunch and dinner.

The old man still tried to convince Guy to leave Sharon even though it was obvious that they were both deeply in love and for Troy, the disappointment associated with losing his world title shot brought things to a head. He was tired, he was bored and he needed a break from boxing.

While the media documented the end of Australian boxing's so-called 'royal family', there was a great feeling of solidarity among Troy, Guy and me. This was a point my baby brother made to the *Australian*'s Cameron Williams a month before Christmas when he said: 'Whatever happens, the boys will stick together . . . we might not be the Waters family, but we'll always be the Waters brothers!'

My father did not handle the bust-up very well and he was still too stubborn to listen to Guy and Troy's demands. At a time when they wanted more freedom, he demanded they return to the farm within a fortnight to commence heavy training or not to bother returning at all.

He told the *Daily Mirror* that we three were in danger of turning our back on the type of glory reserved for a special few.

> *'My boys became famous not only in Australia but in America, Europe and England – they were even featured on USA Today. I had such big plans for them. I went to the unveiling of a statue in honour of Dave Sands and saw Clem, the last of the fighting Sands brothers. He walked up to me and said: 'I always thought my family was something. But congratulations, without a doubt yours is the Royal Family of Australian boxing.'*

I eventually returned to the boxing gym because I was dead broke. I didn't have a cracker and needed to get some quick money together to try and ease the tensions which had started to form on my homefront due to our financial pressures and my harsher attitude to life.

As hard as she tried Kelly could not communicate with me any more because I had changed in too many ways. It had become too easy for me to snap at almost everything she said and the more I thought of it, the more trapped I felt.

Our marriage was on the rocks, but I was still a breadwinner. I was in a real bind because I could not find work and in the end it turned out my fists were the only tools available to me. Guy and Troy had returned to the farm to train for their Commonwealth title defences early in the new year, however, the troubles were far from over. Apart from matters which concerned boxing, Guy refused to talk to Dad while Troy wondered why he was involved in a sport which offered heartache and torment.

Rather than follow Troy and Guy's lead and return to Kulnura I turned up at Johnny Lewis's gym in downtown Newtown, an inner-city Sydney suburb, even though I knew it would cause Dad to spit. Maybe I wanted to punish him by going to the other side.

While I commenced my training for a crack at the NSW cruiserweight title against American Jack Johnson, Troy considered relocating to Britain where he could at least make enough money to fulfill his dream of buying a house by the surf and sand. 'There are junior clerks working for the government who earn just as much as I do in a year,' he told the *Sunday Telegraph*.

As for Guy, his relationship with Dad deteriorated even further when the old man blamed Sharon for his poor showing in a Commonwealth title defence against Uganda's Yawe Davis at the Blacktown RSL Club in Sydney's outer west. It was not the most exciting bout Guy had ever been involved in but what finished off the night was when the crowd booed and hissed the judge's decision to award him the bout. Their response proved to me how ignorant the mob can be.

Few – if any – of Davis's blows broke Guy's watertight defence. He caught them on his gloves and countered well enough to rattle up a points victory. However, the crowd who paid their $15 for some cheap entertainment were disappointed not to see blood and they reacted badly.

Behind the scenes Dad told anyone who cared to listen that Sharon was responsible for Guy's below par performance and when those claims found their way to the press, Guy demanded the right of reply. He told the *Sunday Telegraph*: 'It was written in the paper last week that I was running around looking for a flat with my girlfriend Sharon and I was not tuned into the fight. I don't like it because firstly it was not true and secondly it seems as if Sharon was indirectly being blamed for a not so crash hot performance. It sounds as though if I fail in boxing some people will always want to blame her.'

Sometimes Dad blamed himself for the bust up. Oh, he didn't blame himself for bashing us or treating us like a species of sub-humans who were bred to fight. Instead, he cursed himself for allowing us to taste the poison fruits of society! 'Originally my boys only went out on Friday nights,' he complained to the *Daily Mirror*. 'What's happened is they've gone down to the bright lights of Gosford and met all the backslappers. Just eighteen months ago Troy wanted to buy a property just around the corner from mine. He would have been the king of the mountain looking down over Wyong and Gosford. Next thing I know he wants a beach house!'

Ultimately, Dad's ego put the final nail into our family's coffin when he offered my forthcoming opponent, Jack Johnson, a fight plan to use against me. Dad wanted to prove he knew me better than I knew myself, but by doing so he only highlighted what we had already realised. The old coot would stoop to any level when it suited him.

HONOURING THY FATHER, WARTS AND ALL

Chapter Eighteen

'What do you know about God? Up here, I'm God. I'm the only God you need to know.'

Ces on religion

As much as I loathed doing it, I had no choice but to return to the fight game. I was penniless and, because I had a wife and a one-year-old daughter to support, I was desperate. Apart from coming to the realisation that boxing was the only trade I was qualified for I also found it soul-destroying to register for the dole. Believe me, being forced to line up at the local social security office every second Wednesday was a humiliating experience.

I wasn't the first fighter to find himself down and out; the fight game is littered with greater champions than me who hit tough times. For instance, I remember the time I saw a television special on my hero George Foreman when I was a teenager and it made me cry. George's wife had left him and he was filmed preaching on a street corner to people who did not want to listen. When I saw him, he was overweight and playing the tambourine and I wondered how on earth that could happen to anyone.

Well, I found out the hard way and it battered my pride. Whenever someone in the dole queue recognised me as Dean Waters, the former heavyweight champion of Australia and the Orient Pacific region, I stared them down mean and hard. It was a victory – albeit a small one – when they blinked their eyes and turned their heads away.

I felt humiliated because all my life I had been brought up to believe I would one day be the world heavyweight champion – the king of the jungle. Instead, I lined up behind the dole-bludgers, the desperate and the undesirables as I waited for my government pay cheque. It took me quite a while to look at myself in the mirror. After I cashed the dole cheque I would return home and loaf about. In time I piled on the kilos and I was soon carting a heavy belly *and* a bad-assed attitude about.

When I finally accepted I literally had to fight my way out of trouble I sought out Dad's arch-rival, Johnny Lewis, who made it crystal clear that my blubber had to go. He envisaged my starting my comeback campaign as a cruiser-weight, which meant I had to lose twenty kilos in five short months. The only way that could be achieved was through hard yakka and mad dieting.

To help get me back on track, Johnny contacted a fitness guru based on the Central Coast, former Newtown Rugby League star Bobby Laningan, and his instructions were to flay each ounce of fat from my frame! And Bob followed those orders to the letter – I often finished my training sessions in pain. My first training run was a nightmare: it was only two kilometres but it felt like two hundred! I gasped for air, my lungs hurt when I inhaled and I dehydrated very quickly.

However, I stuck with it and Bob increased my workload every week. The runs lengthened to four kilometres, he added sprintwork, I worked with dumbbells and medicine balls which made my flab-covered stomach muscles feel as if they were on fire.

Without a doubt the toughest test of all was having to sprint up The Skillon at Terrigal six times each session. The Skillon is a tourist attraction because the grass-covered cliff appears to kiss the sky. It was a dreadful test and it was just as well for the camera-wielding tourists that I did my training there at the crack of dawn because not only would I foam at the mouth when I reached the top but I'd come close to vomiting before falling in a heap.

Even at the worst of my existence, I would think of Dad but as a born-again Christian they weren't always angry thoughts. I tried to forgive him rather than condemn him. The more I learned of the grandeur of God the more I wanted to share it with people, even my uninterested father. I became quite scared for Dad's soul. I was terrified he would spend eternity as a piece of spiritual coal helping to burn the fires of hell. I even climbed into my car one day and drove back to the farm to allow him the chance to know God forgives all. Predictably enough he threw it straight back in my face. The old man dismissed me as a born-again hypocrite and he even threw mud at Jesus Christ. 'You know, the more I think of it the more I believe I have evidence Jesus Christ was a homosexual!'

It infuriated me and I felt anger build up inside me as he spoke.

It isn't up to me to judge my father's soul; however, in the months leading up to his death I heard he told a select few of a 'visitor' he had to his caravan at some ungodly hour. Dad would tell his listeners the apparition was dressed like a Quaker from the American mid-west and it had urged him to touch hands with the Devil. Rather than reel in horror Dad reached out.

Nevertheless, I tried to tell Dad that finding God had saved me at a time when I could not forgive myself for committing a terrible crime. I had wanted to commit suicide but my religious beliefs – and my fears for how my baby Rebekka would be brought up without her Dad around – saved me from pulling the trigger. I'm eternally grateful I did not take the easy option because despite some terrible times I would have missed some great moments.

In the weeks leading up to my fight with Jack Johnson at the Bankstown Sports Club I spoke to the *Australian*'s Jeff Wells about my newfound faith and the fight. He could not understand what I meant when I told him the 'big fella' would be in my corner. For all he knew I could have been talking about Arnold Schwarzenegger!'

'The big fella, THE BIG FELLA', I yelled. 'When He's in your corner you can't go wrong.'

However, my father, the little goblin, was in the opposite corner feeding Johnson with everything he needed to know about me, and the Yankee journeyman was smart enough to absorb all that Dad had to say. News of Dad's treachery created an outcry – it was enough to help Guy turn his back on Dad once and for all – but I tried to ignore the hullabaloo by throwing myself into my training.

I enjoyed myself at Newtown – there was always a good mixture of characters walking in and out of the place. One of the most colourful was the Balmain and Australian Rugby League forward Steve 'Blocker' Roach. I like to think I had an affinity with Blocker. A big man, he played his sport with every ounce of his energy and in the process he forged a reputation as a rough and ready character who wasn't scared to whack his opponents on the chin with a full-blooded punch. He was regularly suspended for his rushes of blood, and the big bloke's penchant for walking on the wild side of the game made him a crowd favourite.

Anyway, the international footballer was at his peak in 1990 and he kept in shape by undergoing some gruelling boxing training under Johnny's gaze. While he lacked finesse, Blocker certainly boasted plenty of power and, as part of my warm up to the Johnson title fight, he whacked on a pair of gloves and volunteered to dance around in the ring with me. I appreciated the chance to work with someone bigger than me and before long we were trading leather.

Let me tell you, Blocker boxed the same way he played his football. It was an all-or-nothing effort and he threw his punches like a threshing machine at full speed! While I was always in control of the session, I admired the way Blocker kept coming back from some heavy blows. Before I unloaded a bomb which snapped the air from his lungs and forced him to double over, he showed plenty of ticker and I can remember thinking to myself how hard it would be to meet the bloke on his own turf – the footy paddock!

The night I fought Johnson for the NSW cruiserweight title, I was determined to beat more than just another opponent. I wanted to KO Dad's sense of superiority over me. After all, he had fed Johnson's camp with secrets of how to beat me.

It was a hard fight. Johnson was a cagey cat who was blessed with skills, but lethargy was my main enemy as the fight wore on. I didn't have the stamina needed to complete a title fight and when I look back on my diet – I was eating just one Weet-Bix biscuit with half a cup of skim milk for breakfast – it is little wonder I did not have the juice in the tank. I just couldn't get started. I was like an old car on a cold morning that takes a while to kick over, and Johnson made the most of his opportunities.

He quickly attained a points lead and it continued to grow with every round. In the last round I needed a knockout to win and I uncorked a monster punch which sent Jack flying halfway across the ring, and I watched as he hit the canvas. I knocked him down a second time and it broke my heart to see Johnson climb back to his feet, jelly legs and all.

I was gone. I had climbed my Mount Everest only to lose my grip a few feet from the summit. The bell rang and I'm certain I heard a distant cheer all the way back at Kulnura when the American was awarded the state title on a superior points position.

The press described it as a shock victory; I saw it as anything but! I had been through mental torment and physical torture on my comeback trail. While I entered the ring confident in my fistic ability I would honestly have seen it as a huge surprise had I won the crown.

I was beaten but I was far from defeated. I had no intentions of retiring and I was glad to hear Johnny Lewis thought I still had something to offer when he told the television news crews who packed Bankstown Sports Club: 'Whatever he wants to do I'll be very proud and want to be a part of him. I wish whichever way he goes he takes the right one.'

The next day Jon Harker from Channel Seven was back at the farm with my Dad in his quest to find out how the hell a father, any father, could go against his own flesh and blood. While Harker and *Sportsworld*'s very accomplished Bruce McAvaney described it as a sad story, McAvaney said what everyone was thinking when he told the audience he couldn't imagine why Ces flooded the Johnson camp with information on me.

In a mad fifteen or so minutes with Harker, Dad spoke about my having a nervous breakdown being one of his reasons for hatching the plan to help Johnson:

> *I want to speak to him. I love the fella and his brother Guy more than they'll ever know ... I'm 63 years of age and I don't have a lot of time left on this earth and I want to put the best time in for my sons to help ...* [I told Johnson] *to stay in the middle of the ring and Dean will have to work. Dean can't work because he isn't strong enough ... I proved a point, I know my son better than anyone else. I told everyone he was going to lose that fight and lose it against a man who wasn't entitled to be in the same ring as him ... I gave other advice to make Dean realise I know him better than anyone else.*
>
> *Going to Lewis was an act of betrayal. It has torn me apart, they were the opposition. It would have been worse for Dean if he won the fight because he would have thought he was doing everything right when he's doing everything wrong. He's got this religious thing. I think Dean, over the last few months, has suffered a nervous breakdown; only I have noticed. I don't want the boys to eat humble pie ... all will be forgotten. I love them. I will be here when their so-called friends are gone. I love you, Dean. I love you, Guy.*

We didn't return and Guy fought his first world title bout against WBC light-heavyweight king Dennis Andries with

Lewis, and not Dad, in his corner at Adelaide. Andries won his title back from Guy's arch-rival Jeff Harding in a slug-a-thon in Melbourne and he promised Guy risked a real hiding when he entered the ring. He told the *Daily Mirror*'s writer: 'If I connect right with either hand, he's going to get hurt. If I hit Waters he stays hit. Permanent. I'll just take care of business.'

My brother had never had his heart in boxing and I have no doubt that was reflected in his bout against Andries. Guy gave his best shot against a good champion, but the truth is he did not throw enough punches to win the bout and he was left to ponder that, as he sat teary-eyed in the dressing-room and tried to come to grips with a lost opportunity. Dad also rued the fight as a lost chance – he refused to watch it and told everyone who cared to listen that Guy had denied him his golden opportunity to be in the corner for another world title challenge.

Dad's desire for a reconciliation didn't have any effect on me at all. While I deeply regretted the rift had occurred there was no hope of my returning to the fold to live with him. Too much had passed between us and, anyway, Dad did not want a father–son relationship, he wanted to restore the trainer–fighter, drill sergeant–private bond because that was what would help him attain his world titles.

When Guy and I did not come running back to his outstretched arms, Dad spat us out like cold porridge and rarely missed an opportunity to give us a pay, saying such things as: 'I'm afraid in the case of Guy and Dean they are in danger of becoming the kind of people I always taught them to stay away from. They mix too much with glory-hunters and backslappers.'

Hard times had fallen upon Dad. He was forced to sell

the farm as a part of the divorce settlement with Christine. It broke him. He saw the sale as not only the end of an era but the demise of an important part of Australian sport.

'This has been a kind of boxing El Dorado,' he told the *Sun-Herald*. 'It's been everything I could have wanted it to be.'

When it was obvious the farm was lost, Dad blamed us. He said we should have ploughed our cash into a health farm–training camp for elite athletes and wealthy business executives with pot bellies.

'It would have been a foundation for their future,' he moaned. 'Not only would I have stayed and they have stayed but their children and their children's children. It would have been a dynasty for the future. And that's gone. The chance has gone. It was a big dream.'

My father told many people, the press included, that fate had conspired to crush his dreams. While Dad knew the real story behind Allan Hall's killing – I can't call it a murder, while I may have pulled the trigger I was not my own person then – he persisted in telling people he was just a victim of circumstance.

Even though the magistrate had cleared us, Dad covered his tracks by spreading the theory Hall had links to the jailed international drug-dealer Bruce 'Snapper' Cornwall who was imprisoned for twenty-three years in 1987. The Federal Government confiscated more than three million dollars of his assets, including a million-dollar stud farm on the Central Coast.

'I don't have any doubt it was a drug-related murder,' he told *New Idea*. 'It stinks to high heaven. There's a lot about this case that has been ignored. So what did we have? It seemed to me there was a circle of drug-dealings going on and Hall was in the middle of it!'

Some people believed it, and others sympathised with Dad when he finally was forced to sell the farm and all his belongings to pay off the divorce settlement. Dad moved to a nearby patch of dirt where some neighbours agreed he could stay in his caravan until he found somewhere else.

In time he – and his horde of animals – became a permanent fixture there and he managed to stay put by threatening to hurt the owners if they kept 'pestering' him with their orders to push on! That was Dad.

However, in time, as a nightclub bouncer, I too became a menacing figure in my own way, who developed a dangerous liking for the fast life; in the fast lane. It was the beginning of my downward spiral and for a bloody long time I didn't give a damn about what I did or who I hurt.

LOSING IT

Chapter Nineteen

'You can get further with a kind word and a gun than you can with a kind word.'

Ces Waters

I was an angry young man and my hair-trigger temper won me very few friends as a doorman at a number of nightclubs around the Central Coast. My religious beliefs were pushed to the back of my mind and I declared war on society. Even though I didn't start any fights, I finished plenty and there were numerous occasions when I punched my anger out on an unfortunate soul in a hotel car park. It was barbaric stuff as I fed plenty of would-be tough guys a knuckle sandwich and a bit of what Dad once referred to as 'toe pie'. I was in a moral vacuum and had lost all concern for the consequence of my actions.

During my wildest times I did stupid things like roar past Toukley police station in a V8 Commodore Calais at one hundred and sixty kilometres an hour! Cops? I hated them. In my book they were nothing more than a pack of low dogs.

The only copper I had any time for at all was a Detective Dennis O'Toole who seemed a decent bloke. O'Toole was involved in the Hall case and he knew I was guilty as sin but he couldn't prove it. However, he at least spoke to me with some respect. As for the rest, well, I dismissed them as scum and sometimes as I sped along the highway with those old demons dancing in my head I vowed to clip any copper who dared try to pull me over.

My home life suffered as a result of my anti-social approach and it was obvious that my marriage to Kelly was on the rocks. We argued – Lord knows we argued – and there were times when I hated myself for my behaviour because I was becoming like my old man. My temper made me a public enemy because whenever I was challenged a terrible sense of rage swamped me.

The nightclubs became my sanctuary. I was king there. I had a power over people because the blokes realised I was someone not to tangle with, while some of their girls threw themselves at me. Maybe they were drawn to me because of the tough-guy image or maybe they just wanted to cling to someone with a profile. I did not give a hoot about their motives, I just bedded them and in my arrogance I failed to consider how my infidelity would affect Kelly.

Up until I started work on the doors I did not think I had anything to offer girls. Even when I boxed for national titles I figured women saw me as worthless and it was quite a big deal if one of them spoke to me. However, as a bouncer I found myself within reach of a smorgasbord of talent and I sampled as much as possible.

Long before I had one night stands I suggested to Kelly I should see other people because she was really the only woman I had ever been with. However, the mere thought of that made her cry and when I saw her reaction I dropped off for a while.

However, after a few weeks I stepped up the campaign and I pestered her until it reached the stage I took a supposed friend's advice and saw the girls on the sly. While the sex was meaningless, it felt as good as any conquest could.

I would regularly come home late from work with some girl's lipstick on my neck and face or I'd smell of the latest woman I had rolled around in bed with. Kelly did her all to make our marriage work even though I constantly tested her with my infidelity.

Drugs, however, became a big problem. I was introduced to them at a wedding reception, of all places, when someone enticed me to drop some acid in the toilet with him. He had brought it back from overseas on a small triangle of cardboard no bigger than my finger nail. When nothing happened I shrugged my shoulders and said it did stuff all for me.

However, an hour later it kicked in and, whoa, my head began to buzz! The world spun like an out-of-control carousel and I wanted to get off – but it kept spinning! I screamed and then howled with laughter and I could feel everyone's eyes shift towards the direction of the commotion at my table. My buddy urged me to calm down, but I was out of control!

I didn't care what anyone thought and I proved that point by drooling all over a barmaid who had the biggest set of breasts a bloke could ever lay eyes on! I sat licking my chops like a wild dog, however, it suddenly dawned on me my wife was next to me at the table, watching my shameless display with disgust. When Kelly saw my glassy eyes she demanded to know if I had taken some drugs; I responded by laughing like a maniac.

Our relationship was all but dead and I buried it a few weeks later when I finally came clean about being unfaithful, it seemed wrong to live a lie. However, when I saw the look of betrayal in her eyes, I felt terribly small. I saw Kelly's hurt and anger and there was nothing I could do to ease it. After seven years I was out the door and I was too far gone to care as much as I should have.

Rather than mope about and curse the demise of my marriage I pressed the self-destruct button in my mind and did crazy things like borrowing a Yamaha 750 jet ski with my good buddy Steve Ferguson at Lake Murmona, near Newcastle. The water was rough and choppy and we were sent flying into it when I did a sharp turn while travelling at top speed. Under normal circumstances a jet ski will come to a sudden halt when its rider falls off but when Steve and I took our tumble the wind and the choppy water pushed it away from us. I have never been much of a swimmer so I 'volunteered' Steve to retrieve the jet ski but after he swam about thirty metres I heard him yell for help.

I knew he was not joking so I ripped off my jumper and pair of happy pants and swam towards him. When I reached him, Steve was pale and his terror was obvious . . . my good mate thought he was going to drown. I tried to calm him down by telling him to float on his back while I somehow retrieved the jet ski.

Now, I have faced some tough physical challenges in my life, like running twenty kilometres along goat tracks for training and punching the heavy bag for fifteen rounds, but nothing matched that swim. However, my desperation pushed me because I feared Steve would drown if I didn't get him back on the jet ski. I was in a mad panic and I felt *every* bloody stroke. My lungs burned and I gasped for air.

I reckon I reached the jet ski just a stroke or two before my energy level was about to give out.

While I wanted to rest the thought of Steve slipping beneath the waves spurred me on. It was when I returned to pluck Steve out of the water that I faced my most terrifying moment – I couldn't see him anywhere and I feared he had drowned. In desperation I screamed his name out over and over and when there was no answer my head filled with terrible thoughts, such as how on earth I could break the news to Steve's family that he'd drowned while stuffing around. My mind was in overdrive but I prayed for the first time in a long while that he was okay.

Forget what I have said before about my winning title fights over people like Dave Russell being the greatest relief of my life – nothing has matched the instant I caught sight of my great mate bobbing among the waves twenty metres from me. I started to cry with relief and because Fergo lacked the energy to climb back on the jet ski he clung to the side as I powered towards shore. However, his weight made the machine lopsided and the bloody thing started to sink!

We were still a long way from shore and there was no way we would have made it if we had to swim. I cut the engine and fought the waves to drag Fergo back on the seat and what spooked me was the fact he felt lifeless. He had trouble hanging on so when the jet ski's engine finally kicked over I made my way to a nearby island so we could rest and recharge our batteries.

I was exhausted and Fergo lapsed into an on-and-off sleep-like state. As much as I would've liked to have stayed put where we were safe, it was getting late and the last thing we needed was to make our way back to shore in the dark. As it turned out the trip to the mainland only took five or so minutes, but because I was terrified of us going back in the drink it felt like hours.

Later that night Steve and I were on the door at the Cessnock Workers Club and after our brush with disaster it felt great to be alive. Fergo made the most of the moment to play the drums with the band and I couldn't help but smile at his exuberance. We'd survived and while the incident shook me right up I was even more determined to live my life as one non-stop party.

Melbourne is a happening town. Forget that crap people tell you about the wet weather and the cold climate: if you want to party then the Victorian capital is the place to be!

I headed south of the border in a bid to rekindle my boxing career under the guidance of Keith Ellis. His brother Lester was an IBF world champion throughout the mid-1980s and I figured he could help me fight my way back to the top of the heavyweight pile.

However, my intentions were side-tracked when I was employed as a bouncer in some of Melbourne's best nightclubs along the famous King Street strip. I not only enjoyed the pick of the girls but I also had dibs on the best drugs.

One of my problems has long been the fact I can never do anything in moderation. Everything I do, like the time I jumped the dam on my motor bike, has always been over the top. It was like that with my quest for drugs and girls: I couldn't throw enough gunk into my bloodstream while as for girls, I viewed them as pleasure machines.

Drugs and sex made a frightening combination because I'd set challenges for myself – like the time I spent nearly twelve hours having sex while high.

The drugs opened a new world to me. They helped me

escape my terrible, dark secret of killing Allan Hall and they allowed me to befriend a new group of people, some of whom were heavy duty dudes. Many of them had me pegged as a hard bastard.

One bloke told me his chief ambition in life was to shoot someone dead and in a bid to prove his seriousness he produced a loaded .44 Magnum and waved it under my nose! Another bloke, a Mr Black, told me about a robbery he had planned and asked if I wanted to play a part in it. He had worked at a certain service station and was familiar with its layout, but I wanted to keep my nose clean. Sure, the money would have been handy but I had a bad feeling about his plan and I warned Mr Black to be careful who he trusted. To be honest, I forgot all about the job until he rocked up to the club where I was working at about 2.30 a.m. the next morning grinning like the face of Luna Park! I knew he had done it and it sounded as if he had done a thorough job to cover his tracks because he erased the service station's surveillance camera's video tape.

After I finished my shift I went around to his house and found him counting out $11,000 on his kitchen table! He filled me in on all the details, like the way he held an angle grinder towards the attendant and threatened to do terrible things if he didn't hand over the day's takings. I laughed because I'd never heard of anyone holding up a service station with an angle grinder before and I was also pleased to hear Mr Black did not hurt anyone during the robbery.

After a quick drink I left him to count his money and make his plans. It had been a busy night on the door of the Braybrook Hotel so it didn't take long to fall asleep when I returned to my place. However, my sleep was disturbed by a series of crazy dreams and one of them was that my mate's accomplice had given him up to the cops. It spooked me and when I woke at 8 a.m. the first thing I did was phone to tell Black of my nightmare. When he answered the phone I discovered my dream had come true because he had trusted the wrong bloke. It turned out his pal spilled his guts to the coppers when they put the squeeze on him and the boys in blue were already with him when I called.

In between shifts and orgies of drug abuse I had other people make propositions to me, like one guy who offered me very big money to gun down a heroin dealer. I hit that idea straight on the head: I said he had me wrong because I wasn't into that sort of thing. However, I was running around with some blokes who wouldn't have thought twice about knee-capping someone if they crossed them – the harder cases I knew would not have worried about snuffing someone out if they had to. They lead a dreadful life because they were always looking over their shoulders.

I remember in one sober moment I was in a limousine with a hard bastard and he told me that the number of enemies he had – and knowing what they were capable of – made him feel so ill he vomited with fear every day! However, he could handle himself and he told me of the time a bouncer at a nightclub did not show him enough respect. Rather than punch the tripe out of the doorman, he humiliated him by pulling his pants and undies down and spanking his arse until it was red raw. The bouncer quit on the spot because he knew he'd lost everyone's respect in the space of a few smacks.

But he had enemies and he was scared. I was getting the same way in the sense I was on a few hate lists but, rather than heed his warning, I continued on my downward spiral. I was trapped in the hazy drug world and I abused my power on the door of the Pulse Nite Club in King Street. I loved the authority, I loved being able to intimidate people and, as far as I was concerned, the more the punters hated me, the better I was.

I wasn't the only one who had such scant regard for the public. I'll never forget the time I walked into the kitchen of a pub and I saw another bouncer urinating in the deep-frier where the chips were cooked. I asked what the hell he was doing and the bloke said of the patrons, 'Fuck 'em, they're a bunch of cunts anyway!' I made a mental note never to ever eat at that establishment again. While I never pissed on anyone's food, I was far from clean because I urinated in a big-mouthed security guard's coffee! The bloke rubbed me up the wrong way and he did nothing for our chances at becoming friends when he threatened to put my head through a glass trophy cabinet! However, I impressed him when I made him a cup of hot coffee and I smirked as I watched him drink every drop because I added more than milk and two sugars! These days, as a Christian, I shake my head in disgust at the things I did.

There was one night, when I was at my lowest drug-induced ebb, I spied a big burly bastard trying to break into a store. Normally, I would not have worried about it but it was a particularly quiet night on the door and I needed to entertain myself. I crossed the road to confront the bloke and when he started running from me I went into a mad rage and chased him with a few of the other boys.

We cornered him in an alley and in his terror the poor bugger struck out and hit me flush on the jaw. It hurt like mad and I saw red and laid into the bloke. He bled like a stuck pig yet I continued to bash his head into the pavement – crash, crash, crash. His face was pulped and when the police and ambulance arrived on the scene they thought the bloke had been taken to with a metal bar because his injuries were so horrific.

I treated it as just another day at the office but when the drugs wore off the next morning I heard the man I battered was a patient from a nearby psychiatric hospital. Apart from his mental problems the patient was infected by the potentially fatal hepatitis A disease but, rather than fear I had contracted the AIDS-like condition from his blood which had splattered all over me, I felt hollow. I figured if I contracted the disease then I deserved to die because I had turned into the same type of brute as my father.

I felt an overwhelming sense of pity for the man and a familiar sense of loathing for myself. I didn't pray to God back then. I figured with all the terrible things I was guilty of I had no right to call on Him and ask for His forgiveness. Instead I escaped by taking drugs and they included just about every pill and tablet on the market – cocaine, LSD and amphetamines – and the chemicals clogged my bloodstream.

I was even geared up to take heroin one afternoon after I had been in the brawl with the police. I went to a mate's place, he was a real mover and shaker and had some great contacts. He phoned his people and told them in code he had a mate with a 'Ferrari' but he was after a 'slower' car. I was lucky because the place was raided by about eight carloads of police before the courier arrived and they sent me on my way. I had a few close calls like that.

Another drug-dealer I spent some time with was shot dead in his driveway while other abusers I associated with overdosed or lost everything. One bloke I knew looked the spitting image of Mel Gibson before the bloke hit the drugs – after a few months of constant abuse he looked like a zombie. I'm sure God looked over my every step of that troubled time although I looked pretty bad.

At my worst I bloated up to one hundred and thirty-two kilos after two solid years of drug-abuse and I owed my life to an experienced drug-taker who had advised me at the beginning of my drug taking days not to fall into the same trap of most habitual users and stop eating. My buddy said that was the worst thing I could do because it would weaken my immune system and leave me open to the kind of diseases and infections which kill a lot of drug-dependent people. The worse torture for me was I could never switch off and fall asleep unless I swallowed handfuls of sleeping tablets.

While I knew my life was in tatters I lived for the high the drugs gave me. I loved the feeling of euphoria which came with a hit because it made me feel stronger and I'd bullshit to myself that I could do anything. When I was on a high I spoke at a million miles an hour – I would tell people I was set for a return to the ring and I was going to win my titles back. I was going to conquer the world and nobody, not even Iron Mike Tyson, was going to stop me.

All those powerful thoughts counted for nothing when I came 'down' because my mind would be corrupted by sick and perverted thoughts, thoughts which scare me even to this day. Not all of these crazy thoughts were sparked by a cocktail of drugs.

I remember one night when I was on the Central Coast I watched a television news story about a 16-year-old kid who killed himself because he had been raped by some low animal. The bloke who abused the boy was only given a light smack over his hand and in his suicide note the boy told his parents he must really be a big girl because he was crying as he wrote it. By the time the segment finished I was in tears. I felt a real rage against child abusers and I even thought of trying to find just one to punish. The story affected me badly and for the first time in my life I felt a murderous hatred towards my father. I remembered the beatings, the feeling of worthlessness, the lack of dignity and being badgered to kill Hall. I entertained the idea of killing my father. It could have been so easy just to go the farm and make Dad repent for his sordid life and then do away with him BANG ... BANG.

However, vengeance wasn't for me and in time those thoughts disappeared as I learned more about Jesus Christ. Prior to that brain explosion my father and I had a fearful row because I knew he stashed kiddie porn under his bed. I had stumbled upon it when I lived there and it appalled me. If ever I was going to raise my hand to him that was the time. Instead I told him of the disgust I felt for him. 'What kind of fucking animal harbours that filth?'

My father replied he was simply minding it for someone, yet I could tell the old coot was lying through his teeth.

When I returned to Melbourne big Keith Ellis informed me the first step of my comeback program was to spar with a local bruiser at an inner-city Turkish club. Keith reasoned it would be a tremendous way for me to ease my way back into the fight game. There would be a big crowd on hand to watch the session because I was a former Australian champion and my opponent had a reputation as a banger. I thought it was a grand idea and I felt genuinely excited when Keith and I turned up to the front door of the clubhouse – I could sense a new beginning.

I had met a wonderful woman back at Cessnock named Renee and she was the kind of girl a bloke would be more than happy to come to his senses for. As it turned out Renee was my little ray of sunshine amid numerous storm clouds and as time went by she was to play an important part in getting me back on the right track.

When Keith and I entered the club we took little notice of the two Turks – they had to be brothers – arguing with the security guard about not being allowed into the place. However, they grabbed our undivided attention when we stood in the foyer and one of them smashed the bouncer square in the face with a schooner after he called the Turk a 'mother-fucker'.

When the guard went down the pair were onto him like a couple of hyenas on a crippled water buffalo. The ferocity of their attack stunned me. I didn't want to get caught in a fight which wasn't mine so I followed Keith's lead and left the place immediately. I wanted to be well away from the joint when the fists – and knives – were flying.

Once we made good our escape we actually ran down an alley to ensure we were well out of harm's way, but, you wouldn't believe it, the bloke who glassed the bouncer jumped out in front of us! His thumb was hanging from a sliver of flesh – the glass must have almost chopped it off when he drove it into the bloke's face – and we were then joined by his brother. To anyone who didn't know us it appeared as if we were one happy little group of people but I could sense these blokes spelt real danger.

Well, a fella can be unlucky because just as I prepared to give them the big fend I heard a terrible commotion from the alley. About eighty crazy-eyed Turks were running towards us wielding sticks and knives. They wanted blood and, in an attempt to ensure they didn't take any of mine, I started to run.

Fear is a tremendous motivation – I ran like the wind

and I could hear Keith and the two Turks weren't far behind me. I would have run all night had I needed to, but not Ellis. He was out of nick and the sprint had him huffing and puffing like a steam-engine. I heard him curse aloud – big Keith said he'd rather go down fighting than suffer a heart attack while running from a mob, so I left him.

The other brother decided that was a good idea and he too prepared to dig in and make a stand. (As it turned out the mob let Keith leave but they battered the other bloke.) I kept running and try as I might I couldn't shake the bloke who had started the nightmare. It didn't take long for the mob to close in on us and, in an attempt to revive my running partner, I screamed at the top of my voice: 'Run. Fuck you, run!'.

We ran our separate ways and when the Turks crossed my path I waited for one of them to stick a knife in my ribs. I was terrified and I remember saying to myself, 'God, if you want me to die I'm going to die now. Help me please!' Instead, the bouncer walked up to me and screamed: 'Where is he? Who is he? Where the fuck did he go?'.

I told him I didn't know the bloke from a bar of soap and with that the bouncer went ballistic. He said I was dead meat and as I looked around me it appeared as if the Turks were waiting for a signal to move in for the kill, but I wasn't going to allow that.

I took a tip from Dad's book and put on my brave face even though I wanted to crap my pants. I told them it wasn't my fight and the trouble back at the club had nothing to do with me. I had them bluffed with my nonchalant attitude, though the bloke with the severed thumb didn't enjoy such good fortune. As I searched the streets for Keith I heard the distant wail of an ambulance which I figured was called for a couple of Turkish blokes who had been left for dead after a mob attacked them.

That was one of many adventures I'd had with Keith. Our friendship stretched way back to when I first started boxing and he was even at my last fight in 1990 when I made my return to the boxing ring against the Soviet Union's former world amateur heavyweight champion, Dimitry Eliseev in Perth. It was billed as Australia vs the Soviet Union because Lou Cafaro, Tony Miller, Shane Riley and I were pitted against the pride of the USSR.

I entered the ring fifteen kilos heavier than my rival, and, to tell you the truth, had I not squandered the purse after it was advanced to me I wouldn't have bothered to turn up. I had been hitting the drugs far too hard and I was ripe for yet another beating.

I realised long before the referee read the instructions that the battle was going to come down to kill or be killed so I opened with a tremendous salvo which rocked the Soviet. I smashed his nose in the opening round and I was happy to see his blood stain the canvas floor.

However, the Russian also hit home early in the fight when he collected me with a wide right hand and the damage was shocking. My left ear drum exploded – I heard it pop – yet at the end of the round Troy paid no attention to me when I told him I was suffering. He just waved his hand and said not to worry about that because I had smashed the Russian and looked good. His attitude to my pain summed up the way we three boys had been brought up; we were trained to fight on even if we lost an arm during the heat of the battle.

I returned determined to give all or nothing when the Soviet delivered a series of blows which sent me crashing into dreamland. I was in a trance-like state. Everything was pitch black and while I wanted to pick myself up I had no power in my limbs. And I hurt. Actually, I finished the fight with my jaw broken on one side and fractured on the other; a burst eardrum and a gash which needed five stitches across the bridge of my nose! In my dream world I could hear Guy asking if I was alright while Keith's voice sounded very distant as I heard him yell for someone to get me up off my back because he said the champ should not be left on the canvas.

As I was assisted from the ring a mug punter stood and yelled at the top of his voice, 'As weak as bloody water, too!' While I was too far gone to care, my little brother, who had seen me take a terrible beating, screamed, 'What the hell do you want?', and I think Keith had to restrain Troy from doing something silly.

When I recovered my senses in hospital I had a metal plate in my jaw and my ear-drum was burst. I looked like the elephant man, but the Soviet's best shots were nothing compared to the beating I was giving myself over the shooting.

RENEE

Chapter Twenty

'Dean loves Renee!'
Dean's message to shoppers after he commandeered a supermarket's microphone

When I was caught up in the drug web I thought I could handle even the most serious situation without any hint of a problem. It didn't matter if I had to bluff my way out of trouble with a mob of mad Turks, deal with underworld figures, match wits with the cops or even dish out some back-street justice to would-be tough guys, I could fix things, no sweat. Heck, people could talk to me about a robbery they had plotted and I wouldn't even raise an eyebrow!

However, when it came to dealing with my emotions I was hopelessly out of my depth. I found it hard to talk openly to anyone about my feelings until the night I worked on the door of the Cessnock Workers Club and met a girl named Renee Baccus.

I was back in New South Wales to see my brother Troy

fight on a Kostya Tzsyu bill at Newcastle but he was forced to withdraw from the fight at the last minute with an injured hand. However, I decided to stay around for a while to earn some money working on the door at Cessnock, though most of my interest focussed around Renee.

She was a nice, quiet girl and the night I worked up enough courage to talk to her I asked: 'Why haven't you ever asked me to drive you home before?' And her response was a beauty because she asked why I hadn't asked her to ask me to drive her home. Anyway, I did escort her back to her place that night and as it turned out she had no idea of who I was and that meant she did not know about my boxing background, the Hall shooting, the Waters family fall-out, my father or even my wild streak. I was just Dean, the big log who tried to look mean and hard on the door.

We stayed up all night, drank coffee and spoke about everything and anything. What really struck me was it was all so very decent . . . I saw her as a really nice person who I could quite happily talk to. My mate Steve obtained Renee's phone number for me, but I lost it on my drive back to Melbourne when I pulled up at a Goulburn service station to fill my tank up. I left my wallet behind and when it dawned upon me a few hours later that I had left it a few hundred kilometres back up the road I didn't give a hoot for my cash or credit cards. Instead, my greatest concern was the fact I'd lost Renee's phone number and because I figured I might not get it again I backtracked all the way to Goulburn and my efforts were rewarded when I discovered someone had handed it in at the police station.

Perhaps I should have stayed in Cessnock because on my return to Melbourne I hit the drugs big time. I had a lot of emotions to bury, and top of the list was my pining for Renee.

However, I turned my back on the girls who I'd bedded before my trip back home because I did not want to spoil something which felt so special with a cheap and meaningless romp in the back of a car or the doorway of a building. Instead I phoned Renee *every* day for thirteen weeks and the calls stretched into the early hours of the morning. I did other things to surprise her – like send post packs crammed with chocolates, roses and even exotic coffee. The coffee was a symbol of that first time we spoke until sunrise, however, I bought Renee beans from Kenya and Brazil because I maintained my girl was too good for the boring, old instant stuff from off the supermarket shelf!

One of the special things about Renee was I never felt as if I had to reassure her there was no chance of me getting back with Kelly by rubbishing my ex-wife. I did not need to boost Renee's confidence in that regard because, as I have already said, Renee has a real depth of character. She realised I held Kelly in such a high regard because she is the mother of two of my kids, Rebekka and Courtney. Indeed, Renee later told me later she found the fact I held Kelly in such high esteem an attraction to her.

When it became painfully obvious I needed to be with her I made arrangements for Renee to fly south and help bring some cheer to another bitterly cold Melbourne winter. She had never been in an aeroplane before and because I did not want her to make the trip alone I booked myself onto a thirteen hour bus trip to meet her at the Mascot domestic terminal. However, I wanted to surprise her and I dressed as a loser-like figure. I wore an old army jacket, a long red haired wig and I banged my head away to some psychotic heavy metal tune being pumped into my ears by a Walkman stereo. My mate Steve and his girlfriend took

Renee to the airport and I was to later learn that he pointed out the long haired loser to them and laughed as they walked past me.

Renee had more pressing things on her mind than to think twice about the loony, things such as how would she survive her first flight! However, when Steve noticed the lunatic was following them he pushed the girls in front of him and I laughed to myself as I saw them run off! After a few moments of quick walking I reached out and grabbed Steve. Man, I'll never forget the look of horror on his face, but I knew Steve would have a swing at me if he thought he had to protect himself and the girls. I ripped the wig off and said 'It's me! Dean!' and I could see the look of relief overcome him! We hugged and when Renee saw me she squealed with delight.

The interesting postscript to that little game was my madman's outfit looked so convincing I drew the attention of the Airport security force and they asked me a few times whether I was alright. I appreciated their concern – maybe the guards feared I was going to blow the joint up - so I told them the truth when I said, 'This is what love will drive you to.' However, when I took the wig off they became very concerned and asked for me to produce my airline ticket to prove I had a reason to be there!

Well, I did and our flight over Sydney was marvellous ... even though the weather was bleak, I had my head resting on Renee's shoulder 16,000 feet up and I was happier than I had been for a long time! Indeed, it was as if we were in our own little world when the aeroplane flew above the clouds because while the world was grey and dull below we seemed to have our own fairytale kingdom above the clouds because everything was fluffy and white. It felt so good I was tempted to say to Renee there and then that I loved her, however, I bit my tongue because I did not want to rush things.

We had a marvellous eight days together. On my birthday we went and saw a performance of Romeo and Juliet and while I had trouble getting my head around some of the old English, I enjoyed the experience. I was dressed in the first clothes I had ever bought for myself and I had a beautiful girl next to me. It was a wonderful evening because I felt as though I at least looked as if I fitted in with the crowd. Our time together was filled with romance because apart from hitting the restaurants and night clubs I was like a puppy dog eager to please. I did some silly things like lift Renee on my shoulders in the shopping centre and yell, 'Who's the prettiest girl in the world?' And I would make Renee yell her name out at the top of her voice. On another occasion when we were at the local supermarket I commandeered a cashier's microphone and declared: 'Dean loves Renee!' It was a wonderful time and I didn't care what anyone thought.

A week after Renee returned to Cessnock I was involved in an all-in brawl and suffered a bad head gash. However, when I told Renee of my latest war wound she booked a seat on a coach and came all the way down to make sure I was alright. It was wonderful and we decided she and her kids should live with me. Our first home was in a room at the Werribee Hotel and I'm forever grateful to the owners Maureen and Tony Hall because they allowed us to stay there rent-free until we found a suitable place.

Werribee is known to Melbournites for two reasons – its sewerage outlet and its high crime rate. However, it was there where poor Renee was also given an insight into my terrible drug-induced mood swings when our honeymoon period ended. She learned I could not have a disagreement without it turning into a bitter and explosive argument. While Renee called it the 'devil' inside me, I thought of it as a legacy of the example my father had set. I was harsh if something went wrong ... if a cup broke or a bill wasn't paid I would do my 'nana. In my book there was no such a thing as an honest mistake, everything was pre-planned and deliberate.

It was such a terrible way to live, and it was especially hard on Renee because she felt as if everything I had done to win her heart over was a lie. She began to wonder whether I was a monster who had trapped her. I had no idea of how life worked. I remember losing my temper once when there was no food in the fridge and when she told me she had no money I gave her ten bucks and told her to get in a cab and buy some groceries. Her brother, who was down visiting, laughed himself silly at that because he thought I was joking. It was no joke, I just had no idea of how things like that worked.

Renee ran away a couple of times but I always tracked her down – sometimes at women's hostels – to beg her forgiveness. I pleaded for her to understand I needed time to come to grips with my new life and that I was trying my hardest to do things like understand her children's imagination. Sometimes they would say the sky is green or a shark was swimming in the pool but rather than go along with them I would say they were lying. The sky is blue and there was no shark. It was the same harsh, inflexible attitude my father had raised me with.

However, I did have one saving grace which Dad lacked and that was I could sometimes hear myself rant and rave and I would stop mid-sentence and ask Renee why on earth

I had to always explode about nothing? I could see myself carry on and I figured I should be locked in a nuthouse.

While I blamed the drugs for my behaviour I knew the real reason why I was climbing walls all the time ... I was living with a terrible guilt. I had started to think about turning myself in to the authorities for killing Hall, but that would have meant surrendering my freedom and losing twenty-five years with Renee and that scared me so much I fought hard to repress doing what was right. However, my day of reckoning came when we returned to the Central Coast and I lost my temper so badly Renee took the kids and went to a women's refuge. It was the lowest I had ever felt and when I thought I had lost everything I started to cry. I was dribbling and blubbering and I started to bash my head into a wall because I looked around and realised I not only had nothing, but it seemed as if I had lost the best thing that had ever happened to me. In my desperate attempt to try and win Renee back I threw thousands of dollars worth of drugs down the toilet. I wanted to get my life back and I needed Renee to help me.

VIVA LAS VEGAS

Chapter Twenty-One

'He was very negative, not having the strength, speed or fitness to defeat a boxer of Norris's class and ability ... one of the things that surprised me was the ease with which Norris penetrated Troy's defence.'

Ces Waters' account of Troy's fight against WBC world champion Terry Norris

I took time out from my grog- and drug-induced haze and sobered up for the long trip to Las Vegas where Troy was preparing for his World Boxing Council title shot against the flashy Jamaican, Simon Brown.

My baby brother had become the toast of the American boxing scene after his valiant effort against 'Terrible' Terry Norris, the man many critics described as pound-for-pound the world's best fighter. Norris's manager called him the Michael Jordan of boxing while his record noted he ended the great Sugar Ray Leonard's career.

And when Troy entered the ring against Norris in San Diego to a chorus of jeers and boos from the crowd, the champ made it clear he thought Troy had a death wish by accepting the fight. Some hecklers took that sentiment to heart because they sledged Troy, calling him a 'kangaroo-fucker' and shouting out such things to him as that he'd better have written his will and that they had already booked an ambulance to cart his corpse to the morgue. They were confident Norris would fulfil his prediction and murder the Aussie so and so!

However, on his way back to the dressing-room – just twenty or so minutes later – those hecklers were among the eleven thousand admirers who gave Troy a standing ovation as a tribute to his class, courage and big right hand. Sure, he lost the fight when a wicked blow ripped opened the skin under both his eyes – he was chopped up badly – but my brother proved that even in defeat a fighter can enjoy his sweetest victory.

Troy had become the first fighter in four long years (since 1989) to sit Norris on his backside! If ever you get an opportunity to see a video of the bout, watch the faces of the people at ringside when Troy unleashed his monster right hand and Norris hit the deck: they were stunned! And the American commentary team of former world champion Bobby Czyz, Steve Albert and Ferdie Pacheco shared their disbelief when they exclaimed: 'Norris goes down! Unbelievable! What a turn of events! He's in trouble! It came out of nowhere ... Oh my God!'

It just wasn't meant to happen. Unfortunately Norris rallied and the fight was stopped when Troy received cuts under his eyes which required twenty-four stitches.

Because Bruce Kennedy had hyped the fight up at the press conference when he recited an Ali-like ditty which suggested Troy's big right hand would leave the champ in La-la-land, Norris made it clear the bout had become personal, when he gloated Troy's career may have ended.

'I destroyed your boy tonight,' he skited to Kennedy. 'He's so cut up he might never fight again.'

However, a cable report on the fight captured the mood of the moment when it stated: 'After being battered from pillar to post – and dropped twice – Waters, like a gunboat sinking, let fly with a vicious salvo sending Norris crashing to the canvas in the second.'

And Ron Firmrite of the prestigious American publication *Sports Illustrated* wrote of Troy's ambush: 'The champion had had such an easy time of it in the opening round that he came out in round two looking for a quick kill. Instead, midway through the round, as Norris nailed him with a straight right to the temple, and for the first time since Julian Jackson knocked him out on 30 July, 1989, Norris went down. In thirteen consecutive victories since the Jackson loss, Norris had scarcely been beaten. Now he was hurt . . .'

The mob couldn't believe Norris had actually hit the deck and they crowded outside the dressing-room for Troy's autograph and to get photographs with the man who hammered the hammerer. The flamboyant boxing promoter with the electric-shock hairstyle, Don King, was all over Troy, shouting out such things as: 'The Glamour with the Hammer' and 'The Thunder from Down Under!'

Veteran Australian fight identity Ern McQuillan junior, who was connected with the likes of Vic Patrick and Tony Mundine, gushed to the press that a star had been born. And while Troy was bitterly disappointed to have lost the bout, he clearly enjoyed a victory of a different kind when he said:

Norris couldn't knock me out – he knocked me down twice – but he couldn't KO me. It took a cut eye to stop

> *me. Norris has a mighty reputation ... he's beaten some of the best including Sugar Ray Leonard. I guess they couldn't believe that an unknown from down under could sit him on his backside. I was one punch away from being the world champ and a multi-millionaire.*

Troy further underlined his potential a few months later when he fought Robert Wangila, the Kenyan 1988 Olympic gold medallist, at the renowned Los Angeles Forum in front of sixteen thousand cheering and foot-stamping Mexicans who called America 'home'.

Wangila was a renowned KO merchant and he landed some tremendous shots on Troy. However, Troy took Wangila's best blows and retaliated with a stinging series of body shots which tattooed the African's liver. As a tribute to Troy's tenacity the crowd started chanting 'Mehico, Mehico, Mehico'. According to Troy's trainer, Charlie Gergen – a German-born Aussie who was once described as the world's most disqualified boxer – the mob afforded Troy that honour because they thought he boxed like a Mexican!

Unfortunately fate proved how cruel life can be because while Troy went onto another world title shot after that victory, the East African idol died from a brain haemorrhage in his very next fight.

Troy wasn't the only one proving America was the land of opportunity because in only his third fight in two years Guy was also given a crack at Virgil Hill's WBA light-heavyweight title in snow-covered Bismark, North Dakota. Guy promised he would display an aggression Aussie fight fans had not yet seen in him, however, as if it was part of the curse which seemed to plague us boys whenever we had a *really* big fight.

As Guy braced himself for another crack at the world title things were chaotic back on the homefront because Sharon was forced to undergo a caesarean birth when her blood level shot up to a dangerous level. However, because Sharon wanted to give Guy every possible chance to win the bout she insisted no-one tell him of her problems. While Guy was beaten by Hill his disappointment was placed straight on the backburner once he heard of Sharon's operation. Guy was far more concerned about the health of his wife and baby daughter than a lost opportunity and he made that clear when he told *Sun-Herald* reporter Paul Kent that his biggest regret wasn't seeing Hill raise his arms in triumph but it was not being present for his baby's birth!

Three months after Troy proved 'Terrible' Terry was only human, the quietly spoken Simon Brown knocked Norris out in the fourth round of their encounter. I have no doubts whatsoever that Troy softened Norris up for the kill – my brother proved he wasn't invincible and I'm sure that gave Brown some confidence.

A month after Norris's defeat Troy was signed by Don King to fight for Brown's crown on the inaugural Grand Slam of Boxing bill at the massive MGM Grand Hotel in Las Vegas. Troy's reputation was growing at such a rate in America that many critics questioned Brown's wisdom in making his first title defence against the Aussie wonderkid.

Nevertheless, Brown was prepared to back himself and when I touched down in Las Vegas, Troy's name was up in lights alongside some of the sport's hottest warriors including Mexico's Julio Cesar Chavez and Puerto Rico's Felix Trinidad and Hector Comacho! While I felt a genuine sense of pride when I realised just how far Troy had come since our days at Finsbury Park I couldn't help but feel bitter about the fact that my own career had crashed and burned the night Allan Hall died.

As I saw the likes of Sugar Ray Leonard and Thomas Hearns saunter around the MGM I wondered how far I might have gone had Dad not made me his assassin. I feel as though I never fulfilled my potential, it sometimes feels as if my talent disappeared into the mist. However, it wasn't the time or place to feel sorry for myself. My little brother was scheduled to fight the bout which I believed would set him up for life and I was there to offer him my total support.

It was not difficult to get caught up in the carnival atmosphere of the build-up to the fight night and a lot of my attention focussed on the man many boxers believe to be the Devil himself, Don King. Big Don wore a jewel-encrusted crucifix which would have been worth enough to feed a Third World nation for a year and I laughed when I heard the man who has long been accused of being a blood-sucker and a leech saying he wore it to keep the 'vampires' at bay!

Don was keen to see Troy make it because my brother had four assets which could have translated into big bucks and glory in America – he had good looks, he was articulate, he could throw a dynamite punch and, most importantly, he was Caucasian. 'He might be white but he can fight,' screamed King at the press conference. 'He's the Thunder from Down Under, the Glamour with the Hammer, he's a terrific fighter and he'll soon be the champion of the world!'

They were honey-flavoured words and to tell you the truth I was a bit wary of King's interest in my brother because I was well aware plenty of fighters had been burned by the self-proclaimed King of the Ring. On the other hand I had heard people in America say King was a great man, they pointed out he had received the Martin Luther King Junior Humanitarian award, the Black Achievement award, the Black United Fund's Man of the Year award and the Promoter of the Century award.

However, he had more enemies than friends. Former heavyweight champion Larry Holmes said King boasted such a bizarre hairstyle because it hid his devil horns! Others, like Australia's Jeff Fenech and another former world heavyweight champion, Tim Witherspoon, were among those who loathed King. They warned any fighter that to sign a contract with King was to all but sign your life away.

The Witherspoon account for his 1983 WBC title fight (against my old sparring partner Greg Page) made frightening reading. By the time Don and his handlers took their numerous 'unspecified deductions' from Witherspoon's US$250,000 purse he was left with a pathetic US$41,000. And when Tim fought Frank Bruno in 1986 for US$1,700,000 – enough to set anyone up for life – he finished with a lousy US$90,000, just five per cent of the promised purse.

I was worried Troy's then manager, Bruce Kennedy, appeared to have fallen into bed with King and appeared happy enough to go along with whatever King desired. Bruce obviously thought he was doing the right thing but I was deeply concerned Troy could finish up another King fighter left with nothing more than black eyes and empty pockets! And I really started to worry when I heard Kennedy say he didn't care if King made US$50,000,000 out of Troy's blood and sweat because it would mean Troy would enjoy a much greater earn at the end of the day. I'm the first to concede I am not a businessman but I was scared King would take that kind of talk as an invitation to fleece all he could from my brother's hide.

However, I bit my tongue and kept those thoughts to myself because the last thing I wanted to do was distract Troy from his fight. My Dad had done his best to do that with a poison pen letter which reached Troy a few nights before the fight.

The letter left me feeling as shattered as it did Troy because it showed that even though we were thousands of miles away in the USA we could not escape his venom. Troy, Guy, Tracey and I had realised Dad was getting on in years and he made it clear he did not intend to go to his grave quietly. And our fears that he would go down with all guns blazing were reinforced when Troy received the letter which had been pounded out on an old typewriter as the dreadful bushfires of 1993 threatened to reduce Kulnura to ashes.

ATTENTION TROY WATERS

TROY as this is the last letter I will ever write to you I hope you possess the courage to read it. However I will keep my copy just in case certain people keep it from you, then I can always pass it down the line as proven evidence I did in fact send it to you.

First of all I want you to realise that it is not just me that realises you are a self-centred selfish person. You have knocked me to just about everybody you have attached yourself too [sic] *and everyone of them a bandwagon jumper or percentage hunter looking for glory on the backs of two boxers I spent time creating and taking to the top.*

Besides being the best boxing trainer in this country and one of the best in the world as is now accepted by most in the Australian boxing industry, I have been a darn good father doing what I have always thought best for my children. But I cannot be blamed if my children turned out to be carbon copies of their mother.

SHE LIVED FOR HERSELF AND A GOOD TIME. And all the time making out she was running away from me. No mother deserts her children no matter what the circumstances. If she leaves she takes the children with her.

My book is now finished and it is being edited in England and New Zealand and will be published in those countries plus Australia. Mark Erikson is going to try the USA as another outlet. In the book you and your brothers are described as you really are and I can assure you Troy the myth of the Waters boys will be well and truly shattered.

Do you know people still stop me in the street and tell me what lovely boys I have got? When I told one old lady that not one of those lovely boys bothered to enquire as to my health after I had two heart attacks in four weeks (brought on by the stress of worrying about my lovely sons) she just would not believe it. And then your statement to one person that it was not a proper heart attack that I had. I think the heart rehabilitation unit at Gosford would have something to say about that.

However Troy that heart attack brought forward some wonderful people and I still treasure the faxes from all over Australia and abroad. As I write this I am surrounded by bushfires, the worst in living memory, do you know my phone has never stopped wringing [sic] *with calls from people concerned about me. More now than ever do I realise what mean, selfish human beings my kids are. I have had plenty of time during the research for my book to study each one of you and I can say that I sincerely hope you don't have any children for you can only make a poor father as you have been a lousy treacherous son.*

Do you remember a couple of Xmasses ago you and your brothers rang to wish me a merry Xmas. I had in my cupboard half a tin of beans. I would have had only that if it had not been for friends. Do you realise how low you have sunk? Not only in my estimation but in the estimation of a lot of decent people.

Also I don't think you fully understand how you have deteriorated. As a boxer, and your choice of handlers is to say the least pathetic. They can never take credit for you or your brothers in a million years as it took me over twenty years to mould you as an athletic family and everybody knows that and those who are in any doubt will be enlightened in the book.

You are without family Troy, me and mine don't wish to know you and your brothers, you all had time to apologize [sic] *and make up, now that is beyond repair you have run out of time.*

I did read an article by you and in it you said that you would not mind a father–son relationship but not a trainer relationship. Why did you not tell the full facts Troy? You would not be able to handle early nights very early mornings no females real hard grind no late nights no poker machines.

And joke of all jokes you once knocked me for having a military style camp up in the mountains yet people stop me in the street and comment that Troy is trying to copy his old style of training by doing it in the mountains of the USA. But you will never be able to replace Ces Waters and everybody knows it.

Ian Batty and I watched your fight with Norris for

which you were ill prepared, a fight you could have won and should have won. But you let him get away like you did with Rosi like you did with the Canadian in Santa Domingo and like you did with the shotput in Queensland when you were in High School and I am the only living soul in the world who knows why it happens.

Your loss to Rosi was pretty predictable when one considers that a year leading up to that fight you were rebelling with your smart brothers who are anything but smart.

But all this aside Troy you will never be truly happy and as the years go by you will have to live with your conscience and the knowledge that like your brothers you betrayed the best friend you will ever have. You will never know what I gave up in England to give you kids a chance in Australia because I did not want you brought up in London.

I flatly refused to hand you all over to the London Council for adoption when your mother deserted you, and yet years later you deserted me. You left me with all the debt accumulated over the years even going back to Terrey Hills with debts I got into to buy you clothes when you were at school.

After selling the property and paying off debts I was left with nothing and nowhere to live and I can tell you Troy it even made the editor of the book shake his head. However you will read it one day.

Do you know Troy that when you left me to go over to the winning side (your words) I did not even know until I read it in the local paper. Why? When my sister treated you like royalty (and she did not have to let you in her home after the way you treated me) you came back to Australia and never even sent her a thank you letter.

When Ian Batty had you at his place for a couple of days you left him saying you would see him next week and you never did contact him again. Denzil who has been more than a good mate to you had you at his place and believed you were a friend. You dropped him like a cast-off garment, and you have even been to Queensland and never even phoned him. Believe me Troy that man has been more to you than you deserve. From the very outset I have kept you and your brothers safe in the ring in many ways and you have taken everything for granted.

Well Troy you have the friends you deserve and let me tell you the way you deserve as birds of a feather flock together.

Just to think I would not give Don King and Bob Arum four options on you to fight Matthew Hilton, because I did not want to sell you down the river. I should have not held out for two options and your security, rather I should have thought of my pocket instead of my son. Wake up Troy you love yourself and nobody else. Guy can always use Sharon as an excuse in our fall out, Dean is a very sick person and I can even find it in my heart to feel for him, but for you Troy I only have contempt and it gets worse the more I hear people talk about you.

The word is you are a user and you are certainly not the person you used to be and I only have hate for you and will never recognise you as my son. You never had a mother now you don't have a father.

It is also a relief to know other people know that I am not just talking on – they have had some of you.

Troy Waters only has loyalty to Troy Waters. Any money you make will pass through your fingers like water and your bad luck will be more than you can handle and will stay with you till the day you die. I will pass on like any other mortal and I will be remembered for what I have done and you will be remembered for what you have done. Your treatment of me will never be forgiven.

Do yourself a favour Troy and stay in the USA because you will never shine again in Australia once my book is published. It would be in the interest of the family name Waters (most are in the USA) if you change your name by deed poll perhaps to your mother's maiden name Newman because you most certainly behave like a Newman. That would probably be the only decent thing you would have done in recent times.

Your coming fight with Simon Brown, you will never outbox him because you have lost most of your boxing skills having been in the hands of idiots so long, your only chance is to knock him out because that is the one thing I have always said from the early days that you have the punch to KO anybody up to Light Heavy.

He could knock you out and he has the skill to outbox you and it is odds on you will not have a good fight plan because no matter who you have around you and no matter what crapology you are fed by Americans or ex-Australians in the USA you have not got anybody near you who can come up with the good credentials. All you have is con men and dollar hunters but you deserve them Troy.

Having said that let me say that I, being in a far superior class than that garbage you have around you, would not train you again if you made me a golden handshake of approximately two hundred thousand dollars – about what the court would award me if I had taken you to court for breach of contract, and believe me Troy you would have lost in any court battle with me. The whole of Australia knows the Waters story too well and they also know that without me there would not be a Waters dynasty and do YOU really believe a High Court judge would let you and your brothers off the hook?

As far as I am concerned Troy you are a grub and I never want to see or hear from you or your brother Guy again. As far as Dean is concerned he is to be pitied but as sure as death and taxes you will all meet your Waterloo. You will never know true happiness any of you and you will all be exposed one day as the counterfeit human beings you all are.

John Marr is going to make a feature film based on my book. Those who play the part of the Waters boys will have to be real creeps and I will interview all applicants to ensure the ones we get come over as nice blokes but are in fact greedy arrogant self centred human garbage living only for themselves in fact clones of Gloria Newman. I close wishing the worst luck in the world and hope you show this to all your friends?

Ces Waters, one time father and great friend

While I had intended to keep myself clean of drugs for Troy's sake while I was in Las Vegas, I found there were times when I craved a snort of cocaine to help me get through the day – and night. I was desperate and even put out a few feelers to the right sort of people. However, I resisted the temptation to take it any further because I was terrified Troy's growing reputation in America would be ruined if a team of drug cops kicked down the door of my room and found me with a bag of white powder.

I found it was near impossible to switch my mind off and go to sleep without the assistance of some chemicals so I stayed up at night watching movies, eating ice cream and ringing Renee to speak for hours at a time. I was a complete mess but I fought to keep myself together for Troy.

It's funny how God works because I enjoyed some relief from my demons at the press conference when I heard a journeyman named Dan Ward use his fifteen seconds of fame to quote the gospel and give thanks to God for giving him the opportunity to fight former world champion Thomas 'Hitman' Hearns. Big Dan was on fire and his faith in the Almighty moved me. For a few moments his conviction took me to a higher level.

After he finished speaking I took time out to shake the bespectacled Ward's hand and said Jesus would look after him in the bout. I said he would do his best because he had faith. Dan gave his all on the night but it was not enough to ruffle Hearns who was on the comeback path and chasing a world cruiserweight title. The 'Hitman' needed just two minutes and nine seconds in the first round to send Dan into orbit. However, it was Dan's best and I admired him for it.

There was plenty of nightlife – and mischief – waiting to be enjoyed in Las Vegas. However, I turned my back on it and tried to relax. I was amazed by the glitz and glamour of the place but I didn't want to experience too much of it. Instead, I planned to return there with Renee one day and I wanted to savour the main sights with her.

Troy had been based in Los Angeles for six months and in the build-up to his fight I found that everything I had heard about it being a crazy place was true. He spent most of his time in California at Redondo Beach with Gergen. And through his training at seedy gymnasiums in South Central Los Angeles – where the infamous LA riots took place – Troy rubbed shoulders with gang members and gained a frightening insight into their mentality when he spoke to them about their lives.

The worst gang Troy heard about was a mob called the Smileys, a mad bunch of mongrels who give their victims a permanent smile. Their tactics are to bash a victim, male or female, until they are helpless. They then open the victim's mouth, place it on a gutter and stomp violently on the back of their head. If it doesn't kill them the action causes the corners of their mouth to split right up to their ears, their jaws are busted, some teeth are smashed and the scars leave a permanent smile. Joining the Smileys involves a terrible initiation which includes a new member's mouth being cut with a flick-knife to look like The Joker's from *Batman*!

In other parts of Los Angeles, life and death can be determined by such minute things as the colour of the T-shirt a person puts on in the morning. I heared from Troy that a colour gang shot a ten-year-old boy dead just because he wore a blue T-shirt into their red zone! It's insane, and it is something which can't be allowed to happen in Australia.

However, Troy said his biggest fear while in Los Angeles wasn't being 'scoped' (watched with evil intent) by the gangs. Instead, gun-toting cops were a far greater hassle. When Troy was walking back from the supermarket one day with an Afro-American and a Latin-American boxer – a former world champion named Sammy Fuentes – they were suddenly surrounded by four police cars crammed with armed cops. One of the police drew his pistol and ordered the three to hit the pavement and they were searched. It turned out the trio fitted the descriptions of a few blokes who burned a house down and LA's finest took no chances.

On the eve of his fight against Brown, Troy made it clear to the Australian Associated Press correspondent who covered the fight that he was in a 'desperate' mood. He said defeat would be a disaster and would probably end his career.

'This is my third shot and if I'm not successful I doubt whether I'd want to continue with boxing,' said Troy. 'All I can say is that if by the end of this fight I am not the world champion then they'll be taking me home on a stretcher, because I am going all out, I'm putting everything on the line for this.'

Troy boxed brilliantly under the intense glare of the MGM's bright lights. He counter-punched superbly and his defence was rock-solid. He went punch for punch with the more fancied Brown and in the eleventh round my spirit soared when the champ's eye was cut after an accidental head-clash.

After twelve heated rounds the thirteen thousand-strong crowd went wild and cheered for Troy, though their unbridled enthusiasm did nothing to swing the judges Australia's way. Brown won the bout with scores of 114–114, 116–112 and 118–111.

Troy was beaten but his US agent, the highly respected Don Majeski, was floored by the response the defeated corner received, saying, 'You can lose a fight but you can win the crowd and Troy has done that.'

According to Don King, thirty-nine million people watched the fight on pay television and he promised that they'd be seeing a lot more of the youngest of the Waters brothers.

'Troy Waters, the Glamour with the Hammer, the Thunder from Down Under, is getting better with each title fight,' King crowed. 'He is developing into quite an attraction and will one day be the world champion. He is a terrific fighter and will be used on more of my programs!'

As was the case with the Norris fight, Troy may have been defeated but he was far from beaten. While a number of American well-wishers said he was unlucky not to have been awarded the crown, Troy chose to pay tribute to his victorious opponent by saying Brown was not only an awkward customer but he fought extremely well. I was proud of the way Troy handled the defeat. He took it like a man.

Troy wanted me to stick around in America with him for a few days to take in some of the sights before I returned to Australia. The Superbowl was on television the following day and he promised it would be an event well worth watching. However, I didn't give a stuff about the NFL; all I wanted at that stage was to return home to be with my Renee. I missed her terribly for the fortnight I was away and hours after the fight I hugged Troy farewell and said I was proud of him.

I then threw my gear into a bag and flew to LA International airport to get a seat on the first available Qantas flight back to Sydney. The next day, twenty-four hours after coming so painfully close to winning the world title, Troy lost himself at the Redondo Beach Fun Pier playing computer games and drinking cherry cola with a mate from Sydney. But if the judges had seen the fight through my eyes, the kid would have been a world champ sipping the best French champagne and dining on the finest fare. I don't know why, but it just wasn't meant to be.

COMING FORWARD

Chapter Twenty-Two

'1. If the defendant fails without reasonable cause, the proof whereof lies upon him, to appear in accordance with his undertaking of bail and surrender himself into custody, he shall be guilty of an offence by imprisonment not exceeding twelve months.'

Dean Water's notice of undertaking of bail for assaulting two Victorian police officers

I was terrified I would die young in Melbourne. I had made some terrible enemies by playing god on the doors of various nightspots and I watched in horror as one by one the blokes I knew from the drug trade came to grief. A bouncer acquaintance didn't help soothe my fears when he spoke about the time he was shot by a disgruntled punter!

His bullet wound made me think long and hard about the way I had treated some people because I was certain some of the patrons I roughed up over the years would pay to see me get badly hurt. The drug world had become just as dangerous and that was rammed home when the bloke who'd taught me everything he knew about the trade was gunned down three weeks after he murdered someone. He was shot in his driveway and his death rattled me so badly I wondered whether my body would be found at the bottom of the Yarra River.

Rather than change my life by cutting back on the drugs and the aggression I continued to play the part of an angry rebel because that kind of behaviour allowed me to escape the memory of my having been a good soldier and blasting a man to death.

But I was destroying myself in the process and while I knew the only way I could gain any sense of redemption was to confess everything to the police I was scared of having to spend up to twenty years in prison. The thought of losing everything was a stumbling block and I found the best way to live with my guilt was to drop a pill because their chemicals made the world seem slightly more bearable.

The people I mixed with shared my outlook on drugs and I can hazily remember such incidents as the morning I was in the bouncers' toilets – it was about 2 a.m. – and a DJ staggered in as drunk as a skunk. His hands shook as he dragged a massive bag of amphetamines out from his coat pocket and I watched in amazement as he buried his head into it and snorted as much chalk-white powder as his nostrils could suck up. He was like a psychedelic ant-eater and once the drugs kicked in I watched in horror as his face appeared to melt: it distorted, then twisted, his eyes ran like two taps and then he stopped breathing. He spooked me because his eyes had the glassy look of a mullet in a fish shop's front window.

My mate Shane and I were terrified he was about to croak; however, after about twenty heart-stopping seconds he came good! Actually, once the hit kicked in it seemed to dull the effects of his drunkenness because I would have sworn he was stone-cold sober as he jived his way back towards the dance floor!

As much as I loved Renee and our little family, I was still a selfish bastard. When she became pregnant with our first child, Evander, I wasn't emotionally there for her. Despite her not having any family in Victoria I was still all for the boys and our wild nocturnal adventures in seedy nightclubs. If they wanted to go out and drug the night away I would be there with bells on, but if Renee needed something, *anything*, it was always a hassle and I'd roll my eyes and get angry. I really wish it was possible to turn the clock back because I would handle the entire situation differently.

The nine months leading up to the birth of Evander in 1994 were nothing for me to be proud of. Even on the night of his birth I allowed myself to be talked into a night on the tiles instead of going straight to the hospital to be with Renee and our new-born son.

I'm glad I was at the birth because, as was the case with all my kids, it was one of my life's real highlights to see them enter the world. I took Renee to the hospital at 7.30 a.m. and Evander was born by caesarean process an hour or so later. I was like a Japanese tourist taking photos of the entire event, but when I saw Evander for that very first time I felt a tremendous, natural high which I can't properly explain.

However, I also drove the doctors and nurses mad. Normally when a baby is born they put one identification tag around its wrist, well, I insisted they put one on each limb! There was no way I was going to risk losing the little bloke and until I left for work I watched over him like a hawk. I did silly things. For instance, because I thought the nurse was treating him too roughly when she tested his limbs were healthy I ordered her to stand aside and I took over ... he was my little boy and nothing was going to hurt him.

Unfortunately, rather than go straight back to the hospital after work I did the wrong thing. My pal Chris made it clear I *had* to celebrate the birth of my first boy with a drink and after twenty-four minutes we had drained a large bottle of Sambuca! Then we moved onto bourbon, gin, beer, vodka and whatever else we could throw down my throat until the world started to spin and I had to defy gravity just to retain my balance. However, rather than freak out I just laughed as I tried to satisfy my seemingly unquenchable thirst.

Needless to say I did not make it to the hospital that night. My last conscious memory was of raising my arm in mock triumph when I saw Chris on his hands and knees behind the back shed, vomiting as if there was no tomorrow – and the way we'd hit the bottle there should not have been one! I then staggered into his lounge room and crashed out on his couch.

I only opened my eyes the next day because the sun streamed down through the blinds and it felt as if my eyelids were about to burst into flames. It was a far from ideal way to stir from an alcohol-induced slumber – after I regained my senses and saw my mate's wife glaring at me with a look which could have killed a brown dog, I had a sudden compulsion to chunder all over their floor.

It was a dreadful battle not to embarrass myself and as I pushed past her and bolted for their front door I knew her loathing for me had intensified. I made it to their front lawn to up-chuck what seemed to be two weeks' worth of food. Lord knows I was so crook I had to crawl on my hands and knees just to climb into my car so I could get to the hospital to be with my family.

However, I had not seen the worst of my hangover because once I was inside the vehicle the heat and the stench of my vomit hit me like a frying pan. I started again and was soon caked in vomit. Adding further depth to my despair were the hoots and catcalls I received from people who passed by as I heaved into the gutter.

While I felt lousy, poor Renee had done it really tough in hospital. Instead of being with her when she really needed me, I was out on the drink. It shamed me because instead of worrying about her own health Renee fretted for me because she feared something bad had happened. While a nurse had got it right, saying I'd probably spent the night wetting my baby's head, Renee asked for them to call the police and hospitals to ask if they had me in a cell or hospital bed because she could not believe I would be out on a boozy night out.

When I eventually returned to the hospital to see our little bundle of joy I looked so bad Renee thought I really was sick, but I did not deserve her sympathy. I deserved whatever curse she could summon against me in her weakened state. Despite my seediness I looked lovingly upon Evander and it didn't take very long for him to become the apple of my eye.

I had always thought we Waters boys weren't destined to sire males as a form of punishment for the way Dad had raised us – after all, I had fathered two girls, Guy had one and Tracey had two. And while I have fought hard not to fall into many of Dad's child-rearing traps, I sometimes hear myself calling the little bloke my 'special boy'. Though that is one of the very few of Dad's examples I intend to follow.

*

The birth of Evander and my responsibility to Renee and her two kids Madeline and Julian should have made me re-evaluate my life, but I didn't. My existence was still one rolling party.

I hated the cops, I loathed my father, I treated the patrons at the nightclubs I worked as though they were scum, I gobbled down drugs, drank grog and trod many wrong paths. Worst of all there were times when I roughed Renee up.

I had reached the lowest point of my existence and I sickened myself. The only way I could sleep was to hurl down handfuls of Mogadon – a strong tranquilliser – and I was forever on edge during my waking hours.

I had an evilness inside of me which I could not control and whenever Renee tried to help quell it I responded by lashing out at her. I was at my most dangerous and I guess God decided to intervene the day I was as high as a kite, thanks to a hit of LSD, and I decided to steal a car parked 200 yards from a major police station in broad daylight.

I was with a big-mouthed acquaintance who was all piss and wind and who, when it came to the crunch and I decided to go ahead and steal the car, lost his nerve and deserted me like a rat. He left me posted as I attacked the vehicle but I didn't care because, in my wild state of mind, I did not need him or anyone for that matter. Unbeknown to me, the Commodore had a silent alarm which I'd tripped during my attempt to prise the driver's door open.

I don't know how long I was hard at work but my thought process – and it was way out, thanks to the LSD – was interrupted by two blokes who asked what the hell I was up to. I told them to keep moving and that's when they told me I was under arrest – they were police.

I surprised myself by repressing the urge to smash the

nearest copper's jaw with a solid whack of my elbow. When I sized him up and saw how small he was I just slapped him with an open hand and he shocked me by hitting the deck like a stunned mosquito! His mate then jumped on my back and I brushed him off as if he was an unsightly flake of dandruff on my coat collar. It would have been so easy to hurt them but for some reason I was too scared to go the whole hog. A garbageman who witnessed the rumble yelled at my two opponents to lay off. 'Hey!' he yelled. 'One-on-one man, make it a fair fight!' However, the garbo realised he had made a terrible blunder when one of the policeman yelled at him to shut up because they were cops! Unfortunately for me he later made amends for his error of judgement. It was wild and I do remember the urge to pocket the police badge I saw hit the pavement; however, I didn't have time for that. I ran across a park and it must have looked like a scene from a John Candy movie because I was one hundred and thirty-two heavy kilos, as fast as a sloth and I laboured just to catch my breath! Believe me, I was a shot duck after just fifty metres and the bloody garbageman – who had witnessed the sorry incident – tripped me over.

I crashed face-first into the ground and it knocked the wind from out of me. But I was soon running, er, waddling, for my freedom again, and when the 'stunned mossie' attempted to ring for backup on his mobile phone, I slapped him down. I then made another futile dash for freedom; however, it came to an end when I was whacked square in the back of the head with a walkie talkie. It didn't hurt but I was more stunned to see bits of plastic and wire fly everywhere!

However, it had the desired result because after another wrestle outside a block of flats I hit the deck like a back-breaking one hundred and thirty-two kilo sack of spuds. I was at their mercy. There was no way I could get back up and push on. My lungs were ready to explode and I had expended any energy left in my bloated carcass.

Once they had handcuffed me one of the officers – not the mossie – became Mike Tyson and laid the boot in. The bastard also ripped my earring out during his attack and then promised to give me something to *really* think about once we returned to the cells! I was so high on LSD I didn't give a stuff, though the paddy-wagon trip back to the station gave me an idea of what I could expect because the driver hit every kerb and speed bump at full speed.

Once I was dragged into the cells I was made to get on my knees – I was so stoned I didn't think twice – and then I felt an almighty whack across my back with a baton!

When I demanded they undo the cuffs because my hands were numb, 'Tyson' just whacked me across the head and screamed I was dead meat.

I didn't care by then. Instead of cringing and begging for mercy I just stared at him as if he was a coward. I think I may have slurred *he* wouldn't have been so brave if I could defend myself. The sergeant, who was well aware I had punished two of his men, sneered I didn't look so tough but he changed his tune when I demanded to contact my brother, the famous boxer Troy Waters. Once the police realised who I was – and I dare say, what I was capable of – they brought me in a coffee and a biscuit and when I refused to touch them the walloper in charge said he hadn't spat on them. It was as if not spitting on food and in drink was their idea of being kind. I didn't want to be friends with them so I countered: 'No, you wouldn't have gollied on them, you probably pissed on 'em instead!'

The real tragedy of the moment was I was living out the same life as my father had long bragged about but I could not see it at the time. I was doing everything by the Ces Waters textbook of crime and dealing with coppers: when the police wanted to know who my accomplice was – and I was as dirty as hell on him for leaving me posted – I refused to 'dog' on him. I just played dumb even though the yellow bastard did not deserve any loyalty.

My interrogators gave up and after a few hours I was placed on sixteen charges ranging from the attempted theft of a motor car to assaulting two police officers and possessing a drug of dependence.

I was released on bail and one of my conditions was I could not leave Melbourne, which was a real problem because Renee and the kids had relocated to Newcastle. For the first time in my life I really looked at myself in the mirror and felt not only low but also terribly scared of what the future held.

A good mate named Mark Finn gave me the run of his house during the six weeks I waited to go to court and, just two days after being arrested, I decided to give myself a pep up by buying some drugs from a contact named Leon. He was as mad as a cut snake and had even spent time in an asylum because of his drug dependence. Leon was the bloke who had been a dead-ringer for Mel Gibson until the drugs took their toll and left him looking drawn and sickly but when it came to getting drugs, any drugs, Leon was the man. I told him I wanted to snow-cone – to smoke grass filtered with heroin – and I was lucky fate intervened because as I waited for him to get the wheels in motion the coppers raided the place.

I had smoked some grass with Leon to kill time as I waited for my package to arrive but the party ended with a knock on the door – we received the shock of our life to see eight coppers on his front doorstep! It was a raid and even though I was stoned to the eyeballs I denied taking anything when they grilled me. It wasn't me they were after and I felt a surprising sense of gratitude when they told me to be on my way. The last thing I needed before my court appearance was more trouble!

In time I was fined a juicy $4,000 for my LSD-inspired actions and the judge said I only escaped a stiff sentence because I refrained from hurting the officers. However, the experience made me realise I had hit rock bottom. I knew it would not be long before I ended up in prison – if not for drugs, then assault or even theft if I ever became that desperate for cash.

The idea of going to prison scared me and I feared I would not survive life behind bars. I had spoken to a few hard cases about prison and it was everything I feared. Indeed, one bloke from whom I sought some information about life on the inside advised me I should carry a sharp object everywhere with me if I ever landed a prison sentence. My mate was once one of Australia's most wanted criminals and he said it was a necessity because the day would come when I'd have to defend myself from an ugly situation, like an attempted gang rape.

While it wasn't the sort of thing I wanted to hear, it helped me come to grips with what I would face if I gave into these feelings which had started to surface – the need to confess to my role in the death of Allan Hall.

You see, I had decided if I was going to do time it was not going to be for something as meaningless as drugs; it was going to be for the blunder which had destroyed everything I could have been.

CRY FREEDOM

Chapter Twenty-Three

'I have absolutely no doubt that Dean shot Allan Hall because of the continued badgering and demands of my father and his confused state of mind over loyalty; and at the same time the fear of what our father would eventually do if his commands were not followed. I totally accept that Dean's will at the time of the shooting was overcome by the will of his father.'

Troy Waters' statement to the court

I was angry that I could allow my father's death from a sudden heart attack to upset me in the way it did. Dad had often told people he would like to die within sight of a boxing ring and I guess he did the next best thing because he passed away at a post-fight celebration at the Newtown RSL. His latest protégé, a junior welterweight named Danny 'Boy' Pierce, had won the NSW title and my father dropped dead while the celebratory sandwiches and party pies were being served.

After our big split a number of boxers had made a pilgrimage to Dad's bush camp, including some talented bangers like heavyweight Jimmy Thunder, cruiserweight contender Steve Unterholzer and Pierce. They wanted to be taught by him and Dad put them on the right path as only he could. Dad even fulfilled his life's dream when he guided Thunder to a World Boxing Federation title.

Now he was dead and while I didn't cry all that often it was like a tropical monsoon when my emotions got the better of me – fast, hard and sudden. While I had long pictured Dad as a crazy-eyed ogre, I couldn't help but feel a dreadful sense of loss. After all, he was my Dad and despite all the terrible things he had put us through I still had some love left for him.

I am grateful I made my peace with him a few years before he passed away. I didn't know it at the time but, when I phoned Dad to say I had forgiven him for everything he had put me through, I was actually farewelling him. It was a surprising conversation and I remember it fondly because it was the first time in my life that Dad kept quiet and listened to my side of a story – there was no berating me, no insults, no nothing. He was just an old man listening to his son. I'm grateful Dad at least gave me that one gesture to hang onto for the rest of my life, the simple fact that one time he showed me some respect.

I'm certain any warmth Dad may have felt for me after that call evaporated in the lead-up to his death when I took the hardest step of my life and confessed my role in Allan Hall's murder. It angered Dad because he too was charged with the murder.

While Dad could never understand my actions I had no choice but to come clean because life had finally reached the stage where I could no longer live with the guilt – it had squeezed most of the goodness out of me and I was more often than not so drugged out of my mind I was living in a twilight zone. I knew it was only going to be a matter of time before I did something *really* silly.

Nevertheless, I was terrified of doing what was the right thing because I lived in fear of being separated from Renee and our kids.

And then there was Dad. Even though he was seventy we were still terrified of him because people close to Dad said he planned to go out with a 'bang'. We took that as meaning he planned to kill us and we often walked on eggshells. I feared he would try to get to me by hurting Renee and the kids. My decision to step forward was greatly helped by the wise words of my Christian Life Centre pastor, Kevin Brett, the night I confessed everything to him in 1989. Kevin had told me the day might come when I would not only feel the need to confess, but would have the courage to see it through. Well, judgement day had finally arrived, but I had no intention of going in blindly.

I sought Kevin out to let him know of my fears. Because he understood where I was coming from he arranged for me to meet with a member of his congregation, a Gosford solicitor named Manny Conditsis. All Kevin promised was Manny was a decent, straightforward bloke who would do his best for me, and he was spot on.

From the moment I met Manny he impressed me with his straightforwardness. There was no bullshitting with him – he wanted to hear the whole truth and nothing but the truth, so I spilled my guts. I've never really needed anyone to fight any of my battles for me, but this was different and I was glad to have Manny at my right hand because he has a goodness to him.

Nevertheless, telling him of my dreadful secret and desire to step forward was a tough slog: I was a nervous wreck. The years of drug abuse had taken their toll and I downed jug after jug of water as I revealed what it was like to be Ces Waters' special son. The abnormality of my life wasn't lost on Manny, whose face reflected his horror at my stories.

And Manny was patient. He nursed me through some terrible times and I'll never forget the time I turned up to his office as high as a kite on a cocktail of acid, LSD and pot. I would start crying uncontrollably as a result of the substances in my body and Manny asked whether I was on anything. I told him the truth but rather than browbeat me he put a friendly hand on my shoulder and said a prayer for me. It was an important moment of trust and friendship because I'm certain most other solicitors would have turfed me out onto the street, but not Manny. Few people know how much he helped me because at the time of my decision to come forward I did not have a job or any money to pay my legal bills. However, because Manny was more interested in seeing the right thing done he put aside thousands of dollars worth of work and he prepared my case. Manny soon became a close friend and when I think of him in relation to that period of my life I think of a man who was asked to walk one mile but he ran two.

While I had no right to make any demands I told Manny I wanted to know what I faced if I turned myself into the police because Renee and I needed to brace ourselves for the worst-case scenario, and it was a bad one!

After consulting a retired judge Manny said I faced a fifteen-year sentence and the severity rocked me. I had figured I was entitled to some leniency because I came forward after being found not guilty by a magistrate and, after all, the case couldn't be closed without my confession.

I felt cheated and when I made my feelings clear to Manny he said in the eyes of the law I had killed a man and deserved to face the consequences. According to Manny there would be no escaping a number of years in a cell and if I really wanted to do the right thing I had to throw myself at the mercy of the court.

Well, I didn't like his verdict and I told Manny to forget the matter because I had already served eight years in the toughest prison known to mankind – my mind – and that had all but destroyed me. While I walked out of his office feeling as if I had been cheated by the system, Manny must have sensed something else. As I stormed down the street, he stored the documents away in a safe hiding spot for the day when I returned to do what I'd already termed the 'right thing'.

My downward slide continued for another year until it reached the stage where Renee reasoned if it took fifteen years in prison to get rid of the self-destructive streak consuming me then it was time well spent for both our sakes. She just wanted us to grow old in peace and, because I knew she would wait for me, I phoned Manny to say I was ready to take the worst the court could throw my way. I felt a huge burden lift from my shoulders when I confessed all to Detective Inspector Dennis O'Toole. My only concern was incriminating Damon. While his life had plummeted terribly since that fateful June night, he also had a family to care for and I thought he should know what I planned to do so he could make his own arrangements.

I was terrified because I knew there was no backing out, but when O'Toole asked me who the other shooter was I refused to co-operate even when he said it would look bad for me in court if I didn't give him my accomplice's name. I was happy enough to take the entire wrap and when Dennis said he already knew who the other gunman was I figured he was lying. I told him I didn't even want to hear the name, but Manny intervened and asked him to reveal it. When I heard Damon's name my blood ran cold but I tried not to let it show on my face. However, Dennis pressed on with his assault when he said even if I did not co-operate they would be arresting Damon in relation to Hall's murder after I came forward.

Unbeknown to me Damon's mentally ill brother Craig had told the police everything about the case when he suffered an episode two years earlier. However, the video was misplaced and it took an unbelievable two years to reach Dennis.

Once I realised it was all over for Damon and me, I decided not to surrender half-heartedly but I sought Damon out before making a full confession. I went to Damon's house and told him the game was up, that the cops knew. I told him even though we had vowed to try and forget that dreadful night I could not live with the guilt any more and it was obvious he couldn't either because we both cried long and hard. Both our lives had been destroyed. I warned Damon that the police already knew he was my accomplice and they were going to get him. I also said I would have to tell them his name the following day . . . but I also advised him if he did not want to plead guilty then he should just tell the police the same story which Dad had started to spread; that I was mad and had suffered a nervous breakdown. The next day Julie Cooper, Damon's wife, listened to the radio report of my surrender with disbelief. And with that Damon made the most difficult phone call of all when he phoned the police and turned himself in.

Detective Inspector Dennis O'Toole is a special man. Before I met him I had a deep and utter loathing for the police but Dennis's sincerity has helped alter my perception. Don't mistake this for suggesting O'Toole is a light touch because he is far from it ... he's a tough cookie who gets results by being fair dinkum with even the most vicious crim.

He was one of the cops involved in the investigation which nabbed John Glover, the infamous granny-killer. Glover preyed on defenceless old women on Sydney's North Shore and, interestingly, O'Toole thought my father was not dissimilar to him. He said the only difference was Dad did not have the 'strength' (for want of a better word) to do the killing himself. The way I read his comments was while Dennis thought Glover was a coward because he targeted the weak, Dad was an even greater coward because he had someone else do his dirty work.

O'Toole is blessed with the knack of picking the guilty from the innocent by reading their body language. He told me he knew I had killed Hall not long after I was originally cleared by the judge when I answered a throwaway question from him. I can only vaguely remember the incident but, when Dennis told me there were many people in Gosford who believed I had killed Hall, I apparently shrugged my shoulders and said for them to believe what they wanted to. Dennis said the fact I could not come out and deny it helped convince him I was the killer – but he had no concrete evidence to support his gut feeling.

There were some embarassing incidents for the police and one which made Dennis very angry was when I took the police to the place where I buried the shotgun cartridges after Hall was killed. They had brought with them a metal-detector but because it was new no-one knew how to work it. I even tried to get it to work as it turned out the search was a fruitless venture because there had been a number of floods through the area since 1988 and the water had washed the bullets away.

I was driven to Gosford police station in an unmarked police car and behind my dark glasses and the heavy beard on my face was a feeling of strange serenity. While I did not know what my immediate future held, I knew it was better than living with an all-consuming lie. I had no regrets even though I knew the demons would be dancing a storm in Dad's head when he heard the news.

As I anticipated, my father was outraged to learn of my confession. He told people I had suffered a break-down and he even went as far as to tell *Sixty Minutes* reporter Jeff McMullen that he was concerned I could become suicidal after the attention died down. McMullen covered the trial for the show and, when he interviewed Dad not long before his death, the old man maintained his innocence and tried to turn the glare of the blame from himself by questioning my state of mind.

> *I still believe there are bigger tragedies to come ... I still think the Waters family story is not finished ... It's very sad and the worst is yet to come.*
>
> [McMullen asked what could be worse than being tried for murder] *Well the suicide of one of my children. That could be worse and it is possible. One day when his mind is clear and he wakes up in a sober state of mind, you'll read Dean Waters has committed suicide ... When he suddenly wakes up and into reality. 'What have I said? What have I done?' It's too late then and I believe he'll die of his own hand.*

Despite an impending battle with the law Dad still spoke as if he was James Cagney by telling McMullen such things as: 'You can get further with a kind word and a gun than you can with a kind word. I have found this to be true. There seems to be a strange respect given to people who are apt to use violence ...'

Who knows? Perhaps my father knew he was on his last legs and he wanted to deliver his own epitaph.

The crux of my defence was I surrendered my will to Dad in the lead-up to Allan Hall's death and there was a steady stream of people who were keen to support my case. My brothers, my sister and people who had an insight into Dad's insane world came forward to tell of bashings, of manipulation and torment to give the jury a full account of the pressures and stress I lived with.

I can't begin properly to explain the fear I felt knowing I was fighting for my freedom or, at least, a lesser sentence than that of murder. My belief that I would receive some leniency from the judicial system took a bad blow when Damon was jailed for a minimum of twelve years with an additional term of six years. His sentence hit me like a sledge-hammer because, while Damon's bullets did not kill Hall, Judge Peter Newman regarded his 'criminality' to be at the highest end of the scale.

It was so unfair, because Damon was brainwashed by my father. He, too, was acting out my father's will even though Dad told McMullen he thought it was bizarre two people could be enticed to kill for someone else when he said: 'It would be very, very strange for two people to admit to doing something as vile and foul as that just because someone asked them to do it. Would you commit murder just because someone asked you to do it? Of course you wouldn't.'

I was adamant Damon had been wronged by the system. He was not a cold-blooded killer, he was someone who had unfortunately fallen under the spell of Ces Waters yet the court didn't believe it, and it made me shed a few tears for my own fate.

When I told the Wyong Court I intended to plead guilty to the lesser charge of manslaughter, Manny read the waiting press a prepared statement and the request was for me to be tried by the court, not the media.

> *I have just indicated to the court that Dean Waters is to defend the charge of murder but is prepared to make and to adhere to a plea of guilty to a lesser charge of manslaughter. It needs to be clearly and unequivocally understood by the media and the community that Dean Waters has come forward after almost eight years entirely of his own free will and to clear his conscience and as a result of him doing so he has been charged with this offence before the courts. He didn't have to come forward. He chose to do so. This case is one that involves extraordinary facts which will in due course be known to the community in the proper way, through the courts. In the meantime, on behalf of Dean and his brothers Guy and Troy and sister Tracey who all support him through this, my plea to both the media and the community in general is not to prejudge this matter nor indeed Dean Waters.*

With that done I left my fate in the hands of the court system, my legal counsel and God. I have no doubt God looked over me during that period of my life and sometimes when I reflect upon it I think of the old religious story about footprints in the sand, which says that God and a mortal looked back over his life and it was in the shape of a beach and the only thing that could be seen were two sets of footprints in the sand.

However, the man was confused because at the roughest stages of his life he noticed there was only one set of footsteps and he asked God why he'd been left alone. However, the Lord told the bloke he did not abandon him at his peril, he had carried him!

And that is exactly the way God looked after me because things worked in my favour during the trial. First the video of Damon's brother went missing and secondly my father died after I confessed. I was glad to have stepped forward before Dad suffered his heart attack because I'm certain any confession would have sounded hollow had I volunteered after he was buried.

I was at a friend's place in the outer western suburb of Sydney when Dad died on 4 April 1997. My sleep was disturbed by a phone call and when I was called to the blower it was Troy, with a real sadness in his voice. I was stunned because even though Dad was seventy, I always figured he would outlive us kids.

While I was sorry for him, I was also annoyed he escaped having to face the authorities over the murder he plotted. And by dying the way he did, within sight of a boxing ring, he also failed to come to terms with the number of lives he ruined. Apart from mine there were Christine's, Tracey's, Troy's, Guy's, Sharon's, Kelly's, Hall's, my natural mother's, Damon's, and so many others.

But you know what really burns me? It's the fact Dad was a little bloke who wanted the world and he left with nothing!

He was always one for short cuts and quick schemes and the only legacy I think he's left, apart from having our family name entered in a few boxing books, is that he hurt so many people with his bitter and twisted ways. There are times when I fear Dad is in hell. But I tell myself that isn't my fault because I did try to open his heart to Christ on numerous occasions but his response was to say he was the only God I needed to know. While it was Dad who mocked God and not me I can't help but feel a chill come over me whenever I think of the fate of Dad's soul.

Despite my fears, I could not cry at Dad's funeral. His body lay in state in an open coffin at the Kulnura Community Centre during a non-religious ceremony and when I looked down on him he appeared so small. I wondered what it had been like for him, death.

Dad despised the thought of his own death, it was distasteful to him and I can remember from my childhood the ritual he would perform whenever we passed a cemetery. He would remove his beanie from his head and mutter, 'God bless the dead and have mercy on the living', and he'd then spit as if his saliva helped ward off the Grim Reaper or the Angel of Death.

Our presence wasn't welcomed at the funeral and I could feel many of the hundred or so mourners drill holes through me with their evil looks. When I looked in their eyes they seemed to be calling me a traitor and a dog because the bloke they knew had died with a murder charge hanging over him.

I didn't care what they thought. The *Daily Telegraph*'s Stephen Gibbs was there and he noted: 'An outsider could have thought it was Danny 'Boy' Pierce's Dad in the red timber box yesterday. He did the crying, he had the rose stuffed down his shirt and he carried Ces Waters out to the hearse. The three brothers watching weren't saying what they thought . . .'

Sadly, there was a lot to say, but I couldn't be bothered trying to explain anything to those who were at his funeral because I don't believe they were interested in hearing anything except that Ces was a saint. However, the man described as the Lord of the Ring, Ray Connelly, alluded to the bad days when he said Dad had '... a sense of purpose which was overwhelming. When he set his goals he did everything that was possible to achieve them. One of the problems about feeling a way of life in that regard is that it can become obsessive.'

Dad's 'mates' didn't allow us to carry his coffin but I returned with the others to Dad's property to help lower his coffin in the grave and what struck me about his 'casket' was it was unnaturally heavy, it felt as if it had three bodies inside it. I originally thought it may have been something to do with the oil and balm the mortician used so his body could be displayed, but I was later to find out that, in a futile attempt to defeat death, Dad had ordered for his coffin to be lined with lead! I had an almost romantic notion of filling Dad's grave in on my own but the number of people from the media on hand made it impossible – it would have looked like a publicity stunt.

So I watched on and offered a prayer before the workmen's shovels struck into the small mound of dirt to bury a madman, an ogre, a lunatic, an eccentric and a breeder of four kids.

A few weeks later I went to another burial.

I watched from the public gallery as my mate Damon Cooper was buried by what can only be described as an inhumane sentence. The judge, Peter Newman, who I don't believe realised Damon was brainwashed by Dad over a period of years, described Hall's death as 'the cold-blooded killing of a man who had done nothing adverse to Cooper'. I felt for Damon, and I pitied his wife Julie and kids Amanda and Rhys because he is not a murderer, he was caught up in something which Dad made impossible for him to walk away from.

I sympathised with Julie when she told the press she felt as if the NSW Legal Aid Commission had let him down. I was fortunate in that regard because I had Manny on deck and when my turn to face the music came around, he was white-hot. The Crown had rejected my lesser plea of manslaughter and insisted Manny and I had to fight the murder charge. In my attempt to prove I was under my father's spell the night I pulled a shotgun trigger three times, I called forward witnesses to tell of the brutality I lived hand in hand with. Troy, Tracey and Guy held nothing back and some of their stories brought people to tears. Others who knew and feared Dad painted the picture of a madman.

Indeed, psychiatrists who thought they had heard it all before were stunned by the facts which were unveiled during my nine days in court. The esteemed doctors, one of whom had over thirty years experience in the field of psychiatry, were in total agreement that I did not exercise my will when I pulled the trigger. Dr Straum, who went as far as to compare my father with Charles Manson, told the jury:

I totally accept Dean's will at the time of the shooting was wholly overcome by the will of his father. The father had control of Dean's mind and in the thinking of Dean – no matter how powerful Dean was – all power was with the father and all right was with the father and it was his role to accept that which was dished out to him.

Dr McMando said to Manny:

Your client has been subjected to constant abuse, ridicule and intimidation for as long as he could recall. This put

> *your client in a state of unreasonable and inappropriate compliance and this is a state which one frequently sees in brainwashed individuals and those who follow cults. He craved his father's understanding and praise, though it was very rarely given. He feared his father's brutality and even feared his father would kill him if he disobeyed.*

While finally, Dr Westmore, who was acting for the Crown, told the court:

> *I mean by account of his will being overpowered or his will being submitted to his father is probably a very accurate description of what was happening at the time psychologically. So in that sense it was out of character and it suggests there was an event of some magnitude happening to him psychologically that pushed him over the edge to commit such an extreme act of violence . . .*

As I waited in a pub near the courthouse for the jury to come to its decision all I could do was join Manny in a prayer that everything would be all right. It felt like an eternity, but we were only there for an hour and a half. In that time, however, I thought of so many things. I thought a lot about Renee and my kids, especially little Evander. It had been very tough leaving my place of a morning because he would run out and kiss me goodbye and on each occasion he would ask if I would be coming back that night. Up until the morning of the verdict I was able to say 'yes' but the day I thought I would be sent to prison I told him I had to go away for a long time to work. He looked sad and when he threw his arms around my neck I could honestly feel my heart break.

Renee was not with me for that final day in court because

we couldn't get anyone to mind the kids and while I missed her support Guy and Tracey did their best to help me put on a brave face (Troy was in America for a fight).

Walking back into the courtroom was a harrowing experience because standing behind my seat were two prison guards. They had not been there at any time during the trial and the best I could do to acknowledge their presence was offer a weak smile at one of them. However, God looked over me because the jury found me not guilty of murder. I would have jumped for joy had Manny not warned me I could still be imprisoned for manslaughter and arson. However, when the jury delivered a verdict of not guilty to both charges I exploded with relief. I held my arms open as a gesture of thank you to the jury and when I saw one of them, an old woman, crying I just started to bawl like a baby. I felt Manny grab me and I could see the look of disbelief on the judge ... he was stunned. And in the press gallery I saw Steve Barrett from *Sixty Minutes* and he was as dumfounded as I was. There were tears, Guy was crying unashamedly and so, too, was Tracey. All I could do was keep thanking the jury and I felt a stream of tears cool my face. The nightmare was over.

FINDING DEAN WATERS

Chapter Twenty-Four

'No matter what I'll always be a survivor ...'
Ces on who and what he was

The jury's not guilty verdict dominated the media for a number of weeks. Some commentators accused the jury of being too emotional while others claimed I should be doing time in prison like Damon. However, I have learnt to live with their thoughts in much the same way I brushed aside the sick joke which asked, 'What do Dean Waters and 007 James Bond have in common? They both have a licence to kill.' I have refused to allow that sort of thing to upset me because I would prefer to instead think of the way I felt after I regained my freedom following eight years of mental hell. Tracey told the dozens of journalists who crowded outside the court that she believed a curse which had long plagued our family died with the jury's verdict and I believe she is right. I have a strong belief everything is going to be OK for all of us now.

Every day is a bonus to me and it is whenever I see the

sunset or I talk to Renee about our kids I am glad I did not end my life the time I stuck a pistol in my mouth and thought about squeezing the trigger in order to end a nightmare from which there was seemingly no escape. If I had taken the easy way out I would have missed so many great things – being Renee's partner, guiding our little tribe of kids, getting to know my daughters to Kelly – Rebekka and beautiful Courtney – better, seeing my brothers and sister achieve so many great things and, of course, being found not guilty of murder.

I often think kind thoughts of the jury who freed me because I'm sure none of those wonderful people can possibly understand what they did by clearing me of any wrongdoing when I was at their mercy. They saved my sanity. When they decided upon a 'not guilty' verdict the jurists did much, much more than simply hand a troubled man his freedom. They also said they understood what I went through ... they realised I was really nothing more than the puppet for an evil puppeteer and that really helps when my mind recalls those three shot gun blasts.

At the time of my writing this book I have taken steps to readjust to 'normality'. I attend a church-run course which is aimed at 'deprogramming' me of the mad demons which danced in my head for far too long, and it is slowly helping. For a while I contemplated making a return to boxing in order to help put food on the table and to pay the rent – I even went hunting for old 'Aussie' Joe Bugner's scalp but I don't think swapping punches is the answer. Instead, the only fight I want to take part in is to be in a position one day where I can help troubled kids – especially the self destructive ones – realise that it is possible to forgive yourself for even the most terrible crime. It is also my genuine hope my life story gives bucketloads of hope to those who need it. My prayers for them include;

> 'I press onwards towards the goal to win the prize for which God has called me heaven-wards in Christ Jesus.'
> Phillippians 3:14

> 'I can do all things through Christ who strengthens me.'
> Phillippians 4:13

I once dreamed of being a world champion, nowadays I dream of being a good father and a good husband to Renee. I want to provide the right example for my sons Evander and Chaquel, daughters Rebekka and Courtney, and my step-kids whom I also love very much, Madeline and Julian. I am determined to do a better job of raising my kids than Dad did with us. Though it isn't easy. I don't think anything my father did to me and the others has rubbed off on me except I sometimes hear myself say to Evander that he's my *special boy*. However, unlike Dad I love my kids for who they are, not what I would like them to become.

I thank God that I met Renee because I have grown, and continue to grow, with her. Apart from helping to provide me with the strength to come forward and confess my crime to the police Renee has also taught me a number of very important lessons and they include the real meaning of commitment and that love is a decision, not a feeling. I have fallen down a few times in life but with Renee's help I have also come to realise that winners aren't those who never fail, they're those who never quit – and we have no intention of doing that. We're engaged and one day we will be married and I want it to work because I don't want to be one of the millions of people who find it easier to bail out of a relationship rather than work hard at it. However,

I don't think Renee and I could have asked for a tougher series of tests to check the depth of our love because there have been some horrors!

The other special person in my life is my brother Guy. He, too, stood by me when it could have been so easy for him to turn away. There have been many times when I have needed him to lean on and he has responded in the most loyal and loving way. He's a good-hearted person and I hope he sees the day when all the tears and all the help have been well worth his effort. These days we spend plenty of time fishing together on his boat and we have had some wild old times, like the day we went so far out to sea we lost sight of land and then there was the day his auxiliary engine packed it in and we needed to get a bloke on a jet ski to get us some help. A reluctant boxer, one of his greatest stands was the day when he stood up to our Dad when it seemed as if he intended to hurt Sharon during one of his rages. And he has had to summon the same courage and strength to help me get out of some terrible messes and I thank him dearly for that.

Thankfully, the bitter hatred I once held for Dad has subsided now and there are even times when I think of him telling me over and over: '*I'm a survivor, Dean. No matter what I'll always be a survivor.*' I think of that line a lot because at the end of the day that's what I am, Dad, I'm a bloody survivor.

We all are.

Acknowledgements

To Renee, no-one has loved me like you. You have suffered more than any person should have to in the name of commitment. You have taught me what love and commitment really mean and I thank you. I know our first three years were rough ... the violence, the fear, the drugs and the mental abuse ... no person should have to put up with that. However, you have loved me through the worst and I am gratefuly you stayed with me. Renee, you had faith I would change and I mean it when I say I want to be what you need me to be, not what suits me.

To my beautiful children Rebekka, Courtney, Evander and Chaqueal and step-kids Madeline and Julian, I love you all and I want to be a good father for each of you. Please remember above all else I believe you are all very special.

To my brother Guy, you have been the most special brother anyone could ever hope for. I think of you as an angel and love you with all my heart. May God bless your life as richly as He has mine.

I offer a special thanks to Tara for leading me to Chritianity in my time of need. Similarly, I thank Pastor Kevin Brett for counselling me through some troubled times. God bless you, Kevin, because you helped me find the courage to do what was right.

To Detective Inspector Dennis O'Toole, a good guy. I thank you for helping restore my faith in people (and cops).

To Manny Conditsis. You are a special friend. When I asked you to go one mile you went two. In the depths of my despair, when nothing seemed to matter any more, you listened to me and prayed with me. Manny, you have been the father I never had. May God bless you.

Mark and Kathy Evans. Thank you for your prayers and food. Love always, Food Monster!

To Lincoln Brown, in my times of need you always dug deep and emptied your pockets (even though there was nothing in them!).

Steve and Simone Ferguson. Stevo, you have not only been a good friend and workmate for years but you've also been a good listener and it helped. Thanks mate.

Tony and Maureen Hall, I will never forget all that you have done for us. Thank you.

To Steve and Cherie Lewis, thanks for your support and friendship over the years.

To Peter Wills and family, thanks for being true friends for all these years.